Dimitar Bechev is a Research Fellow at the European Studies Centre, St. Antony's College, University of Oxford, and Lecturer in International Relations at Worcester College, Oxford. He specializes in the external relations of the European Union, comparative regionalism, the politics and modern history of wider South East Europe (the Balkans and Turkey) and identity in international relations. He is the author of *Historical Dictionary of Macedonia* (Scarecrow Press, 2009). His articles have appeared in *East European Politics and Societies, Nationalities Papers, Journal of Southern Europe and the Balkans, Journal of Southeast European and Black Sea Studies,* and *Millennium.* He is the academic coordinator of the Oxford branch of RAMSES2 Network of Mediterranean Studies.

Kalypso Nicolaidis is Professor of International Relations, University of Oxford and Fellow of St Antony's College. She teaches in European integration, international relations and international political economy. She has also held visiting professorships around Europe, including at the École Nationale d'Administration in Paris, the College of Europe in Bruges and Sciences-Po, Paris. She has published widely in journals such as *Foreign Affairs, Foreign Policy, The Journal of Common Market Studies, Journal of European Public Policy, International Organization* as well as in French in *Politique Étrangère, Politique Européenne* and *Raison Critique.* Her latest book publications include: *Whose Europe? National Models and the Constitution of the European Union* (European Studies at Oxford, 2003) and *The Federal Vision: Legitimacy and Levels of Governance in the US and the EU* (Oxford University Press, 2001). She chairs the Oxford branch of the RAMSES2 Network of Mediterranean Studies.

LIBRARY OF INTERNATIONAL RELATIONS

Series ISBN: 978 1 84885 240 2

See www.ibtauris.com/LIR for a full list of titles

MEDITERRANEAN FRONTIERS

Borders, Conflict and Memory
in a Transnational World

EDITED BY
DIMITAR BECHEV AND KALYPSO NICOLAIDIS

TAURIS ACADEMIC STUDIES
an imprint of
I.B.Tauris Publishers
LONDON • NEW YORK

Published in 2010 by Tauris Academic Studies,
an imprint of I.B.Tauris & Co Ltd
6 Salem Road, London W2 4BU
175 Fifth Avenue, New York NY 10010
www.ibtauris.com

Distributed in the United States and Canada Exclusively by Palgrave Macmillan
175 Fifth Avenue, New York NY 10010

ISBN 978 1 84885 125 2
International Library of International Relations 46

A full CIP record for this book is available from the British Library
A full CIP record for this book is available from the Library of Congress

Library of Congress Catalog Card Number: available

Printed and bound in India by Replika Press Pvt. Ltd.
camera-ready copy edited and supplied by the author

This volume is published with the support of the Directorate General for Research of the
European Commission, in the framework of the RAMSES² Network of Excellence, funded
by the 6th Framework Programme (contract CIT3-CT-2005-513366), under the coordination
of the National Book Centre of Greece. This volume is solely the responsibility of the
Publisher and the authors; the European Commission cannot be held responsible for its
content or for any use which may be made of it.

**EUROPEAN
COMMISSION**

CITIZENS AND GOVERNANCE IN A
KNOWLEDGE-BASED SOCIETY

RA𝓜SES②

CONTENTS

LIST OF MAPS

ACKNOWLEDGEMENTS

This book benefited from the generous support of a number of institutions and individuals. We are, first and foremost, grateful to the European Commission which funded the RAMSES2 Network of Excellence on the Mediterranean and made our inquiry into the comparative politics and history of borders, conflicts and memory possible. Within the network, we benefited immensely from the amazing expertise and intellectual depth of a first-rate team of historians, anthropologists, political scientists and students of religion. This volume would not have been possible without the encouragement and the support of Thierry Fabre, a passionate Mediterranean, who has been the driving force behind the RAMSES2 endeavour. We are also thankful to our colleagues at St Antony's College and especially Eugene Rogan and Michael Willis, both at the Middle East Centre, and Othon Anastasakis, director of South East European Studies at Oxford, as well as to Michelle Pace, University of Birmingham, and Alfred Tovias, Hebrew University, for their contribution to various academic events that paved the way to this book. We also gratefully acknowledge the contribution of scholars at the Maison Méditerranéenne des Sciences de l'Homme in Aix-en-Provence such as Marilyne Crivello, who co-convened a workshop on the politics of memory in the Mediterranean in June 2007. Special thanks to Nicholas Purcell, a leading authority on the Mediterranean, for all his ideas about the perennial question of unity and fragmentation around the Sea, shared with us during a conference appropriately entitled 'Mediterranean Unions?', which took place in June 2008. Last but not least, we would like to acknowledge the help of Reem Abou-El-Fadl, our copyeditor, Galina Kostadinova, who translated several of the chapters originally written in French, and Eno Trimçev and Atanas Topalov, who provided editorial assistance.

PREFACE:
AT THE FRONTIERS
OF THE MEDITERRANEAN

The Mediterranean is an elusive space with contours one often fails to grasp. The Mediterranean is more than just a sea in between land masses or a maritime 'continent' whose traces could be easily followed on a map, confounding all attempts at geographical reductionism. It appeals to the imaginary, forming a world composed of multiple narratives, inspiring as well as stirring political angst. A geo-cultural ensemble whose coordinates shift according to historical time and the rhythms of memory, the Mediterranean world defies established rules and entrenched discourses which turn it into a mere border of Europe or even a blurry neighbourhood.

First and foremost, at least for us, the Mediterranean is a site of intellectual curiosity, a source of questions and exploration, a focal point for the development of a comparative field which we have called 'Mediterranean Studies'. This is the principal mission of the RAMSES2 network, one of whose first manifestations is *Mediterranean Frontiers*. Dimitar Bechev and Kalypso Nicolaidis have led a group of researchers from a broad array of disciplines exploring the multifaceted meaning of frontiers in the Mediterranean world. The book inquires into how these frontiers may alternatively become sites of hybridity and connection or sites of conflict and war, and how memories have shaped and have been shaped by these forces over time. This is, indeed, an exciting intellectual agenda promising to draw the attention of a wider readership.

The RAMSES2 network's cross-disciplinary approach lays the foundations for comparative work which, as this book illustrates in a magisterial manner, could prove very fruitful. It offers novel perspectives and helps overcome the prevailing confusion in the media and the day-to-day political talk about the Mediterranean. At a time when the region is once again on the political agenda with Nicolas Sarkozy's Union for Mediterranean, it is more important than ever to broaden our Mediterranean horizons.

The universe of frontiers is the best prism through which one could view the Mediterranean in all its complexity. The volume offers us three angles. The first focuses on the historical trajectories which help us understand the emergence of borders and identity boundaries in the Mediterranean, as well as the role of imperial legacies. The second addresses the question of memories which constitute and maintain the boundary with 'the Other'. The third undertakes to analyze how frontiers in the Mediterranean impact on human lives at present.

The book seeks to rethink concepts such as 'border', 'boundary' or 'frontier' and revisit the relationship between 'Self' and 'Other'. In so doing, the authors hope to evoke a sense of 'we' around the Mediterranean, which distinguishes without merging, separates but at the same time links – this is what animates the book which carves out a new field of inquiry. This is not yet another volume about Europe and Islam rendering the Mediterranean an unyielding fault line between clashing civilizations. Instead, the essays gathered here change the game and open fresh perspectives for understanding the kaleidoscopic Mediterranean world. The figure of a star-shaped polygon, drawn a long time ago by the Algerian writer Kateb Yacine, is an appropriate symbol for such an endeavour, capturing the complex interactions across Mediterranean frontiers.

The Mediterranean has become Europe's new frontier, its horizon, the place, both real and imaginary, where the question of war and peace has come to the forefront yet again. This book is a must-read for anyone willing to expand their horizons and find some answers.

Thierry Fabre

Professor of Mediterranean Studies
Maison Méditerranéenne des Sciences de
l'Homme
Aix-en-Provence

Academic Coordinator
RAMSES2 Network on the Mediterranean

INTRODUCTION:
FRONTIERS, MEMORY AND CONFLICT IN THE MEDITERRANEAN

DIMITAR BECHEV AND KALYPSO NICOLAIDIS

This is a book about frontiers: frontiers dividing and connecting regions, states, nations and social groups, but also frontiers tying together the past and the present. Whether in the Mediterranean or elsewhere, frontiers fundamentally define social relations. The nation-state, the dominant institutional principle underpinning political life in the modern age, emerged in Western Europe at the turn of the nineteenth century. It developed to inextricably bind territorial sovereignty and the forms of citizenship which evolved under it. Yet if modern statehood is characterized by the (claim to) exclusive control within borders, circumscribing authority and separating the orderly 'inside' from the anarchic 'outside'[1], these territorial barriers are also intertwined with symbolic boundaries defining the body politic and its cultural makeup. They are there to sustain shared notions of belonging, blur internal heterogeneity and create a spirit of social cohesiveness. Borders and boundaries are projected into the past through a plethora of myths and officially sanctioned memories, portraying exclusivist identities and territorial attachments as natural and primordial.

Needless to say, this ideal-typical portrayal is far removed from the realities of the 'region' which this book explores. Travelling around the Great Sea, one cannot fail to notice a 'tension between the actual borders of states and other virtual boundaries that frame human communities'.[2] The Mediterranean space – comprising diverse yet overlapping areas such as southern Europe, the Balkans, Turkey, the Middle East and the Maghreb

– is shaped in equal measure by fragmentation and, to borrow a term from Peregrine Horden and Nicholas Purcell, connectivity.[3] This dialectic is becoming increasingly pronounced in this age of globalization: on the one hand, streams of capital, goods and, with many qualifications, people bring riparian countries into closer contact.[4] This state of affairs echoes earlier historical periods when it was possible to conceive of a Mediterranean world which had far more substance than the clichéd images we are offered today by tour operators and restaurant owners. On the other hand, the 'Mediterranean' remains both fuzzy and compartmentalized by borders and boundaries 'hardened' by conflicts between and within states. From Western Sahara, through Algeria and Palestine, to Cyprus, Bosnia and Kosovo, to the painful memories of the Second World War in the Eastern Adriatic, to the scars of Western European colonialism in North Africa or the Armenian genocide of 1915, the politics of the region have been underwritten by strife and violence. Globalization and the expansion of economic exchanges only partly alleviate this condition. Developmental disparities and the differential degree of inclusion into the markets and institutions of the regional mastodon that is the European Union (EU) add a pinch of salt to the vague talk of a 'Mediterranean'. As Kerem Öktem shows in his chapter, the Mediterranean is a veritable region of regions – each with its peculiar dynamics, socio-economic features, historical legacies, and, not least, mental maps of the world.[5] How can we analytically pin down this complex reality? How should we conceive of the interplay between patterns of conflict structured by these legacies, and moves towards integration? The latter has been promoted by noble, yet often dysfunctional, initiatives such as the EU's ill-fated Barcelona Process and its shinier successor, the Union for the Mediterranean, inaugurated in Paris on 13 July 2008.

This book seeks to examine the current policy discussions about security and cooperation in the Mediterranean from a deeper historical, sociological and anthropological perspective. Its title speaks of *frontiers*. While terms like borders and boundaries smack of static exclusion and 'Othering', frontiers is meant to convey the dynamic tensions and practices of contacts, exchanges and coexistence, but also conflict and violence that reflect various facets of the Mediterranean experience. The beauty of the notion of frontier is that it captures social realities that preceded the advent of the nation-state, as well as those of our present which put the nation-state in question. It is applicable to the marches of the Almohad Empire's successor states in the Maghreb, discussed here by Fatma Ben Slimane, the smugglers' paradise of the Negev desert (see Cédric Parizot's contribution), the borderland regimes promoted nowadays by the so-called European Neighbourhood

Policy investigated by Raffaella A. Del Sarto or the ever contested outposts of Ceuta and Melilla whose case is studied by Henk Driessen. Across these different times and spaces, frontiers are both 'lines in the sand' and 'fuzzy', zones of overlapping authority, of transition and contact. They foster not only exclusion, but also connectivity and multiple belongings.

What we have in mind therefore is to subvert the notion of 'border', that is the source of so many of the current conflicts around the Mediterranean, and to analyze frontiers more broadly, and their inherent potential to foster multifaceted human interactions. Our approach is rooted in a deeper, socio-logical understanding of borders/boundaries/frontiers as social structures. They are viewed as institutions and practices at the interface of two state jurisdictions, at the edges of mutually constitutive Self-Other pairs, or at the junction between two or three regions or even continents, such as Asia, Af-rica and Europe.[6] Indeed, the Sea itself serves as such a frontier structure, bridging as well as isolating worlds at its edges. Ultimately, it is also forever 'the next frontier', which can be discovered and conquered, imagined and reimagined with the ebb and flow of history.

The Mediterranean space is bisected by frontiers. This is the starting point in our volume, whose ambition is to add a critical footnote to the dis-cussion on the historical foundations and future prospects of region-build-ing around the erstwhile *Mare Nostrum*. This is the lofty ideal championed by the EU – one of economic integration and peace, embedded in cooperative institutions. However, it is at variance with the colourful mosaic confront-ing would-be *bricoleurs*. Yet claims of Mediterranean unity are nothing new. In addition to inspiring a myriad of travel guides, they have fertilized more than one field of scholarly enquiry. Fernand Braudel, the founding father of this tradition, at least in its contemporary incarnation, chose to write history 'from the bottom up', moving away from, though not entirely ignoring, the conventional divisions imposed by political, religious or cultural difference.[7] The Sea and its edges were conceived as a space of exchange of goods, social practices and ideas conditioned by the constraints and opportunities of the physical environment. In a similar vein, essentialist anthropology developed the notion of common cultural traits defining the Mediterra-nean space, and manifest in traditions of 'shame and honour'. These ideas soon came under heavy fire from critically-minded scholars such as Michael Herzfeld.[8]

Yet the frontier-like character of the Mediterranean is hardly amenable to unification projects, whether political or academic, which bank on (puta-tive) cultural affinities, common pasts, shared environmental destiny, and even economic interdependence. As Nora Fisher Onar's chapter reminds

us, 'clash of civilizations' discourses, as well as more subtle versions calling for a dialogue between civilizations, pervade today's popular images of
Europe's *rapport* with the Muslim communities in its midst, as well as with
the Islamic-majority countries in the southern and eastern Mediterranean,
from Morocco all the way to Turkey.[9] These binary imageries conceive of
the Mediterranean as a fault line between the West and Islam rather than
as a shared space. In all fairness, these discourses did not spring up on 12
September 2001. Huntingtonianism *avant la lettre* was not alien to Braudel,
or to the celebrated Belgian historian Henri Pirenne, who saw the Muslim
conquest of the seventh century as the end of the *Mare Nostrum* of Roman
Antiquity.[10] Seen from this vantage point, the Mediterranean is neither a
region in its own right nor a border: it is a fuzzy space in-between. It is a
void separating the prosperous North from the stagnating South, a great
divide between liberal, secular Europe and an Arab world bedevilled by
economic decay and religious fundamentalism, between democracy and autocracy. Moreover, as Marie-Claire Lavabre and Dimitri Nicolaidis illustrate
through their Algerian journey, this perspective casts the Mediterranean as
the 'interface' between the former colonial masters and their subjects. There
are recurrent questions as to whether a common Mediterranean identity is
possible and, if so, what the implications of this might be.[11] More importantly for us, however, the paramount question is whether this is an appropriate and worthwhile quest – the quest for a common 'we' around that Sea,
for the bond that would make wars obsolete in that corner of the world.
Or should we rather seek conditions for mutual recognition across borders
throughout these shores, whereby actors revisit their shared pasts together,
without trying to weave them into a single narrative?

As in the mid-1990s, some still believe that the winds of the future blow
aside the grim realities and conflicts of the present. The region-building
paradigm promises to settle, if not heal, all those seemingly insoluble conflicts, political tensions and bitter memories.[12] Euro-Mediterranean minis-
terials and President Sarkozy's high-powered speeches stress positive interdependence as a force capable of profoundly reshaping the relationship
between the two shores of the Mediterranean, albeit through 'small steps'
as advocated by Jean Monnet in the 1950s. Thus far, however, integration
has been as much about building bridges as about securing bastions, again
reminding us of the Janus-faced concept of *frontier*. Orchestrated from
Brussels, the process reflects the EU's preference for liberalizing trade but
excluding agricultural goods and labour-intensive services, where the partners from North Africa and the Middle East have a competitive edge over
the likes of Spain, Greece or Italy. Cross-Mediterranean cooperation also

seeks to protect Europe against illegal African and Asian migrants storming 'fortress Europe' through its gates: these include the Spanish enclaves in Morocco, as well as Sicily, the Canary Islands and the Aegean Archipelago. Transformative power this is not. Rhetorically, the EU embraces the promotion of democracy, but in practice, stability tops the agenda. More than one authoritarian regime in North Africa and the Middle East can count on both European and US support.[13] In contrast to its American *alter ego*, however, the EU is largely absent from the radar screen. Talk of cooperation and integration surely means little to the West Bank labourers studied by Cédric Parizot, who smuggle their way into the Negev townships. Instead, these Palestinians from both sides of the Wall reproduce at the most localized level the challenges generated by the twin needs to live as 'brothers' and 'rivals'. For them, smuggling and trespassing help transcend a border that has constituted their worlds in the first place.

Nevertheless, the North versus South polarity rooted in (post)colonial experience does a tremendous injustice to the richness of Mediterranean histories and contemporary politics. This volume's aim is to offer a broader, though not necessarily more optimistic picture, coloured by a kaleidoscope of vivid empirical case studies. The Mediterranean is a repository of multiple historical memories, of which colonialism is but one. The Maghreb and the Levant, Turkey and the Balkans, the Adriatic and the Iberian Peninsula all have their own histories and distinctive relationships with 'core' Europe to the north-west. There are more than two shores to the sea in which we set sail. Acknowledging these divisions and the competing nature of regionalizing discourses, but also the diversity and distinctiveness of smaller sub-regions, should help liberate the Mediterranean debate from tacit imperial longings, quests for domination and neo-colonial designs. This could be a first step towards reimagining the Mediterranean as a non-hegemonic space, in which colonizer and colonized, deporter and deportee can face each other as equals to confront and transcend the divisions of the nineteenth and twentieth centuries.

This volume discusses at length the conflicts and borders emerging in the process of state formation and nation building in various regional *milieux* in the Mediterranean, and the memory traces left by such processes. Memory-laden conflicts about borders are a common thread running through the modern history of the Mediterranean, from the Napoleon's expedition to Egypt through decolonization in the mid-twentieth century, all the way to the break-up of the Yugoslav federation in the 1990s. Yet we should also not lose sight of social conflicts and boundaries cutting *across* the apparent unity of the body politic. Consider the traumatic memories associated with the so-called *Great Schism* in Greek politics reaching its peak in the Civil War of 1946-1949, or the tensions between secularism and politicized religion central to Israeli society, but also familiar to students of Italy, Spain, Turkey and, after the 1980s, the Middle East and North Africa. The main axis of political contestation in Mediterranean polities has not always been the nation-state versus its external 'Others'. Indeed, many of the aforementioned cleavages and divisive identities testify to the flawed vision of homogenous societies pursued by nation builders, as much as to the presence of minorities which are *a priori* excluded from the imagined unity of the 'core group'. For all their symbolic and material power, many nation-states around the Mediterranean have remained rather weak when it comes to effective management of the modernization process.[14] In this context, we need to problematize and study the construction, maintenance and contestation of identity boundaries as dynamic social processes, rather than as ossified givens.

In this game, memory plays interesting tricks. The homogenizing visions of Self and Other, of rupture and conflict, have more than once clashed with dissonant memories of coexistence, diversity and exchange. From the Maghrebi Jews in present-day Israel to the Constantinopolitan Greeks inhabiting Athens, groups 'in-between' have preserved facets of the past which militate against the monochrome depictions of days gone by in officially-sanctioned textbooks. This challenge might not be as potent as liberal optimists would like us to believe. More often than not, divisive conceptions of belonging – paired with rival claims to sacred territories such as Kosovo or Palestine – are engrained in a collective memory transmitted via webs of social practices and institutions. The endless string of traumas accompanying the gradual end of imperial order in the nineteenth and twentieth centuries has been woven into conflicting representations of the past in many countries and regions around the Mediterranean. The noble goal of resolving conflicts through appeals to economic rationality and common developmental goals, as preached by the EU, has more than once run into the rough seas of past grievances, stirred up by the *emotion entrepreneurs* of the day.

It may be that the *memory work* advocated by Marie-Claire Lavabre and Dimitri Nicolaidis, and practised in former Yugoslavia and Israel/Palestine by Brantner's *Women in Black* requires the shaping of what we could call 'trans-memories'. This term refers to shared, if not similar recountings of the stories of the frontiers themselves which have long contained and fostered conflict around this Sea. One of the striking insights to emerge from many of the chapters here is that actors on the ground tend not to ask for recognition (of their or others' suffering, alternative belongings, differences) for its own sake, lest it be instrumentalized by officialdom. Rather we are introduced in many instances to the precarious and faltering pursuit of *just memory* in Paul Ricoeur's words, by those seeking to get memory *just right* (not too much, not too little) and running against grand mythmaking and victim-mongering narratives, especially prevalent in the Mediterranean. To 'get it just right' involves first exposing the 'tyranny of oneness' – whether that of the Mediterranean or of the homogenizing constructs of the nation-states that have recently come to encircle it.

In this spirit, this volume's somewhat quixotic mission is to bring to light some of the hybrid identities and experiences that once flourished in the Mediterranean frontiers, and to listen to their echoes in the realities of strife but also coexistence in the Mediterranean today. Such pervasive hybridity can in turn be seen as rooted in the character of the frontiers themselves, in their original shape as it were. This is a character that may prove more resilient than the lines in the sand drawn by various Northern missionaries. While on paper the 1628 agreement between the regencies of Tunis and Algiers, whose story is presented in Ben Slimane's chapter, may have been less durable than its Western European counterpart two decades later, it can indeed be considered metaphorically as a 'Maghrebi Westphalia'. It did partly revise the long-held practice of overlapping and variable sovereignty explicated in the writings of Ibn Khaldun. Still, subjects continued to roam freely through its 'hardening' territorial limits, and the indirect link between territory and authority persisted. This was compounded when these frontier-worlds became subject to the Ottomans' two-layered sovereignty, where the empire served as umpire rather than adjudicator of local boundary disputes.

There is a wider resonance to this story, whereby ill-defined bonds between centre and periphery meant blurred borders that accommodated overlapping claims to authority. If there is no doubt that the rooting of loyalty in particular and abstract territory as part of a community of strangers is of recent import in North Africa, this did not mean that frontiers were altogether alien before the nineteenth century. They were simply more complex and subtle objects and instruments of politics and power. Indeed, this book explores many variants on the theme of borderlands or *marche*s – akin to those of medieval Western Europe or the *atraf* in pre-Ottoman North Africa. In fact, can we not consider Ceuta and Melilla, or the Maghreb as a whole, to be today's echoes of the medieval *thaghr* (front); coastal cities, located at the interface of external threats? The borders that we explore are actually borderlands, spaces separating political entities. Like frontiers of the mind or the imagination, they invoke both potential encounters and fears of the unknown, but in all cases constitute worlds in themselves and not only inter-faces between worlds.

Of course, open-ended or blurred boundaries are not only synonymous with hybridity and indeterminism, and therefore freedom. They are also the reflection and purveyors of power and domination. What we confront is a *praxis* embedded in a belief that border zones can best serve as buffers, or *avant-poste,* between what the pre-1945 Italian empire-builders called *civiltà* and the rest. In the end, advocates of a truly post-colonial, decentred EU might draw inspiration from these older frontier stories and their current incarnations.[15] European constructs of exclusivity and oneness may well have been appropriated widely, from nationhood and homogeneous ethnicity (the very idea of the 'Turk', 'Italian', 'Croat', 'Algerian') to the struggle against porous borders and illegal migration at present. Yet the syncretic imaginary of the empires that once populated the Mediterranean may serve, all caveats duly noted, as a better guide to the crossing of boundaries at the edges of the *liquid continent.*

Structure of the book

Our journey passes through three stages. We set out to explore the historical trajectory from a world of empires – represented by the Ottoman polity or French, British, Spanish and Italian colonialism – to a world parcelled up into nation-states, each equipped with its grand vision of unity, and aims of catching up with the social and economic models of the West. Thus we survey the emergence of states, borders and national identities, paying special attention to the articulation of shared memories, institutionalized and disseminated into diverse and often deeply-divided societies.

In the opening chapter, Kerem Öktem argues that modernity has actually placed the different parts of the Mediterranean on very divergent trajectories. He distinguishes between the experiences of South East Europe, the Middle East and the Maghreb, and links the notion of 'Mediterranean' to a colonial discourse which legitimized the French expansion into North Africa and the *mission civilisatrice.* The Mediterranean is no innocent label nowadays either. Discourses of Mediterranean vocation are now utilized in cases as diverse as Morocco, Israel and Turkey to reinforce symbolic ties with Europe, and escape from their immediate regional environment, which is imagined as backward and beset by conflict and stagnation.

Human communities define their boundaries with reference to the past. In her *tour d'horizon* covering more than 600 years of Maghrebi history, Fatma Ben Slimane places the current disputes over territorial sovereignty in the region within a *longue durée* perspective. While she dismisses the view that the countries in question are inventions of the colonial era, her chapter shows how the meaning of territorial borders changed dramatically over a period of time – from the notion of moveable and porous margins explicated in the work of Ibn Khaldun, to the exclusivist, Westphalian practices of bounded statehood and fixed limits of state authority which congealed during French rule in the ninetieth and twentieth century. Pre-modern practices and identities tying this part of the world together survive in the age of globalization, and challenge the territorial demarcations imposed by (imagined) nation-states.

The nineteenth century encounter with the West was instrumental in establishing notions of Self and Other. Nora Fisher Onar takes us to the opposite corner of the Mediterranean to narrate the Ottoman and Turkish reactions to Western claims of universal modernity during the Tanzimat period and the republican era. This experience challenges the West-Islam binary that underpins the image of the Mediterranean as the focal point of a confrontation or dialogue between cultural or religious blocs. To quote Onar, 'the conventional understanding of Turkey as stuck between two civilizational essences is merely a construction, albeit a near-hegemonic one, rooted in nineteenth-century discourses and their internalization by the Turkish founding elite'.

Nation-states develop various ways of dealing with Western models, but also with imperial predecessors. Fatma Ben Slimane singles out the Moroccan nationalists' rather anachronistic reading of their country's past existence as an empire through the prism of exclusivist territoriality, which is at the root of the Western Sahara problem. For his part, Dimitar Bechev examines the role of empire in national identity repertoires across the Balkans and the Eastern Mediterranean. The evocative image of imperial power is woven into various mythical representations of the nation's past, from resistance and survival under alien rule, to the *mirage* of former glory and territorial expansion. The chapter ends with a word of caution concerning the misuses of the imperial past and paradigm by latter-day liberal critics of nationalism.

The second part of the volume is devoted to the production, political mobilization and contestations of historical memories, clustered around the physical borders of the state and the identity boundaries of the nation. Are dissonant memories capable of challenging historical canons and national grand narratives of conflict and victimhood? Can they even establish the cognitive conditions for what some have called 'de-bordering'?[16] Marie-Claire Lavabre and Dimitri Nicolaidis dissect the various problematiques associated with the study of collective memory, including the political uses of the past, the *travail de mémoire* aimed at righting past wrongs, and sociological enquiry into 'memory frames'. They apply theoretical insights to the case of Algeria, still haunted by the traumatic remembrance of the 1954-1962 'War of Liberation', as well as the bloody civil conflict in the 1990s. Fieldwork interviews in the city of Miliana near Algiers reconstruct the way personal memories of the colonial and post-independence eras interact with the stale version of the nation's history propagated by the authorities.

Bojan Baskar takes us through the memory of Italy's troubled relations with the Slavs of the Eastern Adriatic since the *Risorgimento*, culminating in the failed attempt at creating a littoral empire during the Mussolini decades. With him, we explore the modes through which the boundary between Italy and its eastern neighbours were imagined as one between civilization and barbarism, and how this in turn led to a strange mixed legacy of Italian victimhood and amnesia. Baskar takes a critical look at the present-day commemorations of the Italians' exodus from Istria and Dalmatia at the end of the Second World War. Rather than fostering reconciliation and mutual acknowledgment of past suffering, this initiative has rehabilitated antiquated stereotypes and tainted Italy's relations with both Slovenia and Croatia.

Part II ends with a chapter by Franziska Brantner reflecting on issues of memory and conflict from a gender perspective, with reference to the cases of Kosovo and Israel/Palestine. She studies the memory activism of civic groups such as *Women in Black* in former Yugoslavia or *Zochrot* in Israel. These groups challenge the hegemonic constructions – needless to say forged by males – of conflict, violence, belonging and otherness. While the political impact of these contestations remains limited, they do open up critical avenues and shift our perspective on the common trope that the Mediterranean can only be understood through conflicts and traumatic memories that reach far into the past and haunt the present.

The last part of the volume shifts the analytical lens to the question of how borders and boundaries shape human life-worlds today, including through the crossing of some of the frontiers described in Part I. Raffaella A. Del Sarto argues that the North African and Middle Eastern littoral is turning into the borderlands or marches of the (quasi-)imperial construct that is the EU. Rather than remaining on the 'outside', they are increasingly drawn into the Union's system of governance, and their elites are co-opted in exchange for privileged access to the European core's material and symbolic resources. The somewhat sad realization is that rather than being the centre of its own world, as the architects of the Union for the Mediterranean would like us to believe, the Mediterranean thus resembles a periphery or a buffer zone for Europe.

No one knows this better than the immigrants from Sub-Saharan Africa who are desperately trying to enter the EU. Henk Driessen tells the story of Ceuta and Melilla, the two Spanish enclaves nestled on Morocco's fringes. This 'Euro-African' edge constitutes a frontier that has changed in meaning over time – from a divide between Islam and Catholicism, to a conduit of the civilizing mission in the nineteth century, to a gateway to the coveted prosperity of Western Europe. It is also the basis of a particular frontier society and economy with all its contradictions and tensions.

In a fascinating parallel reality, Cédric Parizot's anthropological survey of the smuggler economy in the Negev adds further empirical depth to the discussion. By hardening territorial divides between once interwoven communities, the Israeli closure policies during the Second Intifada have resulted in an exploitative relationship between the local Bedouin and the illegal labourers trafficked from the West Bank. Practices of border crossing indirectly condoned by the state have blurred the boundaries between the lawful sphere and informal economy, but at the same time have entrenched the polarization of social identities. The frontier, here as elsewhere in the Mediterranean, creates its own universe, as well as reshaping the social worlds around it.

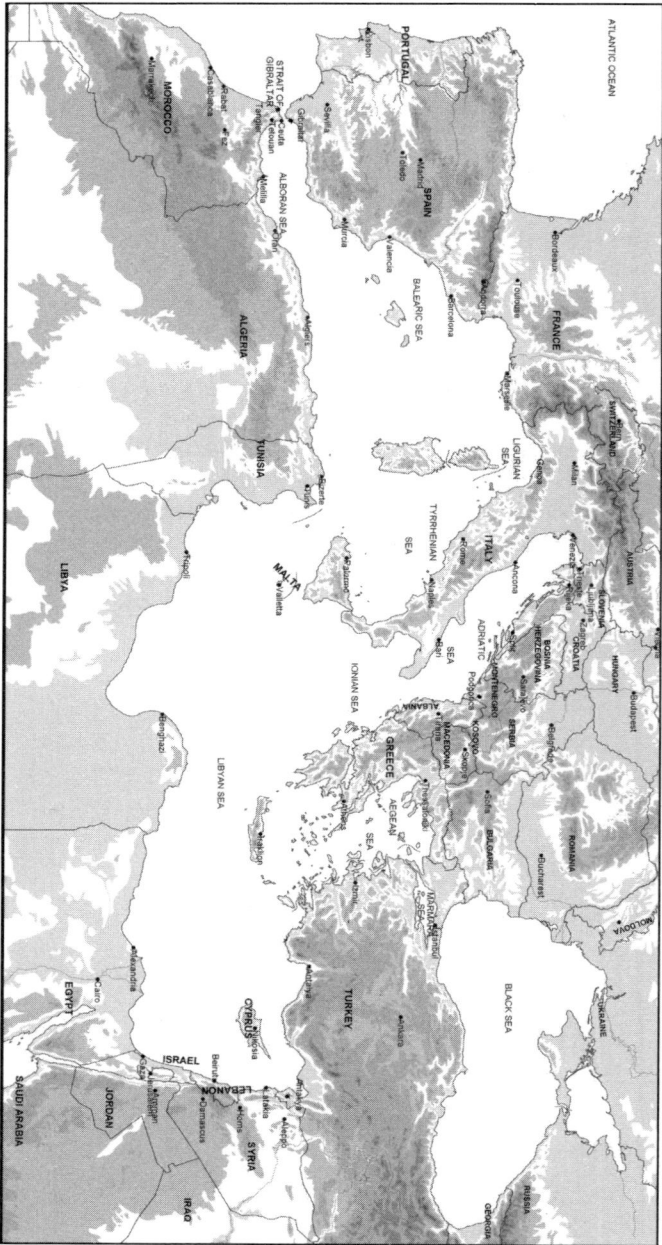

The Mediterranean

Map (c) generated from www.collinsbartholomew.com digital databases, reproduced with kind permission.

PART I:

CONSTRUCTING BORDERS AND MEMORIES

CHAPTER I

THE AMBIVALENT SEA: REGIONALIZING THE MEDITERRANEAN DIFFERENTLY

KEREM ÖKTEM

Among the many public addresses French presidential candidate Nicholas Sarkozy delivered before his election in May 2007, his *Discours de Toulon* stands out as a passionate plea for the future of 'the' Mediterranean. Synthesizing nineteenth century colonial visions of a Franco-Roman Sea with a neo-Gaullist quest for a revived role for France in the world, Sarkozy touched on issues ranging from the assumed primeval unity and common culture of the people of the Mediterranean basin to Turkey's ostensibly non-European identity. Equalizing, in one stroke, the rather different experience of colonialism shared by the *colons* and the colonized, he praised the contribution of 'hardworking' and 'well-intentioned' French settlers in North Africa – the *Pieds-Noirs* – and their Algerian collaborators. The latter, as he conceded regretfully, had been denied due respect when they were expelled to France after independence. He concluded with the enigmatic claim that Europe's future lies on its southern shores, and that France '[would] put the Mediterranean on course to reunification after twelve centuries of division and strife'.[1]

Sarkozy's ill-fated initiative for a Mediterranean Union did not survive his election as President and eventually dissipated into a 'Union of Projects for the Mediterranean' and eventually into a 'Union for the Mediterranean'.[2] This Franco-centric vision of the Mediterranean, however, provides a powerful metaphor reflecting the northern gaze towards the southern rim. Not that these narratives are limited to the north or to the realm of high politics: Turkish, Israeli and Maghrebi versions of Mediterraneanist discourses abound, albeit articulated in social fields other than diplomacy. Their exponents, whom we will encounter in this chapter, are united, above all, by their lack of interest in discussions at the level of ontology. Rather than asking whether a Mediterranean region of primeval unity indeed exists, or whether history might have torn the Mediterranean space apart, they postulate its existence as an *a priori* condition. Similarly, they are not interested in the fragmentations and conflicts of the Mediterranean space, and even less so in the power relations that these discourses promote or hide. For one reason or another, they like the idea of an empty and amenable container that can be filled – according to taste – with their strategic, political, cultural and economic agendas.

Nevertheless, is there a case for a spatial perspective which accommodates notions of unity and fragmentation and at the same time shows interest and awareness of history and geography? One that recognizes the competition between political and cultural regimes of unity, discards the fixation on Rome, and, above all, re-establishes the importance of the Ottoman seascape, so conspicuously absent in Sarkozy's *Discours*? There are good reasons to answer these questions in the affirmative: parts of the Mediterranean world remained under the loose suzerainty of three – at least partly – maritime empires for two millennia, from the Roman Empire and Byzantium to the Ottoman Empire.[3] Moreover, the House of Osman, especially in its founding phase, saw itself as rightful heir to the universal mission of Rome and the institutions of Byzantium, and remained a unifying political structure in the eastern and southern rim for more than four centuries.[4]

This chapter maps the discursive and historical moments that have constructed the Mediterranean both in the realm of symbols, emotions and memory and in the field of international and regional politics, both in space and in time. It looks at three discourses that construct the meaning of the Mediterranean. Located in the realm of imperial politics, historical scholarship and regional identity politics, these discourses partly overlap, and partly compete over conflicting imperial claims to the Mediterranean. It pays special attention to South East Europe and Turkey as an often neglected subregion in the Mediterranean that is nevertheless crucial for the understanding of both division and connectivity in the Mediterranean space.

The chapter then turns to the more recent historical ruptures – I will call them 'regionalizing moments'- that shaped the economic, political, cultural and religious patterns of fragmentation and interaction in today's Mediterranean world. The following foray into the long nineteenth and the short twentieth century suggests that instead of unity and sameness in the Mediterranean, the region was constituted in a succession of four regionalizing moments, ranging from the post-imperial (i.e. Ottoman and Habsburg) to the European (post-Second World War), from the post-colonial to the post-communist. It was during these moments that the continuum of Ottoman maritime spaces dissipated. Regional subsystems emerged with distinct historical trajectories set in motion by events such as Napoleon Bonaparte's imperial *expédition d'Égypte* in 1798 or the emergence of autonomous Serbia and independent Greece in the 1830s. The first event established the North-South division between colonizer and colonized, while the latter prompted the Balkan's albeit gradual and incomplete integration into the European state system and Turkey's torn position in the European borderlands.

Even if the presence of trans-maritime networks vindicated notions of historical and cultural connectivity, and cosmopolitan port societies survived, they were too feeble to subvert the overpowering drive towards homogenization within nation-states, which drew borders across pre-existing regions. The demise of the Ottoman Empire, the emergence of modern nation-states and mandate regimes, and the collapse of maritime economies destroyed the material basis of trans-Mediterranean linkages.

Today, the circum-Mediterranean would be best described as engendering three distinct subsystems: The bi-coastal Western Mediterranean region linking France, Spain and Italy with the Maghreb, South East Europe, and the southern rim countries in the Levante. South East Europe is moving towards EU membership, the Western Mediterranean remains part of a system of economic and human links centred on France, and Turkey is a hinge country torn between European integration, isolationism and regional power politics in the Middle East and the Caucasus. None of these processes seems to put the Mediterranean lands back on the 'course of reunification'. So, is the discussion really only about discourse and colonial constructions of space? Does the 'appeal to unity' obfuscate other political agendas and suggest equality where in fact there is only asymmetry and dependence?

Spaces of empire, scholarship and identity:
Discursive constructions of the Mediterranean

The nineteenth-century English writer Alexander William Kinglake begins his travelogue on the Ottoman Empire at its western border. There, he reminisces about the stark contrast between Europe and the East: 'I had come, as it were, to the end of this wheel-going Europe, and now my eyes would see the splendour and havoc of the East.' In the town he had encountered before the frontier, 'the scenes and the sounds of familiar life; the din of a busy world still vexed and cheered [him]; the unveiled faces of women still shone in the light of day.' However, whenever he chose to look southward, he 'saw the Ottoman's fortress — austere, and darkly impending high over the vale.'[5] Kinglake re-instated the theme of the seminal divide between the Roman Christian *Orbis terrarum* and the *Dar al-sulh*, the abode of the Pax Islamica. Yet, when he made this observation in 1834, he was not travelling from the territory of the nascent Greek state to the Ottoman lands further north. His final stop before the 'splendour and havoc of the East' was present-day Vojvodina, then part of Habsburg-held Hungary. The Ottoman fortress, which he depicted atmospherically in colours of gloom and foreboding, was not in 'Asia', but in Belgrade.

Regional assignations like South East Europe, the Balkans, the Mediterranean or the Middle East are first and foremost social-spatial constructions suffused with discourses of power. We will look at three interrelated discursive arrangements in particular: the Mediterranean as an imperial regionalizing notion, as a heuristic concept in the hands of scholars,[6] and as an escapist discourse of *Ersatz* space.

The Mediterranean as imperial space

World regions were imagined and constructed by European geographers and colonial administrators. They overwrote 'the classical geographical distinction between continents, countries and landscapes with large, abstract spaces (Grossräume) which powerful actors such as 'empires', 'civilizations' or 'races' were bound to invest with meaning, histories and functions.'[7] A prime example was the Ottoman Empire: with its gradual demise, the so-called Eastern Question began to shape the politics of most of the empire in the nineteenth century. The assumption of the time was that once the Ottoman state disappeared, 'Europe would have to take its place'.[8] In place of the empire, yet surpassing it, a new 'Middle East' would emerge that meant not only

> [...] Egypt, Israel, Iran, Turkey and the Arab states of Asia, but also Soviet Central Asia and Afghanistan: the entire arena in which Britain, from the Napoleonic Wars onwards, fought to shield the road to India from the onslaughts first of France and then Russia...[9]

Around the same time, the term 'Near East' entered the debate, initially with David Hogarth's 'Nearer East', exclusively justified with reference to archaeology. This area comprised the lands bordering the eastern Mediterranean together with those on the Persian Gulf, hence including Greece,

the Balkan Peninsula, Asia Minor, Syria, Egypt, Arabia and Persia.[10] Arnold
J. Toynbee popularized the more functionally-minded 'Near East', which,
since the Ottoman demise, applied only to 'Turkey in Europe', i.e. former
Ottoman possessions on the European continent proper, while it excluded 'Turkey in Asia'.[11] British imperial politics positioned Asia Minor, i.e.
roughly today's Turkey, within the Middle East, at least until the establishment of the Turkish republic in the 1920s, when it fell off the radar of
world politics and was cut off from most of its neighbourhood for the
following three decades.

   Unlike in Britain, where the Mediterranean was not the political region
of choice, France's colonization of the Maghreb was based on a legitimizing discourse that projected itself onto the entire circum-Mediterranean,
even if it only spanned its own Mediterranean coasts and the southern rim
territories of Tunisia, Morocco and Algeria. The French colonial project
in Algeria was advanced by Christian proselytism on the one hand and the
secular *mission civilisatrice* on the other,[12] which in itself became a legitimizing
and regionalizing discourse based on the idea of France's role as a force of
enlightenment, by the grace of Rome. The colonial state proclaimed 'itself
as the rightful guardian of the true Latin Mediterranean unit, in opposition to the political rule imposed by the Ottoman Empire, which arguably
drew on central Asian and Arabian modes of social organization.'[13] Thereby
serving the additional goal of de-legitimizing Ottoman imperial rule in the
region, the colonial narrative of the Mediterranean also inscribed the binary opposition of Muslim/Ottoman vs. Roman/French into its policy of
divide and rule. Berber tribes were preferentially treated, based on ostensibly non-Oriental features, and given a state of potential Europeans, a label
vigorously withheld from Arab city dwellers.[14]

   While France clung on to its 'Mediterranean Empire' in the Maghreb
well into the 1950s, parts of the southern Mediterranean and the Adriatic
were targets of the imperial aspirations of Fascist Italy, which was intent on
reviving the idea of an Italian *Mare Nostrum*,[15] Despite these imperial visions
and claims, however, neither country came close to dominating the entirety
of the Mediterranean in the interwar years, nor during the Second World
War. Compared to the Middle East, a political region *par excellence*, located at
the core of the imperial domination of much of the Arab world, Asia and
Africa, the Mediterranean never took on a comparably politicized meaning.
In other words, the Middle East is ontologically linked to the experience of
imperial domination, while the Mediterranean preceded modern colonialism, even if French and Italian imperialists attempted to impose their rule
in their areas of influence.

Yet, even though the Mediterranean has not been a political concept since the fall of Rome until very recently – indeed not before the southern enlargements of the European Community in the 1980s – it did exist beyond its use as a device for colonial domination. It was a scholarly construct for comparative history, anthropological research and intellectual debate.

The Mediterranean as a scholarly space

As scholarly construct, the circum-Mediterranean has been imagined both as historical and cultural space. Before focusing on the Mediterranean region, I would like to explore briefly the German concept of *Geschichtsregion*, as applied to the case of South East Europe. This, as I will argue later, is one of the areas in the Mediterranean with a credible claim to continuity.

In its most inclusive form, a historical region spans the three regionalizing spheres of politics, intellectual discourse and academic research,[16] and combines geographical, political and cultural criteria in different measures.[17] South East Europe, Holm Sundhaussen suggests, can look back on an almost seamless experience of Byzantine-Orthodox and Ottoman-Muslim heritage spanning from the fourth to the nineteenth century. Only in the Balkans did these two legacies mutually reinforce each other to the point of creating a syncretism that distinguishes it from neighbouring regions.[18] Sundhaussen's Balkans have been criticized for a certain degree of historical determinism, yet his spatial nomenclature does underline the need for identifiable structures and networks when making the case for a historical region, whether in scholarly terms or in terms of imperial power politics. A slightly more relativist approach would conceive of a historical region as an oscillating, unfixed space that nevertheless has some degree of uniformity and internal interaction, distinguishing it from other world regions.[19]

Can we find this degree of uniformity and interaction in the entirety of the circum-Mediterranean? Fernand Braudel's total history of the *Mediterranée* does indeed conceptualize the territories surrounding the sea as a 'human unit' with collective destinies, and it would hence qualify as a historical region.[20] Braudel distinguishes between the different time scales of the *longue durée*, *conjuncture* and *événement*, corresponding respectively to the geographical scale of relations between the environment and people, social history and the history of events.[21] The *longue durée* aspect of his work is probably the most compelling, investigating the relations of people with the environment – plains, mountains, islands, coasts and towns – and focusing on 'coastal societies' with seas, ports and coasts as spaces of economic and cultural interaction reaching into the hinterlands. This is also where some faint 'unity of the Mediterranean' may be detected. Yet even in terms of geography and climate, unity was never a given: 'in ancient geographical thought, [the Mediterranean] straddled several klimata, east-west climatic zones; there was little or no conception of a common Mediterranean environment; no place for a region of the kind that Europeans mostly took for granted from the late twentieth century'.[22]

One of the tensions that run through his epic work is the conflict between the claim to Mediterranean unity, and the very fact of the region's political and religious division ever since the Islamic conquest of the sixth century. In fact, this tension, originating in earlier work by the medievalist Henri Pirenne,[23] yet prevalent also in Braudel's work, pervades most debates on the Mediterranean:

> [...] Braudel's Mediterranean is both single and double. Essentially one, it is nonetheless split between its northern and southern shores ... Other observers, from the fourteenth century Tunisian historiographer ... Ibn Khaldun to the late twentieth century 1995 Barcelona Declaration, have also described the Mediterranean as needing to be one harmonious whole, though being in fact split into two contesting halves.[24]

In the absence of a coherent political/imperial project, and beyond the very *longue durée* of the Braudelian seascapes and mountains, to what extent does the Mediterranean still make sense as a historical region, a meaningful regional unit for analysis or an insightful subject for comparative analysis?

The most radical responses to this question came in the 1980s from anthropologists and ethnographers. Criticizing the trend that conceptualizes 'the Mediterranean as a single, more or less homogenous entity', Michael Herzfeld scolded the 'circular logic' that would take for granted a 'Mediterranean culture' and then misunderstand prevalent notions of 'honour and shame' as proof of that very cultural unity.[25] Herzfeld understood this 'Mediterraneanism', a critical term inspired by Edward Said's *Orientalism*, as an 'excuse for illegitimate political ends – for asserting the simple undifferentiated unity, backwardness, environmental exhaustion or whatever of circum-Mediterranean societies as a justification of northerners' political, economic or cultural superiority or domination'.[26] Twenty years later, Herzfeld was stunned to find that 'in an age in which just about every other category has been deconstructed, or at least has self-destructed, "the" Mediterranean has shown a remarkable tenacity in the face of a barrage of critiques'.[27]

The Mediterranean as 'Ersatz' Europe

Indeed, Mediterraneanism has not been confined to academic debate. On the level of intellectual discourse, popular culture and branding, the Mediterranean has held some appeal for identity debates in Israel and Turkey, and to a certain extent in the Maghreb. The former two have developed their own, albeit diverging, versions of Mediterraneanism (*Akdenizlilik* and *Yam Tikhoniut*) as alternatives to the less desirable links with the Middle East as a 'non-western space ... ruled or confined by the west'.[28] Initially an elitist concept for a compromise between Israel's perceived demographic and cultural origins in Europe and its geographical location in the Levant, *Yam Tikhoniout* turned into a cultural metaphor for the need of a 'watered down version of oriental identity'[29] with common cultural points of reference to something beyond the immediate neighbourhood.[30] In the academic context, the emphasis on the Mediterranean de-exoticizes Israel and moves it closer, at least in mental maps and in self-imagery, to the European shores.[31]

The Israeli desire to belong to a political and cultural world other than the one to which it is bound by geography resonates with the Turkish *Akdenizlilik*. Even though *Akdenizlilik* has its intellectual roots in a literary movement of the 1950s and 1960s,[32] its current reincarnation sports mostly pop-cultural and commercial variants. The former is a 'cultural identity that middle and upper-middle class "modern" Turks revert to in order to prove that they are western and European rather than Middle Eastern, Muslim or Asian'.[33] This Mediterranean consists of Greece, Italy and Spain and implicitly ignores the southern shores and the Arab world.[34] The commercial strand of Turkish Mediterraneanism refers to the branding and PR exercises of the tourist industry and the Turkish Foreign Ministry, which seeks to promote Turkey as a Mediterranean – that is less Oriental and more European – destination.[35]

In the Maghreb, the discourse of Mediterraneanism is utilized mostly by states to distinguish themselves from their Arab neighbours. Despite Pan-Arab and Pan-Islamic rhetoric, Silverstein argues, the Maghreb Arab Union serves roughly the same goal.[36] Probably as interesting is the fact that Berber associations, as well as *beurs* (immigrants of Maghrebi origin in France) and even *Pieds-Noirs* (European settlers born in Algeria) now re-appropriate the colonial discourse of the Mediterranean in a post-colonial setting.

Yet all these concepts of Mediterraneanism appear to be expressions not so much of feeling part of a 'multi-ethnic space with common cultural points of reference'[37] but of the desire to belong somewhere else, i.e. to Europe, or to re-imagine something which is lost, like French Algeria. Moving from the discursive to the historical level of analysis, we will now ask how the Mediterranean has come about in the nineteenth and twentieth centuries.

Regionalizing moments in the Mediterranean

If one were to imagine the Mediterranean space as a Palimpsest, as the Catalan novelist Juan Goytisolo artfully did for the imperial capital Istanbul,[38] the many layers of history, culture, commerce, domination and resistance would appear too dense to allow for a sober disentanglement of all these overwritten pages. Acknowledging the historical depth of connections in the Mediterranean, yet questioning the immediate relevance of distant histories, this section retrieves only the uppermost layers of the manuscript in the late nineteenth and twentieth centuries. It identifies four regionalizing moments and a number of regionalizing structures, with reference to Stefan Troebst's 'regionalizing political concept'.[39] The regionalizing moments – post-imperial, European, post-colonial and post-communist – all occurred in the short span of a century, and yet had a profound centripetal effect, destroying the remnants of the last Mediterranean empire and diminishing the importance of the sea as a space of exchange. Setting the riparian states on distinct trajectories towards modernity and bringing to the fore divisions between the colonized and the colonizer, but also within various peripheries such as the Balkans and Turkey, these forces were moderated but not really subverted by the structures of Mediterranean connectivity. These included trans-national networks operated by seafaring communities, remnants of the relatively free mobility within the erstwhile Ottoman space, as well as cross-border minorities resulting from the often arbitrary limits of new nation-states.

The post-imperial moment

The post-imperial moment occurred in different places at different times, and with different outcomes through much of the nineteenth and early twentieth century. Yet, by 1915 and after the end of the First World War, the old empires that had ruled large chunks of the southern and eastern Mediterranean in one way or another, the Habsburgs and the Ottomans, had all but disappeared. The millennial capital city Istanbul was under allied occupation.[40] The countries of the Mediterranean were either colonized or under mandate governance. Others had achieved independent statehood and sovereignty thanks to, or in spite of great power politics.

Europe's 'imperial encounter with Islam'[41] in the Mediterranean was one of gradual economic and political penetration – mainly by Britain and

France, but also Spain and, in a brief yet violent interlude, by Italy.[42] In Egypt, and after Napoleon's short but unprecedented expedition to Egypt, Britain was firmly established as imperial overlord from 1882 on. In the Maghreb, since the late nineteenth century, French emissaries settled French (and often Italian, Spanish, Corsican, Catalan etc.) *colons* even in protectorates like Tunisia or Morocco, which retained a degree of formal independence.[43] Nevertheless, French settler colonialism was at its most destructive and brutal in Algeria, –all talk of a *mission civilisatrice* apart. Algeria's provinces were incorporated into the French state as early as the mid-nineteenth century.[44]

Until 1915, the nominal presence of the Ottoman Empire in the Levant mitigated the humiliation of direct colonial domination experienced elsewhere. This façade of relative independence, however, broke down with the Ottoman defeat in the First World War, and with the establishment of mandate states in Syria, Iraq, Lebanon, Transjordan and Palestine. Britain and French imperial administrations made further inroads into what was by then called the Middle East. Unlike in the Maghreb, however, the societies in the Levant were not subjected to settler colonialism. The sole significant exception was the mandate of Palestine, which became the target of a specific late nineteenth century movement of nationalist revivalism, carried forth through settler colonies. Despite its initial reluctance, Britain confirmed the idea of a Jewish homeland in Palestine with the Balfour declaration.[45] The case of Palestine/Israel as a settler colony *and* a nation state with a secular ideology, homogenized by a concerted campaign of ethnic cleansing in its territories, is an echo of earlier waves of the demographic reshuffling in the Balkans and Turkey. It does, however, remain an anomaly in the colonial/post-colonial southern rim of the Mediterranean.[46] It is only in Palestine/Israel that an entire architectural, economic and cultural web of meanings, institutions and communities belonging to a deported population has been destroyed, entire landscapes buried and superimposed with another structure, that of modern Israel.[47]

On the southern shores of the Mediterranean, in 'Turkey in Asia', the defining post-Ottoman moment was that of European imperialism, with arbitrary borders and mandate states being imposed on reluctant locals in the east, as well as dispossession of native populations enforced in Palestine and to varying degrees in the Maghreb countries. The north-eastern shores, however, witnessed a very different transformation: in the Balkans, new nation-states had been established on the territories of 'Turkey in Europe' as early as the 1830s, whereas the nascent Turkish nationalist government would reach this goal only in the 1920s. It first had to assert its independence against British, French and Italian colonial advances, in order to then follow a comparable course of state and nation-building. This was arguably conducted in an even more coercive manner than it was in Turkey's Balkan neighbours.

'Turkey in Europe', the Ottoman provinces west of the capital, witnessed a long and tortuous process of peasant revolts, nationalist mobilizations, and popular uprisings against the Ottoman overlords. These gradually developed into national liberation movements and eventually into states. According to Misha Glenny, the Serbian Uprising of 1804 in the *Pashalik* of Belgrade 'marked the beginning of modern history on the Balkan peninsula'.[48] Intellectuals of the Balkan enlightenment, intent on 'replacing the old Orthodox conception of Christian time with a new secular understanding of time as national history',[49] prepared the ground for the struggles for ethnically and territorially demarcated nation-states. Greece gained independence in 1830, Romania and Serbia followed suit in the second half of the century, paving the way for the independence of Bulgaria, autonomous since 1878, and Albania. By 1915, the 'Eastern Question', the international management of the 'unpredictable process of Ottoman decline and national insurgence'[50] had largely been concluded. Christian kings, related to European royalty, were now residing over new states, marking the region's integration into the European state system.[51]

The national movements in the Balkans had indeed captured the imagination of the educated urban elites in Belgrade, Bucharest, Sofia, and elsewhere. With the proliferation of new educational institutions and political organization, news of their example reached even the more distant peasant populations. Nevertheless, the attitude of the European great powers was crucial for the emergence and survival of the new states. Greece's independence in 1830 would not have been possible without outside intervention.[52] It is here that the experience of the post-imperial moment in South East Europe differs significantly from its equivalent in the southern rim of the Mediterranean: while the empire's Arab provinces proceeded from Ottoman imperial domination to rule by French and British mandatory powers, South East European polities embarked on the – albeit painful – process of state and nation building. Even if many a western observer was full of contempt for what was often perceived as backward Balkan politics, still influenced by the attitudes and costumes of their 'Asiatic' overlords,[53] European powers more often than not supported the drive to emancipation, no matter whether this was due to the genuine belief that these countries were 'European' by default or culture, or because of efforts to thwart Russia's ambitions vis-à-vis the Ottomans' territorial possessions.

If, with the collapse of the Ottoman Empire, the Middle East was subjected to a new form of alien domination, which proved to be more disruptive and traumatic than the four centuries of Ottoman rule before it, the Balkans instead headed towards self-determination and statehood. To be sure, state formation and nation building in South East Europe was not less traumatic. This trauma, however, resulted not so much from foreign rule, but from policies of the 'unmixing of people' – through forced migration or cultural policies of toponymic codification and language standardization – and from the war between the new nation-states in search of 'unredeemed' territories.

Indeed, most nation-states are built on processes of homogenization, blurring the dividing lines between *demos* and *ethnos*, and often privileging the latter over the former.[54] The late nineteenth and early twentieth century Balkans were very much a stage for interrelated episodes of inter-group massacre and forced displacement. These began with the Muslim exodus from nascent Greece and Serbia, and culminated in the destruction of the empire's Armenians in 1915[55] and the forced population exchange across the Aegean in 1923.

The waves of forced migrations and ethnic cleansing were raging back and forth from the Balkans to Asia Minor throughout much of the nineteenth century. By the time of the collapse of the Ottoman Empire and the establishment of the Turkish Republic, much of South East Europe had become more homogenous in ethnic and religious terms. Initially, 'cities like Bosna Seraj [Sarajevo] … and Sofia were heavily Islamic and Turkish-speaking islands of imperial governance in a mostly Christian sea.[56] Starting from the late 1870s, Sofia was cleansed of almost all vestiges of Ottoman culture and architecture, while the empire's legacy remained, yet became progressively marginalized in Sarajevo, ruled from 1878 by the Habsburgs who had a civilizing mission of their own. In Greece, the Muslim flight to the Ottoman rump state took on epic proportions after the First Balkan Wars in 1912-1913, when large parts of Ottoman Macedonia including Salonica fell to the Kingdom of Greece, quickly losing its cosmopolitan demography and its Jewish-dominated feel. Whatever had survived of the old world of the Ottoman Empire was thoroughly destroyed with the great fire in August 1917, and replaced, thanks to state-planned reconstruction efforts, with a brand-new city that reconnected to an imagined Hellenic and Byzantine past.[57]

While the post-Ottoman Yugoslav territories maintained a degree of ethnic and religious diversity, Greece and Turkey were entangled in a war and a forced population exchange. One and a half million Orthodox subjects of the Sultan were expelled to Greece, while up to 800,000 Muslims were evacuated to Turkey. This event forged Greece and Turkey as modern and largely homogenized nation-states.[58]

During the post-imperial moment, the remaining Ottoman territories' position in the 'Islamo-European borderlands'[59] was ambiguous, despite Ottoman collapse, catastrophic territorial loss and demographic meltdown. As the hinge between imperial domination by mandate politics in the East and integration into the European state system in the West, the rump Ottoman state was subjected to Franco-British and Italian plans for the partition of its territories. The 1916 Sykes-Picot Agreement created the basis for the mandate system in the Levant through 'European deceit over pledges made to the Arabs during the war'.[60] The agreement would have divided Anatolia between British, French and Italian mandates. It would have provided for a Greek territory in the eastern Aegean and Kurdish and Armenian states in the Southeast. After the end of the Great War, successive treaties and conferences – San Remo, Sèvres – attempted to divide the spoils of the Ottoman territories between the great powers. However, in the meantime, the Turkish nationalist movement was evolving into a fully fledged parliamentary government and a standing army, galvanized into action by the Greek occupation of Smyrna in March 1921.[61]

The victory of the nationalist forces, the sack and fire of Izmir, and the population exchange between Turkey and Greece were followed by the proclamation of the Turkish Republic and the abrogation of the Caliphate. This progression created modern Turkey's genetic code of ambivalent obsession and contested integration with Europe. Turkey was spared European imperial domination, yet shaped by the waves of forced deportation and homogenizing policies that turned South East Europe into a continuum of nation-states. It turned on itself in an often reckless and violent project of social and demographic engineering to create – ultimately unsuccessfully – a homogenously Turkish and Muslim, yet formally secular nation-state.

More regionalizing moments: European, post-colonial and post-communist

The post-Ottoman moment had created new spaces of economic, political and cultural interaction that discontinued the maritime bonds criss-crossing the eastern and southern Mediterranean seaports and their hinterlands under Ottoman suzerainty.[62] Yet, more moments of 'disengagement' from a common maritime space were to come after the Second World War and yet again in the 1990s with the fall of communism. This further eroded interaction on a Mediterranean scale, and in its place, created sub-regional systems defined either by internal cooperation or post-colonial domination.

The decades following the end of Second World War saw the gradual emergence of liberal democratic polities and welfare state systems[63] on the Western shores, and an increasing pace of European integration. Spain, the Mediterranean corner of Europe closest to the southern rim countries, also remained the least democratic until the death of its dictator General Franco in 1975.[64] Most of South East Europe came under communist rule and embarked upon concerted programmes of economic development, radically transforming largely agrarian communities into urban-based industrial societies.

In the southern rim, the 1940s marked the end of mandate rule in the Levant, and the discontinuation of formal foreign domination by Italy in Libya, while France stayed on in its North African protectorates until the 1950s. The ensuing nation building projects were mostly of a socialist-statist and authoritarian nature, with differing degrees of attachment to the Pan-Arabist ideals represented by the Free Officers and the Egyptian President Gamal Abdel Nasser. Yet, even the traditional regimes of Morocco and Jordan and cosmopolitan Lebanon were drawn into the maelstrom of Middle Eastern politics with the *Nakba*, the defeat by Israel of invading Arab armies and the ensuing forced deportation of Palestinians in 1948. Indeed this was the 'defining moment' of the modern Middle East[65] and of political identities in the Arab world. None of the political and ideological responses to the Arab trauma of 1948 – Arab Nationalism, nationalism in one state or political Islam – had a Mediterranean orientation, and none of them succeeded in creating a transnational Arab space or national economies that would overcome economic and cultural dependence on their former metropoles. The economic opening of the 1980s and 1990s, and the democratizing discourses employed by Arab leaders cannot conceal that this process has been a 'liberalization against democracy', empowering 'corporate-authoritarian' structures,[66] rather than subverting coercive regimes and strengthening liberal forces.

Europe's post-communist moment on the Adriatic and Black Sea coasts,[67] came with the dismemberment of Yugoslavia, and a new wave of ethnic cleansing and deportations, even genocide in Bosnia. Yet, the 'Balkan Vortex'[68] gave way to EU engagement, fragile post-war arrangements and gradual integration into European structures, symbolized by Bulgaria and Romania's entry into the Union in 2007. South East Europe as a political region re-emerged with Greece playing an increasingly important role as an economic powerhouse. Turkey, with a burgeoning, if still poor economy and a flourishing, if incomplete democracy, appeared as a natural extension of the EU's expansion to the Balkans. However, despite the 2005 start of membership negotiations, Turkey remains at a crossroads when it comes to its European vocation.

The regionalizing moments – post-Imperial, European, post-colonial and post-communist – have created new regional sub-systems, destroyed cosmopolitan port societies and re-oriented centralizing economies from the harbour cities to the hinterlands. The intricate web of relations, especially within the Ottoman seascape, did not survive the age of nation-states, colonialism and European imperialism. Or, did it?

Linkages and connectivity:
Trans-national networks of interaction

Connections in the Ottoman Mediterranean and beyond were infinite, in terms of economic interactions, cultures and communities. Armenians, Greeks and Jews, all Ottoman subjects, together with Levantine merchants and traders, were the diasporic economic backbone of eastern and southern Mediterranean port cities and their hinterlands. Their churches and synagogues remain, yet the communities have mostly been 'repatriated', to Greece after nationalization in Egypt, and to Israel after the declaration of the State of Israel in 1948. A group that has been able to retain a connecting function throughout the region are the Armenians. Even though some of their communities in the Mediterranean go back to the tenth century and Byzantine rule, today they are dominated by the families of the survivors of the *Medz Yeghern*, the Great Catastrophe of 1915. Armenian communities have woven networks of memory, identity and commerce criss-crossing the eastern and western shores, spanning from Bulgaria, Greece, Turkey, Cyprus, Syria, Lebanon, Palestine to Egypt.[69] Whether in the Armenian quarter of Halep or in the Beirut suburb of Bourj Hammoud, the remnants of the Ottoman millet system with its modus operandi of toleration based on separation is still very much in place, creating islands of Armenian identity which is, ironically, complemented by the use of Turkish as a language of everyday life. At the core of these cultural networks, however, appears to be the contested and differential longing for an imagined or remembered homeland – expressed, most visibly in quarters named after cities in Turkey, like Nor (New) Adana, Nor Marash, Nor Sis – and the struggle to come to terms with the genocide, rather than an engagement with the Mediterranean and its host societies *per se*.[70]

Jewish communities, once present on all shores of the Mediterranean, were decimated after the Ottoman collapse, destroyed in the Second

World War, and all but wiped out with the establishment of Israel in 1948. Sephardic Jewry, displaced from its homeland in the Iberian peninsula with the fall of Granada and the *reconquista* in 1492 and dispersed from the North African shores to the Ottoman Empire, France and Italy, had ceased to exist after 1948, even though most Jews from former Ottoman lands were more than reluctant to migrate to Israel.[71]

While the diasporic nature of Jewish communities is generally acknowledged, Islam is more often regarded as 'the great "other"', *le grand contraire*, the opposite: the definer of what Europe was not[72] and hence seen as augmenting rather than traversing the Mediterranean divide. Yet, nothing could be further from the truth: Islamic networks of people and institutions interfused the circum-Mediterranean, thanks largely to the fact that the Ottoman imperial order was, above all, maintained by viziers, military men and religious leaders from the Balkans. H. T. Norris, in his momentous *Islam in the Balkans*,[73] departs from the dominant view prevalent in Ottoman studies that sees Balkan Islam as a territorial extension of the empire, mediated and negotiated through the capital and its institutions. Instead, he makes the case for a Balkan-based 'European Islam' that established unmediated ties with the Arab world. Even if it would be fair to say that 'Anatolian' and high Ottoman influences in art, architecture and religious practice shaped the Balkan world to a greater extent than did the direct contact between the Adriatic and the Maghreb, the latter is nevertheless relevant for the discussion of the Mediterranean as a space of connectivity.

Two episodes of interaction stand out: firstly, the sixteenth century conquest of Algeria and Tunis brought over large contingents of Janissaries and members of the *Bektashi* Sufi-order from Albania and Bosnia. They created, through intermarriage, a new class called *Kul-Oughlu* (Kuloğlu, sons of slaves, i.e. Janissaries), 'whose familial memories of Anatolian, Bosnian and Albanian ancestry and wider Balkan tribal connections were preserved and cherished, and have continued to be down to the present in the major cities of Algeria and Tunisia'.[74] The second, more recent episode is the nineteenth century emergence of Egypt as a semi-independent state. This was the achievement of the outstanding Ottoman commander, known to the world and in Egypt as Muhammad Ali, and to the Ottomans as *Kavalalı Mehmed Ali Pasha* (Mehmed Ali Pasha from Kavala). During his rule as Ottoman viceroy and de-facto ruler of Egypt, Albanian and Turkish became court languages and two *tekkes*, convents of the Bektashi order, were established. Indeed,

[...] Alexandria, Cairo, Beni Suef and other Egyptian towns would harbour Albanians who organized associations, published newspapers and above all wrote works in verse and prose that include significant masterpieces of Albanian literature.[75]

When Egyptians, Tunisians, Algerians or Syrians proudly speak of their 'Turkish origins' today or visit the shrines and mosques of the *Hanefi* rite –the dominant Sunni school of jurisprudence in the Balkans and Asia Minor, though largely absent in the Arab world – many in fact remember their Albanian, Bosnian or Greek ancestors, who had hailed from the distant shores of the Eastern and Northern Mediterranean.

In the Maghreb, French domination led to a different constellation, with European settlers creating the colonial economic boom, and local Jewish communities being somewhat reluctantly enfranchized. This was an option denied, of course, to most members of the Muslim host societies. The settlement policy of the French in Algeria, but also in the Protectorates of Morocco and Tunisia, created a 'melting pot' of southern European settlers and a 'new white race'[76] whose members were French citizens. With the independence of Tunisia and Morocco, and later Algeria, the *colons* and many Jews were evacuated to Southern France, together with the *harkis*, Algerian volunteers in French service. Labour migration since the 1960s from the Maghreb to France has further strengthened the emergence of a 'bi-coastal' network, connecting the two sides, though in very unequal ways.

Neither liquid continent, nor *Mare Nostrum*: just an ambivalent sea

There is no primeval Mediterranean unity, neither in historical, nor in cultural or ecological terms. Whether called 'liquid continent'[77] or 'common heritage'; there is fragmentation and division where one searches for unity. There are many distinct, if overlapping stories, historical experiences, ecological systems, political structures and competing discourses struggling for hegemony. Whether in colonial discourse – the Mediterranean as a French or Italian renaissance of the Roman empire – or in recent debates on the 'Union for the Mediterranean', Herzfeld's initial criticism rings true: the 'appeal to unity' obfuscates other, mostly 'northern' – read European – political agendas, and suggests equality where in fact there is asymmetry and dependence. Above all, it blurs the lines between colonizer and colonized and even calls into question the liberating content of post-colonialism:

Does the 'post' indicate the perspective and location of the ex-colonized (Algerian), the ex-colonizer (French), the ex-colonial settler (*Pied-Noir*), or the displaced hybrid in First World metropolitans (Algerians in France)? Since the experience of colonialism and imperialism is shared, albeit asymmetrically, by (ex) colonizer and (ex) colonized, it becomes an easy move to apply the 'post' also to First World European countries.[78]

Having thus discarded notions of 'the' Mediterranean and acknowledged the colonial origins of French discourses of unity – based in notions of empire, racial supremacy and the use of a West-Mediterranean system as an image capturing the 'essence' of the entire region – we still do not have to give up on the circum-Mediterranean as a space of interaction and research. The regionalizing moments, if not *of*, but *within* the Mediterranean, have created regional clusters and subsets of countries with distinct historical commonalities and patterns of interaction. These subsets of countries are located within the context of a number of other regional systems. One of them is the loosely defined and politically insignificant Mediterranean space, characterized by fuzzy borders, 'microecologies' and 'connectivity'.[79] Others are indeed Europe, the Middle East and the Caucasus and Central Asia.

What then, are the sub-regions of this re-defined and de-essentialized, fuzzy Mediterranean space? They coincide, to a large extent, with classical geographical divisions based on the North–South and the East–West axes: the Western Mediterranean space consists of the Maghreb countries in the South, and Spain and France (and to a certain extent Italy) in the North. The Eastern Mediterranean hosts, on its northern shores, what is now considered South East Europe, with its Adriatic and Aegean (and Black Sea) coastlines. Its southern rim, with the countries of the Levant and Egypt, is clearly defined by the conflict over Palestine and Israel and by the politics of authoritarianism. Finally, Turkey, with the longest of any Mediterranean coastlines, straddles both the northern and southern parts and the political cultures associated with each.

Within this taxonomy, the Balkans or South East Europe and the 'bicoastal' Western Mediterranean system make strong, if divergent cases for regional coherence. We have discussed how the post-imperial moment shaped nation-states and identity narratives through interrelated homogenizing projects and the mutual experience of population transfers, ethnic cleansing and destruction of the heritage of excluded groups. Despite the political divide, since the collapse of Communism and the destruction of Yugoslavia, South East Europe has functioned as both a political space –

characterized by differentiated inclusion in the EU and a trajectory towards liberal democracies – and as an intellectual space of thinking and writing about the region. Turkey is an integral part of this system, yet it also retains a borderland status, which casts doubt upon whether it will be a full member of the EU. Nevertheless, economically, Turkey is strongly integrated into South East Europe, yet also increasingly engaged in the markets of its eastern neighbours.

The Western Mediterranean system is characterized by, for lack of a better word, 'post-colonial' structures perpetuating France's role as cosmopolitan centre. Economically and politically, the region is fragmented, despite the existence of the Arab Maghreb Union, with bilateral trade between its member states at about 2 per cent of the total trade volume[80] and a strong dominance of France both as market for export goods and as source of imports.[81] The pattern of vertical integration with France and horizontal fragmentation within the Maghreb is further exacerbated by the waves of labour migration since the 1950s. These have created additional demographic links between the two shores, yet augmented regional fragmentation. Another factor stymieing integration is the lingering territorial conflict between Algeria and Morocco over the Western Sahara.

Ambivalent sea and many coasts?

This chapter has revisited the Mediterranean through the discourses which have been used to identify, name, control and rule the territories on its shore and through the historical moments, that shaped regional subsystems in the late nineteenth and twentieth centuries. Despite colonial French and to an extent Italian legitimizing discourses of the Mediterranean as a primeval Roman sea, the countries and societies on its shores were shaped by asymmetric historical experiences. These were often conceptualized in binary opposites: the Roman *Orbis Terrarum* vs. the *Dar al-Islam*, the Ottoman Empire vs. Christian Europe, colonization or mandate rule vs. colonizer, North vs. South, and once again, Europe vs. Islam. One does not have to agree with the Manichaean reductionism of these binary opposites in order to acknowledge their discursive, and in fact, material power.

As this chapter has sought to demonstrate, the Mediterranean is a fragmented space, and the countries and societies in its ambit have been shaped by differential regionalizing moments and different pathways to modernity. These have pulled them away from the seascapes and maritime networks on which they once thrived, and have re-oriented them towards national, new regional, or in the case of the Maghreb, 'post-colonial' markets. Mediterraneanism, above all, has been a problematic concept, whether in Herzfeld's term as an 'Orientalizing' and 'colonizing' discourse, or as an escapist, Europeanizing imagery to be found in Israel, Turkey and the Maghreb littoral.

In spite of resilient arguments on primeval unity, and in spite of Sarkozy's *Discours de Toulon*, there is no primeval Mediterranean essence of unity, deposited in a distant past and waiting for redemption. There is no such essence that could be put 'on course to reunification after twelve centuries of division and strife'. The circum-Mediterranean today is a space of ambivalence, characterized more by dividing lines and ruptures, than by connecting networks or a 'common heritage'. Acknowledging these divisions and the competing nature of regionalizing discourses, but also the diversity and distinctiveness of smaller sub-regions, would help liberating the Mediterranean debate from tacit imperial longings, quests for domination and neo-colonial designs. This could be a first step towards the construction of the Mediterranean as a non-hegemonic space, in which colonizer and colonized, deported and deportee, can face each other as equals to confront and transcend the divisions of the nineteenth and twentieth centuries. Considering the situation on the ground, however, there is no reason to believe that the realization of such a vision is imminent.

CHAPTER II

BETWEEN EMPIRE AND NATION-STATE: THE PROBLEM OF BORDERS IN THE MAGHREB

FATMA BEN SLIMANE

Introduction

In the wake of independence, the Maghreb, like the other former colonies in Africa and elsewhere, faced various border problems. Algeria had tensions with its neighbours in both the East and the West. Tunisia claimed a piece of territory located at its southwest border with Algeria.[1] In his speech of April 12, 1957, President Habib Bourguiba accused the French officers of having sought, in 1929, 'to cut as much as possible from the Tunisian and Moroccan territories to make a part of Algeria'.[2] At the other end of the Maghreb, an outstanding figure of the Moroccan national movement, Allal al-Fassi, affirmed that independent Morocco accounted for only one fifth of 'historic Morocco'.[3]

In Morocco, this refusal to accept the legacy of colonial borders pushed the country into a twofold battle: a legal one based on appeals to international institutions (the UN, the International Court of Justice, the Organization of African Unity (OAU), etc.) as well as a military one. In 1961, Morocco's border dispute with Algeria escalated into a war. In 1963, Morocco was the only African country apart from Somalia not to ratify the charter of the OAU, in protest at the *uti possidetis* principle that prohibited newly independent states from changing the territorial status quo inherited from the colonial period. Later, in 1975, Morocco used military force to impose its rights on Western Sahara, following Spain's withdrawal from the province. This action led to the emergence of the Polisario armed resistance movement which pursued Western Sahara's independence with support from Algeria and later Libya. The movement operated from bases on Algerian territory, which rekindled tensions between Morocco and its two neighbours. Maritime borders were no exception. In the 1980s, a dispute broke out between Libya and Tunisia regarding the delimitation of the continental shelf. Today, the illegal immigration from Africa through the Spanish enclaves of Ceuta and Melilla, located on the Mediterranean maritime borders, present yet another problem between Morocco and the European Union (EU).

Border problems are one of the major roadblocks for the project of uniting the Maghrebi countries. In a world of regional blocs, such as the EU or ASEAN, the Maghreb is dominated by national divisions. The Arab Maghreb Union has not been able to hold a summit meeting since 1994, calling into question the very notion of regional cooperation. The present-day image of disunity contrasts with that of a Maghreb held together by its geography and history, which is invoked in political speeches and which shapes the local peoples' aspirations. Moreover, while state borders are 'hardening', serious internal problems destabilize the whole of the region. An Islamist network named 'Al-Qaida in the Islamic Maghreb Countries', defying local governments and the borders separating them, has declared its bid to succeed where states have failed – to unite the Maghreb under the more inclusive principle of the *umma,* the universal community of Muslims straddling borders between states.

What we have here is a clash between two competing paradigms of the state. The first one promotes the territorial nation-state, and corresponds to a modernist and secular concept legitimized through international recognition within the UN. The second one draws its legitimacy from the religious past and the *umma.* It rejects the new world order embodied in the nation-state principle, which it perceives as alien and imposed on the Muslims by Western imperialism to fragment and emasculate their communal bonds. This ideology is stigmatized in the authorities' discourse, which condemns the Salafi movements as backward in their ideas and as terrorists because of their violent actions.

Borders in historical perspective

In all fairness, neither the border question nor the two competing paradigms of nation-states and empire are novel in Maghrebi history. These are old problems which have been given new meanings with each successive change in the historical context. The two phenomena of border conflicts and the threat from Islamist networks point at a crisis experienced by the state in the Maghreb, being subjected to the opposing currents of nation-building and of the globalizing and networked world.[4] But why should borders emerge as a problem in the Maghreb and why should Morocco be the country most exposed? After all, we have heard time and again that, contrary to the Middle East and the rest of Africa, where the borders were drawn by the colonial powers, in the Maghreb's case, there were pre-existing, ancient boundaries which were only demarcated and confirmed in the process of decolonization.

Looking at modern state formation, Robert Baduel questions whether the countries in the post-colonial Maghreb are nation-states. He proposes that the political configuration of state-nation-territory is a European invention dating back to the Middle Ages, whereas, in the Maghreb, the model was only institutionalized during colonization. Thus local states are currently undergoing a crisis mainly because they are themselves recent creations. Taking aboard the insights of political anthropology, the author describes the state in the pre-colonial Maghreb as traditional or patrimonial, and offers us two related paradigms to understand the relationship between authority and territory during this period: the 'segmentary paradigm' and the 'centre-periphery paradigm', both originating from the comparative study of modern state formation. The segmentary state executes its writ over the whole of the country under its jurisdiction, but it also coexists with predating units which it cannot abolish and therefore takes as a model for its own structures. Its territorial sovereignty is thus recognized but limited, and its authority becomes blurred when applied to areas distanced from the centre. In Baduel's view, this account is illustrated by the description of the state-territory relationship given by the fourteenth century Maghrebi historian, Ibn Khaldun. Strongest in the centre, state authority weakens as one moves towards the periphery. Using the centre-periphery paradigm derived from the study of feudalism, the pre-colonial state in the Maghreb is thus further described as centrifugal: 'its space is vague, and the subordinate authorities are more likely to change allegiance if they occupy a peripheral position.'[5] Yet, is the model of frontiers elaborated by Ibn Khaldun in the fourteenth century still valid in later periods? Did three hundred years under the tutelage of two empires, the Ottoman and Sharifian, leave the Maghreb countries unacquainted, until the nineteenth century, with territoriality and borders, both important conditions for the emergence of the state and of national awareness? Bertrand Badie's comparative work on the West and the Muslim world concludes that the phenomenon of territoriality is foreign to Islamic culture. The nation-state model is described as 'imported' by the waves of colonial expansion.[6] Looking at the current spread of the Islamist movements challenging the established geopolitical order, Badie highlights 'the extreme speed at which spatial references in the Muslim world's history change', and goes on: 'one passed from a reference to the Ottoman Empire to a reference to an imaginary Arab empire, even an Arab nation, and subsequently to the reference, probably more salient nowadays, to a Muslim world.'[7]

The Maghreb certainly saw these two transitions in its recent history. However, what were their relative weights? Furthermore, these observations were generated primarily on the basis of the experience in the Middle East while North Africa was shaped much more profoundly by colonialism. Here, the historian Daniel Nordman's work on the formation of the Maghrebi borders in the nineteenth century is enlightening. Looking at the transposition of the concept of border, which had matured in Europe by the nineteenth century, he argues that the novel practices did not match or take into account local ideas. [8]

This chapter investigates the development of the concept of 'border' in the Maghreb during the pre-colonial period. How did the pre-colonial state perceive its space? Did borders and territoriality make sense in the culture and the political practice of these countries? Did they produce identity and political order? How was the notion of territorial limits expressed in textual sources?

Concerning the period in question, I argue that the history of the concept in the Maghreb is marked by three important moments. The first was the sixteenth-century transition from the Maghreb of the dynasties to the Ottoman Maghreb, whose principal consequences were the appearance of new geopolitical entities and a change in the relationship between political power and territory at the level of practices and representations. Between the late sixteenth and mid-seventeenth centuries, a second period ensued, marked by attempts to delimit the Ottoman provinces, as well as by variance in the practices of the Ottoman Maghreb and Morocco. The final period, which commenced with the establishment of colonial borders following the occupation of Algeria in the nineteenth century, ushered in two clashing representations of the concept of border.

Dynastic Maghreb and its marches
(thirteenth – sixteenth century)

The journey back to the pre-Ottoman era aims to elucidate the theory of the state and territory elaborated by Ibn Khaldun, which is used as a model by certain researchers dealing with the Maghreb prior to colonialism. The theory is then juxtaposed with the changes in the relationships in question following the incorporation of a substantial part of the region into the Ottoman Empire.

The dynastic state

Until the beginning of the sixteenth century, three geopolitical entities of unequal size shared Maghrebi space. They emerged after the collapse, in the thirteenth century, of the erstwhile Almohad Empire.[9] These polities had a common geography but each one was individualized by the name of the dynasty to which it submitted.[10] Territory was deemed to be the property of the dynasty, but the dynasty established spatial limits of a particular nature and in special ways. According to Ibn Khaldun, in times of peace, the structure of dynastic space followed a concentric schema reminiscent of the ripples created on the surface of water by a falling stone. If the centre of the dynasty's political power is compared to the stone, its remit is represented by concentric circles which widen as one moves outwards. Dynastic power blurs in the most distant peripheries.

The Khaldunian theory of power cycles is reflected in his discussion of space.[11] To Ibn Khaldun, the zenith of a dynasty translates into the strengthening of central power accompanied by the dependency of the peripheries. This balance, however, is called into question during periods of crisis. The weakening of the centre results in its inability to exert control, and circles disaggregate one after the other starting from the most distant. Once this stage arrives, the crisis favours the outlying areas, one of which assumes a leading role in reconstituting a power centre. Ibn Khaldun developed this theory of statehood and space based on the Maghrebi context of the fourteenth century. But what was this period's notion of border and how was the status of borders defined?

The vocabulary of borders

It is worth looking at the lexicon of dynastic 'borders': *thughur, hudud, tukhum, atraf*.[12] All these names are subsumed into the term *nitaq*, literally meaning 'belt', employed by Ibn Khaldun with reference to the place or zone where sovereign power ends.[13] Each of the names also had a particular political significance, depending on the extent of dynastic power. As the terms had dissimilar geopolitical weight, the vocabulary distinguished between two categories.

Firstly, the words *hudud* (lit. limits), *tukhum* (lit. borders), *atraf* (lit. marches) meant a swathe of land, a more or less broad zone, separating two political entities. All these names convey the sense of a border in times of peace and they are defined chiefly by their distance in relation to the dynastic center. These concepts are close to that of *marche* in medieval Europe. Mindful of their autonomy, the populations of these borderlands changed allegiance depending on circumstances. In this Maghrebi context, the dynasty's authority was ensured primarily by the allegiance of the local community, city, village or tribe which, by recognizing the authority of the sultan through a *bay'a* or oath of allegiance, agreed to pay him tributes.

The most politically and militarily significant word in the frontier lexicon, however, was that of *thaghr* (pl. *thughur*). A given area became a *thaghr* (lit. front) when located at the interface with an external threat. The medieval sources mostly apply the term *thaghr* to the coastal cities, which used to come under constant Christian attacks. However, the statute also applied to settlements in the interior. For example, the town of Constantine, far away from the sea, was nonetheless considered a *thaghr* by the Hafsid dynasty (1229-1574), due to the challenge posed by the rival dynasty of the Zayyanids, qualified by the contemporary sources as 'enemies'. The same role was also assigned to the town of Oujda in eastern Morocco by the local Marinid dynasty (1215-1420). Whether on the coast or in the interior, these strategic cities were equipped with a defence infrastructure and commanded political power. The Hafsid princes in the *thughurs* of Constantine or Bougie controlled fortresses, garrisons and all other instruments of power. Sources tell us that they lived in palaces with courts resembling that of the sultan in Tunis. Profiting from crises eroding the sultan's power, they managed to carve independent principalities out of their administrative districts. Certain ambitious princes even succeeded in seizing power in Tunis.

The dynastic state struggled to keep these regions acquiescent and collect taxes: at times, this necessitated recourse to military expeditions. This brings us back to the schema of the traditional state highlighted by Baduel, who observes that 'the periphery tends to escape continuously from the centre, which is not allowed by centrifugal powers to exert control in ways other than by recurrent negotiation, [and is] therefore in permanent tension with the peripheral forces and at the limits of their marches.'[14] At the same time, the Khaldunian model was upset or threatened by the attempts to revive the Maghreb's unity made by each of the three dynasties, inspired by the past example of the Almohads from whom they had inherited both their territories and their ideology. Until the end of the fifteenth century, all three were attempting to extend their borders.[15] This situation added to the uncertainty of borders and territorial maps.

In conclusion, both at the level of practices and of representations, the uncertainty of borders was a characteristic of the pre-Ottoman Maghreb. Pulled apart by the logic inherited from the pre-existing empires (e.g. the

Almohads) and that of the dynastic states, 'borders' dilated, narrowed or disappeared depending on the circumstances. As a result, the dynastic territories had their own 'variable geometry,' reflected by the polysemy of their frontier spaces.

The vanishing of the marches in the age of the Mediterranean empires

From the second half of the fifteenth century, the whole of the Maghreb entered a period of chaos, as states disintegrated, according to Ibn Khaldun's script. Their borders blurred and frontier communities gained autonomy.[16] The Maghreb went through a geopolitical upheaval whose results are with us to this very day. It was the beginning of the end for the dynasties of the Maghreb, but also for their representations of political space and margins.

The demise of the Khaldunian world

The implosion of Maghrebi space occurred at the time when two rival superpowers emerged in the Mediterranean: Spain in the West and the Ottoman Empire in the East. Over the sixteenth century, the two fought for the control of the Mediterranean. The Maghrebi states, whose power was in constant decline, were unable to prevent the seizure of their principal *thughurs,* located on the Atlantic and the Mediterranean coasts and stretching to Tripoli, by Spain and Portugal. Soon it would fall to the corsairs to unite the region in the name of *Jihad* against the Spanish. As the local dynasties lacked military technology or standing armies, they gradually lost their autonomy, aligning at times with Spain or Portugal, at times with the Ottoman Turks. Two new political actors entered the scene at the two extremities of the Maghreb: the Sufi brotherhood of *Jazuliyya*, which supported the Saadi sharifs (princes) from the southern borderlands of Morocco, and the *Shabbiyya* tribe from Kairouan (Tunisia). They too embarked on a holy war against the foreign forces and their allies of the interior which lasted three quarters of a century.

It is less important to remind ourselves of the vicissitudes of the military history of this struggle over a disputed territory, than to examine the concomitant geopolitical transformations and representations which they generated. There were two contrasting images of space: the one advanced by the Ottomans and the traditional notion, which the dynastic states and other indigenous actors, such as the religious brotherhoods, sought to revive. They are explored in some detail below.

The Ottoman conquest and the establishment of Algiers, Tripoli and Tunis as regencies

The Spanish and Portuguese occupation of Morocco almost never exceeded the boundaries of the coastal cities. According to Fernand Braudel's analysis, the Spaniards were attracted neither by the interior of the Maghreb nor by the prospect of seizing power from the hands of the dynasties in place. They were content to put the latter under their protection, and to control the coasts by fortifying certain strategic points (*presidios*) like La Goulette and Tunis. Their principal concern was to halt the Ottoman advance in the Eastern Mediterranean, and to protect the coasts of Christian Europe against the Moorish-Ottoman corsairs. Therefore the occupied cities were regarded as European border outposts in the Maghreb.

The Spaniards' attitude differed from that of their adversaries, the Ottomans. The Ottoman Empire always viewed the Maghreb as part of *Dar al-Islam*, the Realm of Peace populated by the community of believers.[17] It was thus necessary to shield the weakened local dynasties from the Spanish occupation. In practice, the Ottomans competed with the Spanish for control of the maritime frontier. The cities they managed to tear off turned into anchorage and entry points to the interior. Yet the Ottomans' definitive presence in Algiers, and its later transformation into an imperial province in 1520 provoked violent reactions by the local authorities. It also agitated the two indigenous dynasties, the Hafsids of Tunis and the Zayyanids of Tlemcen, who felt threatened by the Ottoman presence on what they saw as their ancestral land. Indeed, the conflict which erupted between the two powers is coherent with a certain ideological imagery of territoriality. This is evident in the arguments made by the Hafsid sultan to the famous Admiral Hayreddin (Khair-Eddin) Barbarossa – originally a Greek convert – in Algiers, intended to delegitimize the Ottomans' authority.

In one of his letters, Mulay Mohammad, the sultan of Tunis, exhorts his counterpart of Tlemcen to fight the Turks and notes that 'looking at how the Turks usurped the ground of our ancestors, [it would] not be long before they deprived us of our own kingdoms.' The contested area would become the core of the Ottoman *eyalet* (province) of Algiers, spanning the two kingdoms. Contemporary sources named the area 'the remote marches' (*ath-thughur al-kasia*), which the authority of the sultans of Tunis or Tlemcen reached only seldom, and which was not defensible by either of the two in the sixteenth century. Much to the Maghrebi sovereigns' displeasure, Hayreddin Pasha responded that it was thanks to him that Algiers and its surroundings had been liberated and protected from the Spanish encroachments, and that he had, therefore, gained rights over it.

This conflict points at two types of spatial legitimacy: a right resulting from conquest, that of the Ottoman Turks, and a right resulting from historical practices, asserted by the sultan of Tunis. At the same time, the conflict reveals the collision of two territorial logics: that of the dynasties, based on the protection of one's realm, versus an expansionist imperial logic of the Ottomans. At the time of the conquest, the Ottoman frontier in the Maghreb advanced according to the model elaborated in Frederick Jackson Turner's classical work:[18] it pushed forward each time military power succeeded in vanquishing recalcitrant populations, with each conquered city constituting a new point of departure.

Around the mid-sixteenth century, the whole area between Annaba and Tlemcen became dependent on Algiers. The newborn province was primarily formed by what was formerly the borderland of two dynasties. The same evolution is observed on the south-eastern borders of the Hafsid state. Occupied until 1551 by the Knights of Malta, Tripoli then passed into Ottoman hands. As with Algiers, it took the name of a former Hafsid *thaghr* to become the *Tarabuls al-Gharb eyalet* (province of Tripoli of the west). Following the example of the Algerian governors, Turgut (Dragut) Pasha of Tripoli started in 1556 to conquer some northern cities, to the detriment of what remained Hafsid territory. At the beginning of 1557, he reached Kairouan and dislodged the minuscule state of the *Shabbiyya* brotherhood.[19] Between 1569 and 1574, the Turks of Algiers and the Spaniards fought for Tunis until an Ottoman armada, led by Admiral Kılıç Ali, captured the city, ending half a century of Spanish domination and 350 years of Hafsid rule. The Grand Vizier Sinan Pasha, who was part of the expedition, decided to establish an autonomous province there.

Thus, from the chaos of the sixteenth century, the three provinces of the west (*Gharb Ocaklari*), were born – themselves three political entities-to-be (Algeria, Libya and Tunisia). Only Morocco, which witnessed the same process of disintegration, stayed away from the Ottoman advance. The local forces there developed their own strategies to unify the country.

Saadi Morocco: state-building from the margins

The role of the outlying areas in southern Morocco (Sous, Draa, Tafilalt) in the political history of the country is very revealing of the relationship between power and territory. Although distanced from the urban power centers in the north (Fes, Meknes, Marrakech, Rabat), these peripheries were far from being politically marginal. Between the tenth and seventeenth centuries, they constituted a 'laboratory' for the dynasties who would reign the country: the Almoravids, the Almohads, the Saadis and the Alaouites. In the sixteenth century, the Saadi sharifs, coming from the Draa *wadi*, had to fight three forces at once: the Portuguese, who occupied the Atlantic port cities, the Wattasid dynasty, and the Ottomans, who were trying to extend their hegemony into Morocco. The Saadis arrived to unify the land through holy war, with the support of local tribes and Sufi lodges (*zaouïas*). In the north, the Wattassids were removed from Fes in about 1549.

The Saadi-Ottoman conflict, however, was not merely a struggle for hegemony, but also a clash of two imperial ideologies. Mohammed ash-Sheikh, the first Saadi ruler (1545–1554), considered himself an equal, if not a rival of the Ottoman sultan, owing to his alleged connection to the family line of Prophet Muhammad. When an embassy official from Istanbul wrote to demand that he recognize the suzerainty of the Ottoman *padishah*, he retorted that not only did he not acknowledge the caliphate of the 'sultan of the seas' – alluding to the Ottomans' maritime expansion and thus denying Istanbul's claim over people on dry land – but he also threatened to drive him out of Egypt and the Holy Cities.[20] Beyond the political antagonism which animates it, this attitude reveals the ideology which underpinned the Saadis' power. Due to their claimed link to the Prophet, the dynasty and its loyalists always saw power and its relationship to territory in imperial terms. The ruler's most significant titles were *amir al-m'uminin* ('Prince of the Faithful') and *al-Mahdi* ('Redeemer'). The former granted him the power to unite Muslims wherever they may be; the latter rendered this power unlimited, due to the potential universalism of mahdist ideology. The *Mahdi*'s mission was to spread justice on earth and salvation for all humanity.

These universalist claims endowed the Saadis with unlimited power in the imagination of the period's intellectuals. According to his secretary Abu Faris al-Fishtali, Sultan Ahmad al-Mansûr ad-Dhahbi (1578-1603) was 'the heir to the prophetic caliphate who takes care of the defence and the integrity of Islam, and whoever should try to exert power without reference to his legal authority would be but a heretic.' Al-Fishtali continued that as a *Mahdi*, the sultan had 'the legitimate right to exercise suzerainty and tutelage over all people, in the name of Islam.'[21]

It is in this context that one can understand the expansion carried out by the sultan against Algiers or Sudan, both Sunni countries. Oscillating between the domains of the faithful and those of the whole of humanity, the power of the sharifs was subject to no territorial limit, which explains the tensions with the Ottoman Empire.

The Maghreb under Ottoman rule
(sixteenth – nineteenth century)

Compared to earlier imperial polities such as the early Islamic Caliphate, the foundations of Ottoman ascendency were not rooted in a religious ideology. Expansion into the Maghreb, while carried out under the banner of *jihad*, was nonetheless a power political enterprise. This observation is important to any investigation of the region's subsequent evolution. While Morocco was reconstituted once more under the Alaouite dynasty in the 1660s, the three Ottoman provinces obtained relatively clear-cut limits. But what was the nature of these borders, what was their meaning in the Ottoman context and their implications for the Ottoman authorities and populations?

The status of the Maghrebi eyalets

The geopolitical evolution of Maghrebi regencies was situated in the following legal and political context:

– Regarded as imperial marches, the provinces in question enjoyed the status of *salyaneli eyaletler*, owing the Porte only an annual tribute. Within this status, the provincial authorities were granted a broad measure of freedom in the conduct of their internal and external affairs, as well as the management of their disagreements, notably concerning territory.
– While drawing the Maghreb into its orbit, the empire did not fix any territorial boundaries between its provinces, implicitly leaving the task to the authorities representing it on the ground. What the imperial centre prioritized was that the *Gharb Ocaklan* remain under its control, protected from Christian Europe.
– The problem of territorial delimitation in the Ottoman Maghreb emerged in the wake of the conquest of Tunis and its transformation into an imperial province.

The frontier wars

Of the three Maghrebi entities, it was Tunis, the last province established by the Ottomans, that was the most dubious. The disappearance of the Hafsid state and the threat of reconquest posed questions as to how the military authorities could reconstitute the territory and legitimize the new regency. The archives show that it was by force that Tunis sought to bring back its former territories, particularly its cities. The expansion proceeded towards the south and west, leading to military confrontations with the neighbouring provinces.

During the last quarter of the sixteenth century, the Ottomans of Tunis pushed back their borders, seizing interior cities in the centre and the south which had hitherto been under Tripolitania. At the beginning of the eighteenth century, Tunis conquered the island of Djerba and the border between the two provinces was established a little further southeast, with the establishment of a Tunisian fortress and garrison at Biban.

The governors of Tunis also expanded towards Algiers province. The punitive expeditions against the great tribal confederations of the borderland, aimed at curtailing the power the latter had enjoyed since Hafsid times, sparked a war with the Ottomans of Algiers. Following a violent confrontation between the two regencies in 1628, the common border was fixed through an agreement. Historians consider this event fundamental, not only to the relations between the two provinces, but primarily to the institutionalization of the concept of border.

The concept of border

To gauge the significance of the 1628 agreement, one needs to examine its content, and then its form and the vocabulary it employs. [22] The agreement uses geographical and 'non-human' reference points, such as river courses and watersheds, as a basis to delimit the lands of each province. Only the northern confines of the two provinces are demarcated, leaving out the remaining territories in the interior, the steppe and the Sahara. The agreement concerns solely the taxation jurisdiction of the governors in Tunis and Algiers. The demarcation is considered no obstacle for the movement of populations, and a group could change its allegiance after crossing the dividing line. The agreement was an important development in a state of affairs marked by shifting rights and allegiances, as well as political instability. The authorities of Algiers and Tunis sought to put an end to recurring conflicts and clarify the local communities' political affiliations. This explains why the agreement focused only on the north, which had been the theatre of several confrontations, and was populated by the most powerful and defiant tribal confederations, whose loyalty to the Ottoman governorships of Algiers or Tunis was arbitrary.

The vocabulary employed is equally illuminating. The document is not formally named, except with the expression *resm at-tahdid* ('written document of delimitation'), used previously in an accord adopted by the two regencies in 1614. *Resm* (pl. *rusum*) refers to writing, and – in the documents of the seventeenth and eighteenth centuries – it denotes a 'trace' or 'written work', a land right or even simply a valid legal ground. [23] In practice, *resm* is the act produced by a notary sanctioning the right of property; it is the proof (*hujja*) which warrants appropriation. Its purpose is to protect estates in a potential dispute. The word was, therefore, transposed from civil affairs to the field of geopolitics, from the private to the public domain.

In terms of form, however, the agreement does not resemble an inter-state treaty, even if it contains territorial clauses. It is rather a hybrid between a notarial writ and a peace agreement ('*aqd solh*) reconciling two quarrelling individuals. This composite character is confirmed by the use of the verb *aslaha* (coming from *solh*), meaning 'restore' or 'rectify' a damaged object. The damage can affect the possessions of, or the relationship between individuals or communities, and it is in this sense that the word was used in the 1628 agreement. The text states that it was the preacher of the mosque of Tunis who, invoking a Quranic reference, had issued a divine order exhorting the two Muslim groups to settle their differences, heal their relationship, and restore peace. The terminology pertaining to *delimitation* is also embedded in this linguistic context. The word *hdada,* used widely in the document, stems from the local experience. Peasants used this term to refer to a small elevated fence separating two fields which belonged to different owners.

The border concept, therefore, was situated in a *mélange* between tradition and innovation, as well as between social and legal practices. This feature is confirmed by the heterogeneity of the signatories of the 1628 document: about twenty signatures came from the janissary corps, a new political factor representing the empire in the provinces, described in the agreement as pious people who had performed the rite of *hajj*. Also signatories were *ulema* from both the Hanefi and Maliki schools, who headed councils and issued religious proclamations, and who joined other signatories guaranteeing the establishment of peace.

The blurred delimitation vocabulary reflects the novelty of this institution and the difficulty of adaptation to a new status quo. The practice of state borders was new, and the political actors had attempted to forge a compromise between social and legal practices in a cultural atmosphere whose key references were inspired by religion. It was significant that written documents were being adopted for the first time by Maghrebi politicial entities as a method of solving territorial conflict and establishing borders. This marked the birth of the concept of territorial limits giving political authorities in the regencies a right to the ownership, continuity and stability of their territories.

Towards the mid-seventeenth century then, the Ottoman provinces of the Maghreb had relatively precise limits. Admittedly, the situation differed from that of the Treaty of Westphalia in Europe, but it was also discontinuous with regard to the medieval period described above. Unlike the Khaldunian state, whose limits had been fuzzy and movable, the Ottoman period was an era of territorial stability, irrespective of the political vicissitudes the Maghrebi polities went through. Neither the empire nor the local powers called into question the geopolitical order that had been put in place.

The role of the imperial centre

If the Ottoman Empire did not intervene directly in the occasionally bloody conflicts of the provinces, it was nonetheless informed of these developments. Through an exchange of letters and emissaries, the central authorities sought a peaceful solution. They managed border problems by looking at them through an imperial lens, i.e. by regarding them as the internal business of Muslim countries. The Porte considered the regencies in the Maghreb as imperial marches, and was consequently eager to maintain internal peace and safeguard the coasts. This attitude to the border question was at odds with the one in the regencies themselves, however, where it was considered of vital importance.

As Ottoman archives testify, the governors of Tripoli called upon the sultan for support, as they felt they had been deprived of territories that they considered rightfully theirs. They made particular reference to the conquests carried out by the renowned Ottoman Admiral Turgut (Dragut) Pasha in the 1550s and 1560s, starting from Tripoli. As for the Tunisians, they inherited a vaguely defined space and considered it vital to extend its boundaries, as demonstrated by their correspondence with Istanbul. Benefiting from local support, they countered the claims of Tripoli, citing the small size of their territory, and especially the desire of the inhabitants of the provincial towns under Tripolitane rule to come into Tunis' fold. These arguments were sufficient for the Porte to ratify the *fait accompli*, i.e. the expansion of Tunis all the way to the Djerba Island.[24] In the East as in the West, in the cities as in the rural areas, the desires of the indigenous populations, and more particularly of the notables, influenced the space delimitation between the provinces. In pleading in favour of an attachment to Tunis since time immemorial, these populations contributed to the shaping of the regency. Whether established with written documents or imposed by political and tax practices, the order inaugurated in the first quarter of the seventeenth century in the Ottoman parts of the Maghreb continued to be respected – the subsequent wars between Algiers and Tunis notwithstanding.

The Formation of 'historic Morocco'

In the same period, at the western end of the Maghreb, Morocco went through a dynastic change which shaped concepts and practices of territory and borders significantly. Ibn Khaldun's paradigm applies to the transition of power from the Saadis to the Alaouite dynasty in the mid-seventeenth century. The weakening of Saadi rule was accompanied by the decomposition of Morocco into multiple autonomous entities. Several of the coastal cities fell under European occupation once again, much like at the time of the Merinids' decline in the fifteenth century. Once again, disorder worked in the interest of the peripheries. Tafilelt in southeast Morocco, was the matrix of the new power, that of the Alaouites, which emerged between 1666 and 1671. Like the Saadians, the new dynasty, was patrimonial in nature and based on religious legitimacy derived from the bond with the Hashemite family and Prophet Muhammad. As Abdallah Laroui posits, this development illustrates a characteristic continuity in Morocco's history.[25] There is also a notable continuity at the level of territory. It was at the beginning of this period, in particular during the reign of Moulay Ismail (1672–1727), that the Moroccan Empire was established. Its memory would remain alive among Moroccan intellectuals until independence and afterwards, enshrined in expressions such as 'historic' or 'Greater Morocco'. Moreover, Moroccan historians from this period compared the empire with that established by Ahmad al-Mansur ad-Dhahbi, which marked the height of Saadian power – thus continuity was present both at the level of practices and that of ideology.

Like the Saadis, the Alaouite sultan nourished an expansionist project, convinced like his predecessors of the legitimacy conferred on him through the Prophet's lineage. Moulay Ismail carried the title of caliph and demanded to be treated by the European countries on an equal footing with the Ottoman sultan.[26] However, when his armies attacked the Ottomans of Algiers, they were defeated. The sultan was forced to conclude peace with his eastern neighbours and committed in a letter to the Dey of Algiers not to cross the Tafna *wadi* marking the border previously established by his predecessors. The conquests were also directed towards Saharan Africa. The moulay's power extended to Chenguit in present-day Mauritania, where a caravan later went every year to collect taxes and undertake expeditions all the way to the Senegal River. With the recapture of the coastal cities from the Europeans, Moulay Ismail's empire was born.[27] According to the historian Mohammed al-Ifrani (1670–1747), it spread from the *tukhum* (marches) of Bilad al-Sudan (contemporary Western Saharan Africa) and beyond the Senegal River, thus exceeding the empire of al-Mansur. In the East, the kingdom extended to the area of Biskra and the surroundings (*nawahi*) of Tlemcen.[28]

So where exactly did Alaouite power spread to? An examination of the borders with Algiers, as well as the language used, is instructive. The sources point to the recognition of Tafna as a border, and it might seem that such a commitment would have been at odds with the universalist ideology of the sharifs. Yet this commitment was undertaken in a unilateral manner and was deeply anchored in religious doctrine. It was not an agreement between individuals asserting political power over territory, but was declared with the aim of satisfying God and his prophet.[29] These borders must have been about expediency, otherwise the later attacks by Moulay Ismail against Tlemcen are hard to understand. The commitment was not a constraint, as its application was left to the sultan's own judgment before Allah, as the heir of prophetic power. A religious bond like this is governed by a logic other than that which underlies a political treaty: thus it is not surprising that the border was malleable, unstable, and transitory.

Until the end of the nineteenth century, terminology relating to the border in the Moroccan chronicles confirms this observation. To take the example of the frontier with Algiers, the chroniclers classify the city of Oujda, just like the coastal city settlements vulnerable to Christian Europe, as a *thaghr*, an outpost in enemy territory, except that the adversary was another Muslim country. The Alaouites, smilar to the Saadis before them, distrusted their Ottoman neighbours, considering them a threatening Other. As for the remainder of Morocco's territory, the texts make use of several terms, including *atraf*, *tukhum*, and *hadd*, all testifying to the fluidity of territorial demarcations.

The chronicles relate the difficulties which the successors of Moulay Ismail encountered in keeping the peripheral areas of the sharifian empire (e.g. Rif, Sijilmassa, Under and Marrakech) obedient until the nineteenth century. As for the remote areas conquered by the sultan, the authority of the royal government (*maghzen*) was ephemeral. The *maghzen* lacked the technological means and troops required to maintain effective control over such distant areas. The sultan was forced to rely on the honesty of his representatives.

The making of Maghrebi state borders in the modern era

The capture of Algiers in 1830, followed by the extension of French power towards the interior, ushered in the first attempts to delimit the frontiers with the provinces of Tunis and Morocco. This marked a significant turning point in the history of borders in the Maghreb, but also in the Ottoman Empire as a whole. To the Ottomans, the occupation evidenced their empire's weakness vis-à-vis Western Europe, as well as reconfirming the perception of the vulnerability of the marches. The Porte was prompted to reinforce its hold. In 1835, a crisis of the local dynasty of Karamanlis brought Tripoli back under Ottoman control. The empire embarked on the reterritorialization of Tripolitania by fixing the provinces' western borders and extending its influence towards the town of Fezzan.[30] The Maghrebi countries in the neighbourhood of the French colony experienced different problems, however.

The changing notion of borders

Prior to the conquest of Algeria, the Ottoman regency elites' notion of borders differed from the one in Morocco, as well as from the one in the West. Although the political elites in the Maghreb shared a sense of belonging to the wider community of Islam, they were also attached to a locale, circumscribed by its borders. In the north, these borders were written down on paper, while in the steppe areas, borders were more often of a fiscal nature and therefore based on collective allegiance. Fragments of the faded Khaldunian model, still operational in Morocco in the nineteenth century, were visible across the Maghreb until the colonial period. The authorities periodically resorted to military force, or *m'halla*, to maintain order in the interior regions and peripheries. In spite of the turmoil in the three regencies, there was no secession in the frontier areas, nor did independent power centres form in the peripheries. The authorities extended their hegemony with the help of military garrisons, and thanks especially to the professional army of janissaries recruited in Anatolia and the Balkans.

Maritime contact with Europe took place in a relatively well-demarcated space. The Maghrebi provinces were pushed to fortify their coastal cities and engage in piracy to guard themselves from European encroachments, as well as those of the Knights of Malta, whose role vis-à-vis Europe was analogous to the one of the North African regencies in relation to the Ottoman Empire.[31] Starting from the latter half of the seventeenth century, relations grew more peaceful, and separate political and trade treaties were signed with the European countries. These treaties, promoting commercial exchange by limiting the damage caused by piracy, introduced the Maghrebi political elites to a category of territorial waters borrowed from European maritime law. The concept had emerged in the seventeenth century, with the development of international commerce. For the Maghrebi entities, the idea of sovereignty at sea applied to both European states and their mutual relations. In the nineteenth century, however, the concept itself was still fluid. Archives from the Bey's government in Tunis, dating back to around 1816, regard the bombardment of the roads of Tunis by French ships as illegal, because the area in question formed part of what they called the 'waters of Tunis', as delimited by the treaties. Indeed, the treaties concluded since the second half of the nineteenth century contain clauses specifying a safety distance (measured by the range of a gun) for the European ships. The European states required each signatory not to offer either assistance or a safe haven to corsairs originating from other 'Barbary' countries in the Maghreb. The local (proto-)states, for their part, were making a choice in favour of their own 'national' interests over sentiments of Islamic fraternity.

While the coasts were increasingly seen as part of *Dar al-Islam*, the occupation of Algiers posed problems regarding land borders. The wars between the regencies forged, at least amongst the elites, an awareness of belonging to different entities. In the regency of Tunis, for example, ruled by a semi-local dynasty of the Husseinids since the eighteenth century, a notion of the border as a line separating two distinctive polities began to take shape. This slow transition is evident in the archives. *Hadd* (pl. *hudud*), indicating the boundaries with Tripoli and Algiers, supplanted the panoply of words used in former times, indicating a transformation in representations of the state and its territory. By contrast, in Morocco, the Alaouite *maghzen*, like the Ottoman authorities in Istanbul, continued to conceive of the country's territory in imperial terms until the nineteenth century. Aside from the Tafna *wadi* already recognized as the border with Algiers, the peripheral areas' bonds to the centre remained ill-defined.[32]

These divergent perceptions are illustrated by a comparison between the Husseinids of Tunis and the Alaouites of Morocco. In the wake of the French offensive against Algiers, the Ottoman government dispatched Tahir Pasha to the region. He had to enter Algeria by passing through Tunisian territory but was denied access to Tunis' soil by the Bey. The officials' ship was moored at the port of La Goulette and Tahir Pasha ultimately had to return to Istanbul without accomplishing his mission. Just as pragmatic was the attitude of the Bey of Tunis vis-à-vis his counterpart in Constantine, who was similarly denied assistance and refuge. The Husseinids' non-intervention in Algeria was perhaps due to the unequal power and the potential threat posed by France, but it also had to do with the memory of the wars with the Regency of Algiers throughout the Ottoman era. This state of affairs favoured *raison d'état* over Islamic solidarity, and the Husseinids followed their interests.

The Moroccan sovereign's attitude was in marked contrast with that of the Husseinids. In keeping with his duties as a 'Prince of the Faithful', Sharif Abderrahmane (Abd al-Rahman) accepted the oath of allegiance (*bay'a*) of Tlemcen's inhabitants after the fall of the Ottoman power in Algiers. Later, he not only agreed to offer refuge to the Emir Abdelkader (Abd al-Qadir), who led an uprising against the French occupants, but also raised an army to defend his claims. This move had disastrous consequences: the sultan suffered a heavy defeat at the Battle of Isly in August 1844, leading to the French-imposed Convention of Lalla Maghnia the following year. The defeat heralded the end of the imperial dream, and led the *maghzen* into decades of tortuous border demarcation processes with France. As a political and religious figure, Emir Abdelkader shared similar views with the sultan of Morocco. In his correspondence with the British, he is depicted as a sovereign (*amir*) whose territory spanned from Tlemcen in Algeria all the way to Tunis, which owed him allegiance (*ta'at*).[33] The concept here is fluid and reflects an embryonic notion of border – or at any rate, one far removed from that of the French who had just occupied Algeria.

Between France and one's neighbours: border conflicts and clashes of representations

To Algeria's new masters, the border status quo among the Maghreb countries seemed problematic. The absence of any form of control over the movement of populations and goods from one country to the other was unacceptable. French officials interpreted the local governments' tolerant or indifferent mindset at times as a form of laxness, at times as a sign of political weakness and inability to exercise authority over borders. The French attitude stemmed from a political culture developed over the course of at least three centuries of wars in Europe followed by border negotiations, demarcation treaties, terrain surveys and cartographic techniques, all instruments used by states to fix their boundaries. This process reached a stage of maturity in the nineteenth century, with the advent of linear borders intended to close off territories which had become national.

Yet the conditions in the Maghreb were very different. The conception of borders as barriers, and as instruments of spatial enclosure and distinction between people, was absent from the collective imagination, both among the men in power and the local populations. That frontiers should be open was considered self-evident both by the authorities and their subjects. Meanwhile, the French military authorities in Algiers were concerned by the continuous flows across the Algerian-Tunisian border, despite an initial delimitation in 1845. The Bey of Tunis' retort to the French was that the livelihood of frontier communities depended on such mobility.

Frontiers were conceived of as a space of exchanges and various other activities such as agriculture, pastoralism and commerce. These activities also included social exchanges: throughout the Maghreb, populations across borders shared the same religious practices (e.g. ritual visits to holy places) and ties of kinship. The absence of barriers in the collective subconscious was symbolized by the *Hajj* caravan bound for Mecca, which crossed the whole region each year, starting from Morocco and moving eastwards. As early reports by French officials in Algeria testify, these movements took place entirely freely, with no intervention by the authorities in the various Maghreb countries. As a result, there was an atmosphere of mutual incomprehension between the local authorities and their subjects on the one hand, and the colonial administration on the other.

The problem faced by both parties was how to transform undifferentiated borderlands by drawing lines which would split communities sharing similar modes of life and thinking. Where the French pressingly asked where the sovereignty of each particular ruler ended, the answer was always vague. Sometimes it depended on the lands of the tribes subjected to the authority in question, sometimes the allegiance of the tribal chiefs. Both the Bey of Tunis and the Moroccan sultan made use of historical rights: they presented their territories and borders as ancestral heritage. The sovereign of Tunis invoked the property rights of the Ottoman sultan, never referring to the 1628 agreement which had become null and void after the seventeenth century anyway. In short, on both sides of French Algeria, the border reflected not geographical considerations but human contingency or indeed custom.

Conclusion

The demarcation of boundaries, which lasted into the twentieth century, can be read as a history of the transposition or adaptation of a European border model to Maghrebi realities. The process brought into play two modes of representation resulting from two different cultures. It is not surprising, therefore, that among the Maghrebi countries, Morocco – where the imperial dream survived until the nineteenth century – was to experience the greatest number of border issues and feel a victim of territorial plunder.[34] Indeed, the colonial advance towards the south of Algeria transformed the Sahara 'from a territory constituting a *res nullius* into a land of conquest,'[35] and led to the annexation of areas considered by the sultan of Morocco as his kingdom's lands. Around the same period, following the war of Tétouan (1859-1860), Spain forced the *maghzen* to accept the enlargement of the borders of its enclaves, Ceuta and Melilla, into the lands of the neighbouring tribes.[36] Finally, towards the south, Morocco claims ownership over Western Sahara. To this very day, these problems are far from being resolved.

History is indispensable in grasping the border issues in the Maghreb today. To the historian, they illustrate the complexities and ambiguities of the formation of the territorial state and consequently the nation-state and the institution of citizenship. As shown by the study of language and social practices at the borders, this process had its similarities as well as differences from country to country in the region. The divergent legacies left by the Sharifian and Ottoman Empires conditioned the different reactions to the colonial predicament in the nineteenth century. As elsewhere in the Mediterranean, the social structures and contradictions inherited from the imperial era continue to bear on successor states.

CHAPTER III

TURKEY IN THE POST-OTTOMAN MEDITERRANEAN: TRANSCENDING THE 'WEST'/'ISLAM' BINARY?

NORA FISHER ONAR

Introduction

The trope 'the "West" and "Islam"', normatively loaded like most binaries in favour of the former, has become a staple in representations of ties between parts of the world inhabited mainly by peoples of Christian European descent and peoples of Middle Eastern and North African Muslim descent. Rooted in a particular strain of Western thought which dates at least to the Renaissance, this trope was given forceful expression by the ideologues of European imperialism. Supplanted in the aftermath of the two world wars by a West-East dichotomy pitting the 'Free World' against communism, it was resuscitated by Samuel Huntington's 'Clash of Civilizations' piece for *Foreign Affairs* in 1993. Claiming that the great challenge to the 'West' emanated from a monolithic, immutable, and hostile Islamic civilization, Huntington 'successfully captured an array of feelings that had been calling out for a slogan ever since Khomeini toppled the Shah…'[1] Despite its populist appeal, the thesis was dismissed by most serious observers of global affairs as conceptually flawed and empirically unsubstantiated. This changed with 11 September 2001, when it was seized upon by a hawkish White House, a sensationalist media, a cowed academy, and a stunned American public receptive to simple answers.[2] Western Europeans—relatively more resistant to post-9/11 'clashism'[3]—picked up the rhetoric in the wake of the murder of Theo van Gogh, the Prophet Mohammed caricature controversy, the

Madrid and London bombings, and rising anxiety over extending membership of the European Union to predominantly Muslim Turkey. Today, on
both sides of the Atlantic, the binary increasingly shapes and even 'block[s]
other narratives from forming or emerging,'[4] as evidenced by the tenor of
recent debates over immigration, multiculturalism, and Turkey's European
credentials. Today, even advocates of Turkey's accession to the European
Union, including the country's government, feel compelled to evoke the
binary by describing the country as a 'bridge between civilizations', the great
and only chance for dialogue between the 'West' and 'Islam'.

The challenges associated with Turkey's EU bid – many of which are *non
sequitorial* to the West/Islam debate – are thus the latest in a long list of issues captured by dualistic representations of the 'West' and 'Islam'. And yet
the Turkish case gives pause for thought because of the degree of ambivalence which it also inspires. Huntington himself, rather than situating Turkey
squarely in the 'East', calls it a 'torn country', trapped by its Muslim formation, from which it cannot escape, and Western vocation, which it refuses to
renounce. Others, as seen above, eschew this essentialism and assign a positive value to Turkey's liminal status. But for them too, Turkey is somehow
perpetually 'in between'. This chapter turns to the Turkish case as a way
of problematizing the binary. It suggests that Turkey's proverbial place at
the interstices of the 'West' and 'Islam' is simply a conceptual trope which
emerged in a particular set of historical circumstances and which has colonized modes of thinking both inside the country and beyond. Drawing on a
growing literature on 'late',[5] 'alternative'[6] and 'global'[7] modernities, it argues
that Turkey does not hopelessly straddle the 'West' and 'Islam', but rather
is *perceived* to do so, due to the old habit of equating modernization with
Westernization. The near-reflexive understanding of modernity as inherently Western prevents both Turks and external observers from registering
what in fact has been a complex historical process of 'creative adaptation'[8]
to a set of conditions thrust upon the Ottoman Empire by an ascendant
western Europe from the early nineteenth century onwards. This adaptive
process was certainly informed by and modelled on an emergent Western
modernity – indeed, it contributed to the shape of that modernity by being appropriated as the Oriental 'Other'.[9] Yet engagement with the West
was also always grounded in Ottoman-Islamic and, later on, 'native' Turkish idiom, itself the product of the dialectical intertwinement of Western
and Ottoman-Islamic practices in the preceding century. Conceptually, an
internalization of the West/Islam binary was part and parcel of this whole
process, especially after the promulgation of a brand of Turkish nationalism that rejected the Ottoman-Islamic past in accordance with European

Orientalist perceptions of the Ottoman-Muslim world. In reality, however, 'creative adaptation' rendered that dualism meaningless. For contemporary Turkishness is the product of an inextricable intermingling of manifold expressions of the 'West' and 'Islam' over two centuries, transcending the artificial confines of the binary.

This chapter seeks to give a sense of the complex process of 'creative adaptation' by revisiting Ottoman political elites' engagement with Western actors and ideas over the course of the nineteenth and early twentieth centuries. It recognizes that this process was embedded in an evolving set of power relations and material conditions. However, in light of the chapter's main purpose, a conceptual exercise in questioning the West/Islam binary, the emphasis is on the conceptual and discursive elements of the engagement, rather than on economic, social, or diplomatic points of encounter. Rather than offer new evidence, it seeks to demonstrate how reinterpreting available information through the prism of 'creative adaptation' makes it possible to think outside of a box which condemns Muslim Turkey to a Sisyphean imitation of the West, and acknowledges the hybrid vibrancy of Turkey's own trajectory of modernity.

Ascendant Europe, Oriental responses

The Enlightenment left a twin legacy to western European perceptions of the Ottomans. On one hand, it marked an era of rising confidence and faith in the universal brotherhood of man, helping to dissipate medieval and early Renaissance constructions of the 'Turkish threat'. On the other hand, it breathed new secularized life into old religion-steeped fantasies of the decadent and despotic Muslim. This second strand was reinforced by the growing power asymmetry between European players and the Ottomans. In accordance with this trend, anti-imperialist strands of European thought — evident, for example, in Edmund Burke's empathy with the subjugated peoples of Ireland and India — were eclipsed by enthusiasm for Empire from thinkers as diverse as J.S. Mill and Alexis de Tocqueville to Karl Marx.[10] This took the form of what Said famously called Orientalism:

> a style of thought based upon ontological and epistemological distinction... between "the Orient" and... "the Occident"... despite or beyond any correspondence... with a "real" Orient'; 'It is a kind of Western projection onto and will to govern the Orient in which the Orient is *contained* and *represented* by dominating frameworks.[11]

By casting the Orient as irrational, stagnant, and tyrannical/tyrannized in contrast to a rational, creative, and free West, the agents of European colonialism were able to rationalize their domination of the non-European world. Orientalist logic was inscribed into the fledgling fields of sociology, anthropology, linguistics and archaeology, as well as onto history and philosophy. It was transmitted to tantalized European publics by Romantic novelists, artists, and adventurers seeking escape from 'wheel-going Europe' in the 'Havoc of the East'. And it permeated the political discourse of statesmen embroiled in managing crises associated with, for example, Ottoman minority secessionism and the fate of the Turkish Straits, i.e. the Eastern Question.[12] Whilst it did not dominate all modes of thinking about the non-European world – as evidenced by the works and popularity of E.M. Forster and Joseph Conrad – it was a highly salient discursive accoutrement of nineteenth century European colonialism.

Ottoman Muslims across the 'Near' and 'Middle' East – terms coined in 1902 by a British archaeologist and American navy captain respectively [13] – reacted to Great Power encroachment and its ideological corollary, Orientalism, in three veins.[14] One response declared that European incursions were punishment for deviation from the true path of Islam. Advocating a return to the purity and practices of the era of the Prophet (*asr-i saadet*), this response formed the basis of an Islamic fundamentalism which, like its Jewish and Christian counterparts, sought to reject the condition of Western-imposed modernity from which it in fact emerged. A second response also combed sources of Islamic doctrine, but did so in search of principles which could be fused with select Western institutions, to provide a basis for Islamic modernism. A third group believed that autonomy from the West could only be restored by radically overhauling society along Western lines. All three modes of resistance-cum-adaptation were evident in Ottoman responses to European ascendancy. In time, however, the second approach, syncretism, would dominate.

Ottoman engagement

The process began with Selim III (1789-1807), who came to power the year of Napoleon's invasion of Egypt. Selim's response reflected an impulse which characterized almost all subsequent engagement of the encroaching West, namely, a will to internal reform, if need be along Western lines, for the paradoxically conservative purpose of maintaining the status quo. Accordingly, Selim sought to overhaul the military along Western lines, a move for which he was eventually murdered by the traditional janissary corps. As the European powers' presence in the region accelerated, the constituency

for reform become stronger, and Mahmut II (1808-1839) was able to eliminate the janissaries and launch a programme of importation of Western
military and technological expertise whilst foreswearing the adoption of
corresponding political ideas and institutions.

The insufficiency of these measures became evident with the Greek War
of Independence, framed by its ideologues as a fight for 'freedom' from
'despotism' and won in good measure due to the support of the Great
Powers. The experience brought home awareness of two great dangers to
the Empire: burgeoning nationalism amongst the multi-faith and multi-ethnic Ottoman peoples, and European interference in Ottoman affairs (often
manifest in sponsorship of minority nationalisms). Ottoman elites came to
belive that these woes both stemmed from and could be addressed through
evaluating 'ideas circulating... from the Enlightenment and the Western
revolutions,'[15]. Moved by the aforementioned paradoxical impulse to reform in the name of preservation, they accepted that change was 'inevitable because the survival of the state obviously depended on adaptation to
circumstances.'[16]

Ultimately, the will to change was about answering the question: 'How
to become modern while remaining oneself?'[17] The query spurred the Ottoman political elite to a series of programmatic answers – each, in turn,
dialectically constitutive of its successor. The one feature that all of the
proposed formulae shared was a belief in the notion of a universal civilization that transcended the bonds of faith and culture. The Arabic term for
urban, 'madaniyya' was appropriated to mean 'civilization' (Turkish, medini-
yet), and, via the Enlightenment, was understood as 'a state of 'refinement,
grace, order, respect for set rules, a higher form of living etc.'[18] In this way,
generations of Ottoman reformers imbued the 'Western meaning [of the
term civilization with] the political experiences and cultural aspirations of
the Ottoman elites.'[19]

The first proposition came in the shape of the *Tanzimat* reforms (1839-
1871), which effectuated a gradual and piecemeal, but far-reaching transformation of the institutional and sociological structures of Ottoman society. The high-level bureaucrats of the *Tanzimat* sought to placate minority
agitation and stem European interference by creating a modern, centralized state, with an effective bureaucracy that commanded the loyalty of all
subjects. They did so by accelerating Mahmut's functionalist overhaul of
the military, central and provincial administration, taxation, and education,[20]
but also by injecting a number of liberal political ideas and institutions into
the Ottoman political vocabulary. They recognized too that 'change would
not be accepted by the lower bureaucracy and... public without some kind

of Islamic justification.'[21] This syncretic rationale was bolstered by the fact that legal pluralism was a *de facto* reality. For although the sultan/caliph's legitimacy was enhanced by the principle that the state served religion (*din-u devlet*), in practice Islamic law (*şeriat*[22]) co-existed with forms of customary law known as *kanun* and *örf* which had secular origins, as well as with parallel judiciaries serving the non-Muslim communities. By evoking the Islamic concept of *zaruret* (necessity), as legitimising change, *Tanzimat* reformists were able to situate their engagement of the West on a 'pragmatic, worldly, and flexible' platform.[23]

The first step they took was to guarantee Ottoman subjects' life, property, and religion. These principles, reminiscent of the French Revolution, were also solidly rooted in the variant of Islamic jurisprudence to which the Ottoman dynasty subscribed – the Hanefi school. This school sanctions universal human integrity and the inviolability of a number of basic rights including life and property[24]. This was followed by a series of legal reforms formulated by Ahmet Cevdet Pasha, advisor to three sultans, who was both a learned Muslim scholar (*alim*) and part of the *Tanzimat* inner circle. Ahmet Cevdet 'recognized the need for bringing the Ottoman legal and judicial system into step with the times, but advocated the modification and adaptation of the indigenous Muslim law instead of the importation of alien law whenever that was possible.'[25] To this end, he codified the *şeriat* along Western lines in a new civil code, the *Mecelle*, which affected all aspects of life except family law. Women's status was also a matter of reflection and action for the reformers, and when measures could be defended in accordance with Islamic law, women's rights were expanded. For example, although the *Mecelle* left women's traditional status within the family intact, it instituted equal inheritance rights for women under the rubric of property law in 1856, some thirty years before women's property rights were recognized in Britain. The provision was emblematic of Ottoman syncretism, in that it was legitimized by the fact that Islamic law provides for women to retain property after marriage.[26]

Innovations in literature were also deeply implicated in the *Tanzimat* project as 'Westernists...traditionalists, reactionaries, [and] conservatives' became engaged in a quest for self-identity which 'ultimately was taken up by a number of writers seeking to achieve synthesis'; their creative endeavours produced, 'conflicts and reconciliations which in time elided into a new mentality, new state, new styles of life, and even new types of men and women.'[27] The father of Ottoman literary syncretism was Şinasi who called for a combination of 'the wise old reason of the East with the young ideas of the West.' A democrat, he collected popular proverbs to use in poems which employed a combination of old Court forms and stylistic innovations, whilst conveying modern concepts about the universe, democracy, and rationalism.[28]

Şinasi's protégé, Namık Kemal, was one of the authors of a second wave of responses to the question 'how to become modern while remaining oneself?' The movement was both engendered by and a reaction to the *Tanzimat* in that the middle and lower echelons of the bureaucracy and a flourishing provincial middle class were increasingly irked by the arrogance of the high-level bureaucrats. Their behaviour in practice jarred with the liberal, individualist bent of their reforms.[29] These sentiments were given expression by Kemal and an assemblage of personalities dubbed the Young Ottomans. They were at once 'pious Muslims and Ottoman patriots who looked back nostalgically to a golden era of Islam and to the era of the Empire's greatness' and ardent defenders of 'liberal values with Islamic arguments.'[30] They sought to root the adoption of Western principles of government like citizenship and constitutionalism in Islamic values. Kemal, for example, attempted to establish an Islamic foundation for democracy from the notion of consultation (*shura*) between the Prophet and the members of the Islamic community.[31] He interpreted the oath of allegiance sworn by leaders of the Islamic community to a new caliph (*baya*) as a social contract between subjects and ruler.[32] He also invested old terms with new meanings. He gave the word for birthplace (*vatan*) the connotation of 'fatherland', the description of a freeman (*hürriyet*, i.e. not a slave) the meaning freedom, and made the old term for religious community (*millet*) signify nation.[33]

Although many Young Ottomans were initially sent into exile, most 'identified closely with the state they wanted to save through liberal reforms'[34]. When recalled, their labours bore fruit in the notion of Ottomanism: multicultural citizenship under a unified and territorially-conceived Ottoman state.[35] Their activism thus served as both corrective to the perceived deficiencies of the *Tanzimat*, and as a furthering of their predecessors' goal of consolidating under a centralized Ottoman state a polity rooted at once in nascent modernity and its own cultural idiom. In the final reckoning, Ottomanism was unable to woo back separatist minorities and even had the unintended consequence of promoting the Turkification of the Empire by privileging the Turkish language as the official language of education and government. Furthermore, it failed to stem Great Power usurpation of control over many aspects of Ottoman economic, diplomatic, and military life. It did, however, set forth a coherent ideological programme which would be appropriated and overhauled in the context of the ongoing encounter with European ideas and power.

A new era began in 1877-78 when, in one fell swoop, the Empire lost a third of its territory and a quarter of its inhabitants to the nascent Balkan states. A newly crowned Abdulhamid II responded by suppressing the parliament and constitution which, he believed, had empowered minority activism. The move was authoritarian, but was also animated by the conviction that only a combination of force and caution could safeguard the reform process through which the dwindling Empire could be saved. As the sultan himself put it, 'I made a mistake when I wished to... reform by persuasion and by liberal institutions... I now understand that it is only by force that one can move the people...'[36] Working closely with Prussian advisors, Abdulhamid continued military and educational reform along Western lines. He admired the scientific achievements of European civilization, which he thought could serve as a model for Muslims to 'rid their faith of dogmatism and obscurantism.'[37] At the same time, he was a consummate realist who, writing off the loss of the Balkan Christian nations, sought to invest the Caliphate with an ideology of pan-Islamist resonance, to forestall non-Turkish Muslim separatism. This deployment of a pan-Islamist ideal that declared all Muslims a single nation was a supremely modern innovation, which secured for one more generation the loyalty of Muslim Albanians, Arabs, and Kurds.[38] Although he never acted on the rhetoric – he even suppressed grassroots fundamentalists – his evocation of pan-Islamism provided leverage against European powers, whose millions of Muslim colonial subjects placed great stock by the Caliphate. It also helped pacify a pious Ottoman populace disconcerted by the subversion of traditional order.

A new generation of palace scions, bureaucrats and officers – stifled under Hamidian autocracy and educated in the era's secularized, Westernized academies – picked up the thread of the Young Ottoman critique. Many found themselves exiled to Europe and it was in Paris that the son of a member of the Ottoman parliament founded the Committee of Union and Progress (CUP), known in France as the *Jeunes Turcs*. The CUP initially served as an umbrella organization for diverse strains of resistance to Abdulhamid. The liberal faction was led by the royal patron Prince Sabahattin, who was deeply influenced by Demolin's treatise *A Quoi Tient La Supériorité des Anglo-Saxons*. Believing the Empire's ills were the function of an overbearing state apparatus and the communitarian structure of traditional society, he advocated small government and educational reform to imbue citizens with capitalist initiative.[39] At the first CUP congress in 1902, he declared together with Armenian organizations embroiled in the events of 1894-5, that both violence and solicitation of foreign intervention were acceptable forms of resistance to Abdulhamid.[40] In so doing, he became anathema to the Ottoman nationalist cadre within the CUP, who, more typical of the conservative streak of Ottoman reform, sought to strengthen rather than minimalize the state. Galvanized by the Japanese victory over Russia in 1905 – the first victory of a non-European power against a member of the Concert of Europe – they were suspicious that the Liberals wished to replace Hamidian tyranny with British rule. Officers from the Salonica command declared themselves members of the CUP on the side of the nationalists in 1907. When they deposed the sultan in 1908, the Ottoman dynasty and its pretensions to pan-Islamism, not to mention Ottoman liberals, were shunted to the ideological margins.

At this juncture, the Turkification of Ottoman nationalism began in earnest. The term 'Turk' was recovered from the West,[41] yet another example of the appropriation of European constructs. The effort was two-pronged, with one branch inspired by, amongst others, French and Hungarian Orientalists, as well as émigrés from the Empire's periphery. The Kazan Tatar Yusuf Akçura, for one, emphasized Turks' Central Asian origins.[42] He argued that a multinational Ottoman polity was an illusory dream, and that pan-Islamism was a non-starter because it would be blocked by the colonial powers. Only pan-Turkism could provide the Ottoman state with a vehicle for both its preservation and greatness, as such a project would be supported by all the Turkic peoples of Asia, and opposed only by Russia.[43] Acknowledging Islam as the second pillar of Turkish identity, the pan-Turkist emphasis was on linguistic, ethnic, and for Akçura, racial Turkicness. It was encouraged by the German commander Colmar Freiherr von der Goltz, who oversaw the Ottoman military schools and the reorganization of the army. Initially dismissive of the Empire's chances of survival, Goltz came to believe that the country was undergoing 'profound revitalization and change', especially after getting to know 'the new officer corps and the army drawn mainly from the Turkish peasantry'[44]. With inflections of Herder, he believed that the Turkish people possessed a moral energy which when fused with political pan-Turkism could thrust them into the civilization of Europe. Author of many military textbooks, his views were welcomed by both Abdulhamid and the men of action who controlled the CUP in the post-Hamidian era. Politically, however, pan-Turkism amounted to little more than escapism from escalating tensions. These eventually culminated in the Balkan Wars and the outbreak of the First World War, a juncture at which the CUP triumvirate fatefully chose to align the Empire with Germany.[45]

Meanwhile, there was a second strand of Turkist sentiment, which emphasized the Anatolian homeland of the Turks. This view was reinforced by the fact that ethnic Turks were increasingly seen as the one demographic group upon which the state might still be able to rely; their numbers were also augmented by the flow of Muslim refugees from the Balkans and Caucasus, whose number totalled some 7 million by 1914. Although only half of these migrants were ethnic Turks, they were generally amenable to assimilation to the emergent new ethnic identity.[46] Bolstered by the literary and linguistic revival that had begun with the *Tanzimat*, the novel, poetry, and above all the flourishing press was used to disseminate a future-oriented vision in which Turks were at once 'enlightened' and preserved their own values. The trend was further stimulated by the ever greater asymmetry in relations between the dwindling Empire and its western European interlocutors. As an 1880 newspaper column proclaimed:

> We are, at the present time, under the influence of European civilization, but in this we are unable to prevent excesses and deficiencies. Some of us wish to not drink the "milk" of European civilization but are satisfied with its "skin"…We must become civilized while keeping our national customs; that is, we must try to become civilized Turks.[47]

This distinction yet fusion between Turkish culture and European civilization was characteristic of the thought of Ziya Gökalp, a sociologist and active member of the CUP, who became the leading ideologue of a brand of Turkish nationalism which made claims to Anatolia rather than the whole Turkic world. Pointing to the Japanese example, he asked, 'Can't we accept Western civilization definitively and still be Turks and Muslims?'[48] Defining the West as 'the positive sciences, their methods, and techniques', Gökalp's views bore the imprint of the nineteenth-century Ottoman tradition of casting reform as a culturally-neutral cilvilizational goal. Western civilization – often used interchangeably with the term 'modern' (*asri*) or 'contemporary' (*muasir*) – was thereby compatible with linguistic Turkishness and cultural Islam as the tripartite pillars of an emergent Turkish identity. Gökalp embedded his 'syncretic imaginary' in Durkhemian positivism, with its vision of organic society composed of 'non-material social facts, morality, collective conscience and collective representations.'[49] Gökalp's positivism was very much a product of the contemporary European intellectual climate, in which 'evolutionism, organism, and positivist epistemology joined hands to dictate universally valid and ahistorical truths.'[50] Positivism was also instrumentally attractive for Gökalp and his CUP colleagues because it amounted to a religion of science – indeed it had been lauded as such by its founders, Henri de Saint-Simon and Auguste Conte. This presentation was more palatable to Ottoman popular opinion than alternative materialist theories of society in circulation. Its propensity for social engineering won over the Young Turks, who incorporated it into their nation-building programme in the wake of the Allied invasion, the 'war of independence', and the establishment of the Turkish Republic.[51]

Conclusion: Kemalism and the West/Islam binary

Mustafa Kemal (Atatürk), the founding father of the Turkish Republic, adopted Gökalp's brand of localized nationalism. The great distinction between their understandings of Turkishness, however, lay in Kemal's dismissal of Gökalp's original trinity – Kemalism emphasized the ethno-cultural Turkish and the 'contemporary civilization' components of Turkish identity, whilst rejecting the Islamic dimension. Gökalp's own endorsement of Comptean positivism contributed to this outcome because he deemed it necessary to transcend metaphysical civilization in favour of rational civilization. Kemalists, interpreting Islam through the lens of their European Orientalist counterparts, believed that Islam as a master social signifier was irretrievably part of the metaphysical stage of humanity and could not serve as a platform for positive, and hence civilized knowledge. The achievement of 'contemporary civilization' thus required the transposition of Western modernity onto Turkish society to the extent that it had a 'mimetic quality... [having] to be carried out in detail at the personal level, in terms of dress, writing and habit.'[52] In the meantime, Turkey's Republican founders set about eliminating a series of institutions constitutive of the Ottoman-Islamic order (e.g. the sultanate, caliphate, *ulema*, Islamic brotherhoods and foundations, Arabic script and calendar). In their place, they established their own state-controlled Directorate of Religious Affairs, for the purpose of both privatising and minimising the role of religion in society. In time, this stimulated the emergence of a laicized Turkish-Muslim identity as the unifying principle of the nation, whose independence and territorial integrity were to be safeguarded at all costs.

The emergent Turkish identity thus simultaneously enshrined a laicized Muslim cultural identity and negated Islam.[53] This paradox lay at the heart of what proved to be the definitive answer in the series of unstable formulae Ottoman reformers had offered to the question, 'how to be modern while remaining oneself?' And this answer rendered the paradox, indeed the question itself, irresolvable. For, even if laicized Muslim Turks adopted the attributes of 'contemporary civilization', the notion of 'civilization' for most early twentieth-century Europeans 'expressed the consciousness of the West'[54] and remained intimately associated with Christianity, albeit a Christianity increasingly relegated to the background. As Gökalp himself put it, for the 'European... internationality is nothing but Christendom.'[55] And if international civilization, that is modernity, was irreducibly Christian/Western, then Muslim Turkey, however secularized, categorically could not participate.

Herein lies the source of Turkey's assignation to an indeterminate status within the West/Islam binary. As attested to by recent events, that binary – never an accurate description of a complex process of dialectical intertwinement – has severely distorted the debate over the post-Cold War and post-September 11th order, not to mention Turkey's EU candidacy. This paper has sought to problematize the binary by suggesting that the conventional understanding of Turkey as stuck between two civilizational essences is merely a construction, albeit a near-hegemonic one, rooted in nineteenth-century discourses and their internalization by the Turkish founding elite. This paper has argued that two centuries of modernization were characterized by a process of 'creative adaptation' rather than second-rate imitation. The intermingling of norms, practices, and institutions – which might originally have been characterized as Western or Ottoman-Islamic – engendered a hybrid trajectory of modernity that renders descriptions of Turkey as 'Western', 'Islamic' or something 'in between' meaningless. Turkey's liminality is not reflective of an inability on the part of Turks to converge in full with modernity, but rather one of how modernity is defined. Thus the Turkish problematique speaks not of an *aporia* but of what Derrida called a 'blind spot', a point of interpenetration of Self(s) and Other(s), from which it may be possible to dismantle the West/Islam binary altogether.

CHAPTER IV

THE USES OF EMPIRE: MYTHS AND MEMORIES IN THE BALKANS AND THE EASTERN MEDITERRANEAN

DIMITAR BECHEV

We are often told that the Mediterranean mosaic can be traced to the footprints of successive empires: Ancient Rome and its heir Byzantium, the Arab Caliphate, the grand land-based polities of the Ottomans, the Habsburgs and the Moroccan Sharifs, the modern colonial empires of France and Great Britain, the Romanov tsardom followed by the mighty Soviet Union. Empires' fortunes may have waxed and waned but they have also shaped collective identities, notions of belonging and images of Self and Other. While the Mediterranean space defies facile generalizations, it would not be an exaggeration to contend that over the past 200 years or so, it has seen a complex transition from a world of empires to a world of nation-states. Commencing with the independence of Greece in 1830, this tide culminated in the decolonization process of the 1950s and 1960s. During such changes, how do the heirs of empire deal with what is left behind from days past? How do they construct, imagine, and instrumentalize imperial legacies, and enshrine them in collective memory?

This is a difficult question, as the borderline between the past and the present is thin. Legacies linger on in the aftermath of empire, and survive – whether vivid or fading – in institutions, social structures, mentalities and practices. However, when the analytical lens shifts to collective identities and boundaries of belonging, what matters is the *perception* of the past rather than the *imprint on the present,* to borrow an insightful distinction from the Balkan historian Maria Todorova.[1] Herein lies a tension. National states foster a sense of cohesion across time, space and social class. They project clear-cut territorial borders and identity diacritics separating nationals from non-nationals. Empires, by contrast, have fluid frontiers and differentiated modes of individual and group attachment to central authority.[2] The relationship between the two types of polity is fraught with myriads of contradictions.

The chapter examines the *liaison dangereuse* across the Balkans as well as the Eastern Mediterranean, a tentative 'region' comprising Turkey and the Levant. It sets off by unpacking the notions of empire and nation-state. It then investigates national mythologies, in order to build a typology of representations of empire. This will be used to investigate usages of the imperial past by present day liberal opponents of nationalism.

The world of premodern empires

The word 'empire' occupies an honorary position amongst what are termed in academic jargon 'essentially contested concepts': it is multilayered, controversial, politically laden and emotive. One thing is for sure: empire is bad. By the time Vladimir Lenin forged the term imperialism as a label for the 'most advanced stage of capitalism' empire had already acquired an aura of illegitimacy in intellectual discourse. Despite the heroic efforts of academics and pundits such as Niall Ferguson or even Michael Ignatieff to market liberal empire, we continue to associate the notion with domination, coercion, exploitation, or – to borrow from the Founding Fathers of the new colossus – 'taxation without representation'.[3] This is the legacy of the 1848 Spring of the Nations, the Wilsonian idea of self-determination and the anticolonial movements in the Third World following the Second World War. Still, the metaphor is surprisingly obstinate. From President Ronald Reagan's 'evil empire' of the early 1980s to the critiques of America's interventions in the Middle East or of globalization, to recent portrayals of the EU as a 'neo-medieval empire',[4] the concept of empire continues to underscore our efforts to make sense of the complex world around us along with its historical roots and antecedents.

While empire invariably evokes images of concentration of power—which is justified given the meaning of the Latin *imperium* – a more fruitful way to grasp the phenomenon should look at (1) the type of territorial governance espoused; (2) the ideology of empire and the resultant collective identities.

On the first front, Alexander Motyl has argued, rather convincingly, that empires are defined by a complex relationship between a core elite and peripheral elites and societies.[5] This relationship plays out differently in different imperial contexts. The classical premodern empires, from Rome to the Habsburg monarchy, were territorially contiguous in the sense that there was a direct link between the dominions and the centre. The core-periphery configuration was much more visible in seaborne empires which emerged later in history, though one could already see Venice – which established its dominion after the thirteenth century across vast swathes of the Eastern Mediterranean – as a prototype. While the core-periphery structure is visible in other polities, notably in the nation-state, it is important that with empire the distinction is much more clear-cut and engrained in political and social institutions. Moving from premodern to colonial empires, we see that nineteenth and twentieth century Great Britain and France organized political life in the metropoles according to the principles of citizenship, democracy and mass participation, yet ruled their overseas possessions either through local traditionalist elites or authoritarian civilian and military administrations.[6] The ideal-typical empire is grounded on the principles of heterogeneity and adaptation to local conditions: perhaps this is one of the reasons the British have been considered more successful imperialists than the French, who treated Algeria as just another *département*, and who schooled the pupils in West Africa about '*nos ancêtres, les Gaulois*'.[7]

Imperial polities rest upon universalist ideologies. This tendency manifests itself in multiple guises: Rome's promotion of its *ius civile* within the Mediterranean, Charlemagne's claim to be the protector of Christendom through the construction of the Holy Roman Empire, the Arab Caliphate embodying the *umma*, i.e. the community of faithful spreading from the deserts of western India to the Atlantic shores, and Moscow as 'the third Rome'. One should also note the secular myths of *mission civilisatrice* or the 'White Man's Burden' which underpinned Europe's, or rather Britain and France's, domination over large parts of the non-European world during the enlightened nineteenth century.

Interestingly, universalistic aspirations coupled with the differentiation of the imperial core from peripheral domains prevented certain empires from engaging in homogenizing policies to mirror practices already taking root in nation-states. Of course, there have been exceptions in modern times: the assimilationist campaigns towards non-Russian populations in the western domains of the Tsarist Empire in the 1880s and 1890s, and 'Magyarization' in the Hungarian half of the Dual Monarchy in the wake of the 1867 *Ausgleich*. As a rule, these efforts proved abortive. Empires are by definition about mixing peoples and the patterns of conflict associated with 'unmixing' are a crucial part of imperial legacy. Empires are multilingual, multiethnic and multiconfessional. Social class, ideological alignments and closeness to the centre of power are much more meaningful than identity boundaries established around ethnicity and language. Empires are often ruled by elites of different ethnic group than the mass of subjects. To cite a Mediterranean example, the Byzantine state saw more than one emperor of Armenian origin. Nowadays it is inconceivable that a non-Greek would head the Ecumenical Patriarchate in Constantinople – this fine illustration of Romanian historian Nicolae Iorga's notion of *Byzance après Byzance*.[8]

Another implication of imperial universalism is that empires conceive of themselves as the centre of the world, if not its legitimate rulers. This was especially true of the premodern empires. Thus, while Western European diplomats resided in Istanbul from the sixteenth century onwards, the Ottoman sultan would not maintain permanent embassies in European capitals until the Tanzimat era.[9] State doctrine ranked the *padishah* above the European monarchs, and invested him with supreme authority as God's representative on earth. Especially during the period of expansion, the Ottomans never conceived of clearly established borders. Theirs was a frontier state, much like nineteenth century America as famously described by Frederick Jackson Turner, whose margins were rather fuzzy and movable.[10] This presents a curious contrast with the modern Turkish republic's fixation on territorial integrity and the protection of its borders.

Like its premodern counterparts, the Ottomans prioritized the extraction of revenue from loosely attached fiefdoms in the periphery, rather than by ruling the latter in an intrusive fashion. In the Balkans and Anatolia, Byzantium was surrounded by a circle of states which it found hard to control politically but still drew into its imperial orbit through its cultural and socio-economic influence. In a similar vein, the Ottomans exercised indirect control over its Maghreb regencies and parts of the Arabian Peninsula, but also Eastern Anatolia and the highlands of Albania and Montenegro as well as areas in present-day Greece. The Ottoman state drew its legitimacy from Islam, though it incorporated Turkic tribal traditions as well as the institutional legacy of Byzantium – e.g. in the relationship between the Sultan and the land-holding gentry of the provinces.

This does not mean that the empire did not try to emulate the nation-states. The opening up of the Ottoman lands to the forces of modernity and capitalism during the Tanzimat era was manifest in reforms aimed at administrative centralization, economic modernization and the gradual introduction of Western constitutional models. This was one of the sources behind the ideas of Ottomanism – a common identity transcending ethnic and religious boundaries and linked to loyalty to the state – reaching their zenith with the Young Turk revolution of 1908. Similar dilemmas of keeping the pace with modern times were faced by Russia and the Austrian (later Austro-Hungarian) Empire. Both saw recurrent waves of modernizing reform and attempts to reestablish allegiance to the state derived from collective identity rather than traditional legitimation proceeding from the monarch's divinely sanctioned authority.[11]

The premodern empires of the Mediterranean can be better understood if compared and contrasted with the colonial empires of the modern era. Theirs was a world shaped by ideas of exclusive sovereignty, established (if disputed) borders, and delineated spheres of influence – hence hallmark events in diplomatic history such as the Congress of Berlin in 1885 parceling up Africa. Metropoles cultivated 'colonial subjects' as well as new 'Europeanized' elites in the colonies, which absorbed the culture of the centre and carried it back to their native milieu. This dynamic is rarely observed in 'old-fashioned' empires where often the core lands where the dominant group formed a majority were not necessarily the most economically and socially advanced region – as shown by the cases of the Baltic provinces of the Romanovs or Bohemia within Austria-Hungary.

The nation and its myths and memories

The nation-state has in many ways been the antipode of the premodern imperial model. The mechanics of governance are different. Nation-states seek to draw and protect territorial borders, centralize administration, create all-encompassing political institutions, penetrate society, transcend parochial loyalties, and standardize languages in ways that erstwhile empires were either incapable or unwilling to do. In Europe, the rise of the nation-state over time sealed the fate of more than one empire, though this possibly conditioned European imperial expansion in the rest of the world. The Treaty of Westphalia (1648) inaugurated the concept and practice of state sovereignty, chiefly meaning – at this juncture – the exclusivity of princely authority over the respective realm. Westphalia dealt the final blow to the preceding territorial order in Europe established on the notion of universal Christendom and a web of overlapping secular jurisdictions: feudal kingdoms, city republics, federations of free merchant towns, ecclesiastical fiefdoms, dependencies and tributaries.[12] Several decades later, Voltaire was able to sarcastically remark that the Holy Roman Empire – this last vestige of Charlemagne's universalist vision – was neither holy, nor Roman, nor really an empire. It did not last much longer, as Napoleon abolished it in

1806, formally sanctioning what had been a long-standing reality (though Charlemagne is the name of one of the buildings which houses the EU Commission in Brussels).

The French Revolution and Napoleonic wars spread the gospel of popular sovereignty, which in turn paved the way for the emergence of national ideologies and movements across Europe. The nation – a notion as contested as that of empire – was seen by its intellectual and political champions as a group of individuals bound into a community of shared language, culture and, at times, alleged genetic makeup, but also by shared political aspirations. Rulers and ruled, elite and social strata now communicated in a single standardized idiom, and had their loyalties directed to a unified set of institutions providing physical security, economic welfare, education and social protection (thus fostering solidarity across the society). Uniformity, as Ernest Gellner argued, reflected the structural transformations linked with the expansion of markets and technological change in the modern era.[13] Even if one is critical of Gellner's standpoint, it is easy to observe that the ideology of nationalism, much like the imperial visions of major European nation-states such as Britain and France, was married to the discourses of modernity, progress and socio-economic development.

The spread of nationalist ideology also had a tremendous effect on South East Europe and the Eastern Mediterranean, which at that juncture were under the rule of the Ottoman and Habsburg empires. The story is well-known. Throughout the nineteenth century, the Ottoman state – but also the Habsburg monarchy if we forget for a time the Bosnian episode – shrank, eroded by its nationalist contenders. In the Balkans, empires were succeeded by nation-states, though neither the first nor the second Yugoslavia were nation-states in the way neighbouring Greece, Albania or Hungary were. By the 1920s, Kemalist Turkey cast aside the last vestiges of the Ottoman polity, though empire's legacies survived there much longer than it did in the neighbouring countries.[14] In the Eastern Mediterranean and the Middle East, the European colonial powers played a key role in the establishment of Jordan, Syria and Iraq, whose borders they drew using often arbitrary criteria.[15] The classical age of empires, to borrow from Eric Hobsbawm, came to an end with the First World War, though it was not until the 1956 Suez Crisis and the Algerian War of 1958–1962 that this became apparent in the metropoles.[16]

Nation-states in Western Europe, the Balkans, the Middle East and elsewhere, are in the business of promoting a sense of community within complex and often fragmented and polarized societies. True, nineteenth and twentieth century nationalism was a phenomenon having to do with modernization, 'print-capitalism', technological revolution and the emergence of mass politics. In his famous lecture at the Sorbonne in 1882, Ernest Renan, himself a native of Brittany, described the nation as *un plébiscite de tous les jours*. However it was not solely the common will that bound the group together, but also a set of communal remembrances. In order to be a nation, a group of people had to be equally able to recall 'heroic past, great men, glory' and to forget all that divide it.[17] Thus, even in the tradition of French republicanism, the construction and celebration of shared memories is essential. It is not a purely voluntaristic community but one which traces its roots in history, the further back the better. Nation builders use historical material – which according to theorists like Anthony Smith still have to resonate with premodern collective identities and cultural artifacts – to create representations of unity and continuity through time.[18]

Seen from this perspective, national myths cannot be treated as the opposite number of truth. For one, the criterion also tends to be very subjective. In the words of William McNeil, 'one man's truth is another man's myth'.[19] Indeed myths blend – albeit always in different proportions – fact and imagination, description and distortion, emotion and reason. What really matters is the myth's social and political function: its purpose is to keep together a community far larger than the one people find themselves in, and interact with in their daily routine. As aptly shown by Lucian Boia and Stephanie Schwandner-Sievers in the context of South East Europe, myths use the past to forge a sense of shared purpose and identity through narratives of togetherness and destiny.[20] Myths are thus an expression of the nation's Janus-faced nature – rooted in the past but facing the present and the future. What is more, they provide the overarching framework which structures the shared memories of the nation or any other human community, and they create social boundaries between the national self and its Others.

Myth(s) of Empire?[21]

How does national myth-making deal with empires and their legacies? Can we say that there is a distinctive imperial myth within the armour of national myths?[22] The Mediterranean area, not least the Balkans and the Levant, has seen a fair number of empires over its millennial history. Premodern empires such as Rome, Byzantium or the Arab Caliphate, far removed in time, are more amenable to manipulation by national awakeners, historians, political and cultural elites. How have the nation-states of the area made use of those historical memories, reshaped them, and mobilized them for achieving certain political aims? Can we speak about a distinctive imperial myth recurrent in diverse national contexts in the way that 'the white man's burden' appeared in the ideologies of Western European colonial powers?

The short answer to this question is 'no'. The reason is that empire was experienced differently in different national and regional contexts. Various national or proto-national elites, ethnicities and social classes had different positions and faced dissimilar challenges according to how 'embedded' they were in imperial milieus. While patterns of national mobilization within a multiethnic setting exhibit similarities – for instance in terms of stages of development, as famously analyzed by Miroslav Hroch[23] – the managing of imperial pasts can follow multiple scenarios: from rejection to celebration to nostalgia. Perceptions also tend to change through time. The Habsburg monarchy, which was considered Europe's *Völkerkerker* ('prison of nations') by many of its contemporaries, was recast by the political elites of post-communist Central Europe as a beacon of Europeanness and enlightenment.[24] Similarly, the Ottoman Empire – the backward, Asiatic Other of early Kemalism, of Balkan nation-builders or even of the British liberal grandee William Gladstone – now furnishes inspiration and intellectual ammunition to Turkish free thinkers in their criticism of the rigid nationalism of the republic and its persistent failure to accommodate minority rights.

Yet images of empire feature prominently in national mythologies. Collective memories of imperial rule and perceptions of legacy are part of a number of myths from the typology proposed by authorities on the subject such as Anthony Smith, Geoffrey Hosking and George Schöpflin. Here are some of the myths that feature in the repertoire of nationhood:
– Myths of glorious pasts and golden ages;
– Myths of resistance and survival;
– Myths of victimhood, suffering and injustice;
– Myths of renewal and rebirth.

Glorious pasts and golden ages
Myths of glorious pasts and golden ages are fairly common in nationalist constructions and representations of history. In most cases, they are opposed to the rather lacklustre present of the national group or nation-state in question. Appeals to former glory, therefore, are a compensatory mechanism used to bolster the nation's standing among its counterparts. They are a favourite mining ground of intellectuals, particularly in the early periods of nation-building. Thus Greek nationalism – a pioneer in the Balkans and the Eastern Mediterranean – was strongly oriented, thanks to the conscious efforts of adepts of the Western Enlightenment like Adamantios Korais,

towards classical Hellenic antiquity. This articulation of Greekness was in contrast with the one linked with Orthodoxy and the memory of Byzantium espoused by the traditional ecclesiastical and lay elites based in Istanbul. Ultimately, however, the challenge to the narrative of Hellenic continuity posed most famously by the German historian Jakob Philipp Fallmereyer in the 1820s prompted local intellectuals like Constantine Paparrigopoulos (1815–1891) to weave Byzantium and Ancient Greece together into an unbroken millennial thread of Greekness. Nevertheless, the conflict between the racial Hellenic and the cultural-religious Byzantine ('Romaic') myth was far from solved.[25]

Medieval (quasi-)empires provided the best identity resource for a number of other Balkan nations. The Bulgars and the Serbs could turn their eyes to the Tsardoms of Simeon the Great (tenth century) and Stephen Dušan (fourteenth century) as their golden ages. Both polities had their imperial dimension. Their rulers imitated the glamour of Byzantium, claiming the title of Tsar (a Slavicized form of Caesar) and seeking the throne of Constantinople. In the nineteenth century they were 'nationalized' and recast from multiethnic conglomerates into blueprints of modern nation-states. Upon the proclamation of formal independence in 1908, King Ferdinand adopted the title of Tsar, and in a few years his troops were desperately fighting the defence lines of Istanbul in vain pursuit of the imperial dream. Lacking their own medieval empire, the Romanians stressed their historical link with Rome manifest in their Latin tongue. This fed into the sense of antiquity and cultural superiority over the barbaric Magyars and Slavs surrounding the isle of Latinity in the European east, i.e. Moldova, Wallachia but also the disputed Transylvania. Rome inspired post-Risorgimento Italy's drive to spread its hegemony in the east. The road to domination over *Mare Nostrum* passed through the conquest of Libya and the Dodecanese islands in the 1911 war with the Ottomans, and the acquisition of Trieste, the Istrian peninsula, Fiume (Rijeka) and Zara (Zadar) after the First World War, as well as the gradual absorption of Albania into Benito Mussolini's state in the 1930s.[26]

A latecomer in the Mediterranean and still in its nascent stage in the last decade of Ottoman rule, Arab nationalism had its own vision of the golden past. It was dominated by the myth of the Arab Caliphate of the early Islamic centuries. This glorious era came to an end with the rise of Turkic dynasties and especially with the Mongol invasion leading to the fall of Baghdad in 1258. A handful of Arab nationalist intellectuals, mainly from Ottoman Syria, 'celebrated the history of the early Arab conquests, which carried Islam from the Oxus to the Pyrenees.'[27] Despite the references to Islam, Christians occupied a prominent position in the ranks of those ideologues. They saw the ideology of Arabness as a tool to improve their standing in a predominantly Muslim society. One such example is George Antonius, an Orthodox Christian who became the father of Arab nationalist historiography. The myth of the golden age was later contested: in the latter half of the twentieth century, Maronite activists espoused ideas of Lebanese separateness dating back to the Phoenicians.[28] In the early twentieth century, Egypt too maintained a sense of distinctiveness rooted in its autonomous political development at least since the early nineteenth century. In 1970s Egypt, after Nasser's passing as leader of the pan-Arab movement, the Sadat regime reoriented the national project (back) to an emphasis on Egypt's cultural uniqueness.

Resistance and survival

At least in part, what George Antonius called the 'Arab awakening' had to do with alienation from Istanbul resulting from the Young Turks' policies of Turkification in the Arab provinces. This was followed by resentment towards the mandate regime established by the French and the British during the interwar years. Myths of glorious past are inextricably linked with myths of purity and survival in a hostile environment and rough times. In nationalist imagination, empires – invariably dominated by groups of other ethnic and religious background and also conducive to 'mixing' people – are often the ultimate Other. What is essential is to preserve national specificity within the melting pot of empires. In the Balkans, national historiographies have carefully researched every instance of resistance to Ottoman rule, whatever its roots. The study of mutual influences and everyday practices of commercial exchange or religious syncretism comes into the spotlight much more rarely, and almost never in historical texts aimed at mass consumption such as history school books. Of course the opposite is true for Turkish historiography, which has tended to romanticize life under the Ottoman Empire as defined by peaceful coexistence of faiths and ethnic groups. Yet, at the end of the day, Turkish national narratives have also emphasized the survival of the Turkic identity, language and folk culture in the cosmopolitan and Islamo-centric Ottoman environment ready to be rehabilitated and developed to its fullness by the secular nationalism of the republic.[29] In nationalist thinking, primordial nations live encapsulated only to reemerge with the decline of imperial order and their restitution. Even par excellence imperial institutions such as the Orthodox churches, which contributed to the blurring of ethnic lines amongst their adherents, were seen by national historiographies as protectors of the *Volksgeist* and national identity during the dark Ottoman centuries.

The myth of heroic resistance to imperial encroachments is a subspecies of the same survival myth. A classical example is the Serbian myth (also powerful in Montenegro) of fighting the Turkish invaders to the end, but also that of fighting the Teutonic imperialists represented in a different period by the Austro-Hungarians and the Nazis (ignoring, of course, the important role played by the Habsburg Monarchy in the development of Serbian political and cultural institutions and elites). The image of Serbia opposing (imperialist) outsiders such as Germany or the US was also projected strongly by the regime of Slobodan Milošević. One could also draw a parallel with Albanian and Romanian myths of preserving national specificity and independence in the face of recurrent waves of invaders, mainly Slav and Ottoman, and claiming back their ancestral plains and place in history after surviving for centuries in their obscure highland refuges. Similarly, Arab nationalism in the twentieth century was profoundly influenced by the struggle against colonial domination as well as Zionism, which was portrayed as an extension of the West's subjugation of the Middle East. One cannot fail but notice the structural similarities with the Israeli myth of the Masada which again builds on the theme of resistance and survival in the face of imperial power.[30]

Victimhood and sacrifice

Myths of resistance and struggle are genetically linked to myths of victimhood and sacrifice. Empires victimize nations, divert them from their progressive paths of development, and often deny them their rightful place on the proper side of civilizational divides. The *martyrium* myth has strong religious overtones. A classical example is the recurrent image of partitioned Poland as Christ, advanced by Romantic nationalists such as the poet Adam Mickiewicz. This imagery is particularly potent when mingled with the dichotomy of an enlightened West and backward East. In South East Europe there is an abundance of so-called *antemurale* myths. Nearly all nations have imagined themselves as bastions of Western civilization against the encroaching East – be it the Ottomans or the Russian Empire. Examples include Croatia, where the phrase *antemurale Christianitatis* was often heard from the historian Franjo Tudjman, as well as Romania and Albania, where the myth of Skenderbeg, the last defender of Europe against the Ottoman hordes, has been central in constructions of national identity since the late nineteenth century (Skenderbeg himself is a good illustration of the power of imperial memories as he claimed the name and therefore the grand stature of Alexander the Great).[31] Martyr nations suffer for the good of larger social entities such as Christendom or European civilization. Their relative backwardness in the modern era is the direct consequence of their sacrifice at the holy altar of history. Empire, therefore, emerges as the ultimate 'Other' of the nation. The nation is progressive and future-oriented, while Empires represent decay and stagnation and thus elicit memories of humiliation. At the same time, and rather paradoxically, nations claim superiority as their roots are much more ancient than those of the *ancien regimes* imposed on them by imperial overlords.

Renewal and rebirth

Narratives of former glory, victimhood and resistance feed into the ultimate national myth, the vision of rebirth and renewal. Thus the memory of the Byzantine Empire set the scene for the development of the so-called *Megali Idea* (Great Idea) which envisioned the expansion of the tiny Greek state into a hegemonic power in the Balkans and Anatolia.[32] Imperial myths and memories were immensely important as an instrument with which to draw the imaginary boundaries of the successor nation. Imperial rebirth had clear territorial dimensions set by the historical rights of the nation. In the Greek case, these were rather unclear as Byzantine borders ebbed and flowed. Still, the focus on Constantinople as an imperial/national capital made the question of the territorial limits somewhat irrelevant. Hungarian nationalism is at the other extreme. The lands of St Stephen's crown were clearly delimited since the days of the medieval kingdom. Their boundaries were reaffirmed with the emergence of the Magyar quasi-empire within the Habsburg Monarchy spreading from the Gulf of Kvarner in the Adriatic to the Carpathian chain. Even today, one constantly sees images of St Stephen's Hungary when walking in Budapest, a remnant of the interwar revisionism fixated on the restoration of the pre-1918 status quo.

In their attempt to recreate ancient and medieval empires, however, modern states are more likely to fail. The Greek case is again instructive. Statesmen such as Elefterios Venizelos had to confront the complexity and ambiguity of imperial legacy: Greek-speaking or Orthodox populations affiliated with Hellenism were scattered throughout Asia Minor and the Balkans. To rebuild an Empire in the shape of a nation-state was a formidable task, and one doomed to failure at that. *Megali Idea* burned in the flames of Smyrna in September 1922. Ultimately, the Ottoman State proved a better guardian of Byzantium's legacy than the modern Greek heir apparent which, together with the newly-born Turkish republic, was the protagonist in dismantling much of what the two communities had shared for centuries.

Imageries of revival were very vivid amongst the Arab nationalist think-ers too. The very word for rebirth or renaissance in Arabic, *Ba'ath*, was the name given to leading political parties in Syria and Iraq. The promi-nent ideologue of *Ba'athism*, Michel Aflaq, built bridges between the an-cient achievements of the Arabs manifest in the Islamic civilization, and the cause of social revolution and national liberation in the twentieth century.[33] *Ba'athist* strongmen such as Saddam Hussein had the tendency to draw par-allels between their own personalities and the grand imperial figures of the Iraqi past: the Abbasid caliphs, Saladdin (a fellow Tikriti), or even Nebucha-dnezzar II of the Neo-Babylonian Empire. Similarly, modern Egypt, where the nation-building process had a strong Arabist emphasis, also celebrated its pharaonic heritage. For instance, Nasser brought a giant statue of Ram-ses II from Memphis to Cairo in 1955.[34] The nationalist vision struggled to combine pan-Arabism and loyalty to the state and its imagined history.

Conclusion: nostalgic counter-myths?

Nation-states in the Mediterranean have claimed the legacy of preexist-ing empires or defined themselves in stark opposition to the latter. They were driven, in the first instance, by the desire to establish continuity with the grandeur of distant eras. Secondly, nation-builders rejected the imperial order with all its vestiges, such as domination by an 'alien' centre and ethnic and confessional heterogeneity, and constructed memories of struggle and resistance enshrined in textbooks, collective commemorations, popular me-dia and other assorted *lieux de mémoire*.

Both strategies have played a tremendous role in shaping identities and maintaining the boundaries between Self and Other. They have also posed problems. The glorification of the imperial past neglects the profound dif-ferences in terms of political structure and identity politics between em-pires and modern nation-states. When married to territorial expansionism, the imperial vision has proved costly. The drive to redeem one's empire spelled a national catastrophe for Greece but also Italy. It also bred war, po-litical and socio-economic strife, ethnic cleansing and also intra-communal conflict. Ironically, the myths of imperial rebirth have contributed to the utter destruction of the demographic and cultural legacies of empire.

The second mode, that of rejection of empire, is equally problematic. Grand narratives opposing the national Self to its imperial Other(s) have portrayed the past in simplified, black-and-white terms. They have swept aside dissonant memories of coexistence, exchanges, hybrid identifications or even the profitability of empire for individuals and social groups seen as inseparable, and sometimes essential, parts of the nation's sacred past. The classical example, of course, is the Ottoman Empire, whose rule is still vilified in most successor states, from Syria to Albania, and, not least, in pre-1980s Turkey.

This rejectionist stance has been turned around by critics of nationalism. The latter tend towards nostalgia for the imperial age and its cosmopolitanism, contrasting it with the parochial and exclusionist ideology of the nation-states. In the 1980s and 1990s, Central European intellectuals and political activists recast the Habsburg era, particularly the pre-First World War decades, as their paradise lost replaced in the interwar period by petty nationalisms and ultimately by the tyranny of totalitarianism. One finds similar motives in the writings of Orhan Pamuk celebrating the ethno-religious diversity, the cultural richness and ambiguousness of the Ottoman era.[35] Of course, such nostalgic representations are themselves anachronistic in the sense that they project contemporary dilemmas onto the past. Amongst other things, this is very visible in the rather promiscuous usage of labels such as 'multiculturalism', which stem from the particular experience of various Western European or North American societies in dealing with immigrant communities, in relation to the Ottoman or the Habsburg Empire.[36] Imperial nostalgia is about myth-making too, as it appropriates the past selectively to make a political statement about the present. Compared to nationalism, this is a more benign usage of imperial history. Yet it opens up new spaces for contestation and counter-myths.

PART II:

REVISITING MEMORIES TO TRANSFORM CONFLICTS?

CHAPTER V

CAN WE ACT ON MEMORY... IN THE MEDITERRANEAN? THE CASE OF ALGERIA

MARIE-CLAIRE LAVABRE AND DIMITRI NICOLAIDIS

Political actors often try to interpret the numerous identity-driven conflicts around the Mediterranean, with a view to pacifying relations between communities and states. In doing so, they emphasize the weight of history as a major conflictual factor inside, as well as between states in the Balkans, the Middle East and North Africa; they seek to promote a renewed vision of history, and set themselves the task of changing the representations of the Other, especially where national myths have been mobilized in past clashes.

The 'politics of memory' proceed from two assumptions: first, that there is a collective representation of the past of which the individual imaginary is but a reflection, and which one can influence; in addition, that 'work' on individuals' memories, or at least on the interpretation of the 'traumatic' past which is supposedly shared, allows for the development of new individual representations. These can eventually acquire a collective dimension and change the public discourse about the past. This dual assumption implies that there is some continuity between the particular group's narrative about the past, and 'living memory', i.e. shared individual representations and recollections. However, this assumption does not rule out the need to examine the mechanisms from the level of the individual to the group and backwards. How does one pass from the diversity of individual memories to the unity of fixing a story of the past or a shared 'historical memory'? How, in turn, does one get from a memory framed as a collective one, to the multiplicity of individual experiences? It seems that these questions concern the possibilities of influencing both individual and collective memory.

Yet the question of 'can we act on memory?' remains largely underexplored. Not only by 'peacebuilders' but also within the different social sciences dealing with collective memory. Nevertheless, one can summarily distinguish three broad approaches, embedded in different disciplines and theoretical traditions, which take memory as an object of study. The first so-called *lieux de mémoire* problematique, is associated with the name of Pierre Nora and rooted in the field of history, and focuses on the political usages of the past, generally at the level of the nation. The second, that of *travail de mémoire* (memory work), is linked to the name of Paul Ricoeur, and is part of a politico-normative perspective which examines the issue of 'just memory'. The third goes back to the sociologist Maurice Halbwachs and his concept of 'memory frames' (*cadres de mémoire*), i.e. the social and political conditions favouring the evocation and formulation of memories. It is located in the field of sociology. These three paradigms refer to different concepts and contexts. However, they often overlap in the perspective of the practitioners of memory, an expanding and internationalizing field.

This chapter first provides an overview of these three paradigms of 'sites of memory', 'memory work' and 'memory frames'. It then goes on to test the validity of each through the case of Algeria, where all three may be involved. Indeed, on that side of the Mediterranean, where the divide between people and power is massive, it would be futile to account for the shared representations of the past solely on the basis of discourses produced in official politics and the media. Drawing on empirical sources, including fieldwork, we will examine three successive levels of the so-called 'collective' memory: the political usages of the past and their evolution, the militant efforts to construct a 'just memory', and, finally, the social conditions for the evocation and formulation of individual experiences. Thus we attempt to sketch out the issue of memory as faced by present-day Algerian society and conclude by drawing some broader lessons from this case.

The paradigms of memory

The three dominant paradigms of memory which we describe coexist today in France but also, with local nuances, elsewhere. Whilst developed side-by-side and overlapping, each has a history of its own. Although Maurice Halbwachs can be regarded as a precursor (*Les cadres sociaux de la mémoire* was published in 1925, *La topographie légendaire des Evangiles* in 1942, *La mémoire collective*, in 1950, posthumously), he did not father these ideas. On the contrary, it was thanks to the wave or the fashion of memory writing that Halbwachs was rediscovered.

Sociology has not been at the forefront of the study of memory. Historians were the first to take it up as a research subject, focusing excessively on the definition of memory and its distinction from history. The result has been an epistemological debate opposing an academic discipline – with all its professional conventions – to a social phenomenon dismissed from the outset as falling short of scholarly standards for how to read the past. In historical circles, the *lieux de mémoire* problematique is largely dominant, at least in terms of the definition of memory it puts forward. It has been exported widely: to Germany, Italy, the Netherlands, and elsewhere. Although it studies the public narrative of the past, or, even more so, the political usages of the past, first signs of this approach are in fact present in the work of Moses Finley in the 1960s. Finley reflected on the uses and misuses of history, and issued an injunction to historians to view these issues as legitimate objects for research. We remember especially the 'liberating divorce between history and memory' declared by Pierre Nora, and his announcement that memory should become the 'spearhead' of a new historiography. Initially 'counter-memorative' and critical, this project has been perverted, as Nora acknowledges himself, by its success – one to which the nostalgia for a national identity deeply rooted in the narrative of the past has undoubtedly contributed. The profound social, political and economic changes marking the mid-1970s certainly proved fertile ground. Sites of memory are born of a 'sense of loss' and are in some respects resolutely past-oriented and appeasing at the same time: it is noteworthy that, twenty years after this enterprise was first launched, the issues of colonization or communism are still absent. In its radicalized form, Pierre Nora's concept opens a genealogical perspective on the uses of memory. If the historian's intellectual quest is applied to realities as diverse as 'flag', 'Vichy' or the 'conversation', another measure of the concept's success is the fact that it is also used in reference to sites, in the physical sense of this term. That is why 'memory politics' may be applied, tautology aside, to identify 'sites of memory', to illustrate the common past of the nation or to commemorate this or that category of victims in a community of reconciliation.

The second, 'memory work' perspective, was imported from psychoanalysis. It starts from the premise that, like the individual, society is suffering from its past and must undergo memory work, the way one undergoes a period of mourning, in order to achieve 'just memory', proper forgetting and reconciliation with the Other as well as with oneself. According to Paul Ricoeur and, a short time before him, Tzvetan Todorov, this problem clearly relates to a normative register and a politico-philosophical reflection. It is not foreign to the earlier reflections of Henry Rousso on Vichy or Benjamin Stora on Algeria, even though many historians privilege the analysis of 'memory' in terms of the uses of the past in the framework of the nation. It has seen a strong rise since the 1990s in response to the emergence of the no less intrusive 'duty of memory'. In many respects, this paradigm overlaps with 'sites of memory', in that it matches better the present reality of various 'memorial' claims, the political will to settle past accounts and formulate political strategies for healing and resolving conflicts that arise from the past.

The third approach is more strictly limited to the academic sphere, less easily appropriated by political actors, and more demanding in its treatment of the memory phenomenon. This is the 'memory frames' perspective, which derives from sociology but may nevertheless be linked to the other two perspectives. The political usages of the past and memory strategies rest on the belief that social and political actors *can* influence memory to achieve political reconciliation or co-existence within a democratic society. The memory frames approach rather opens a black box, and reflects on the interaction between the public uses of the past and individual recollections, to verify empirically what the shared representations of the past are, and thus answer the question posed above: can we act on memory?

What we wish to explore in the case of Algeria are the three distinctive subjects put forward by each of the approaches: the political uses of the past and other public narratives, the politico-normative reflections on the strategies for settling conflicts originating from the past, and the conditions for the articulation of shared experiences, whether lived or transmitted. We hypothesize that the third mode – the study of recollections and representations retrieved by means of a social survey – is a prerequisite for the other two: the analysis of 'memory politics' and the normative formulations of a 'just memory'. Existing empirical studies suggest that the politics of memory and militant approaches to the past only very partially recover the representations and traces of lived experience.

'National memories': the political uses of the past

On 23 February 2005, French deputies adopted a law concerning 'the recognition by the nation of its contribution in favour of French returnees'. Its fourth article envisioned teaching 'the positive role of colonization' in schools, which sparked off intense debate.[1] The law undoubtedly dealt a blow to the rapprochement between France and Algeria, and demonstrated yet again the extent of the dependence of the Algerian discourse on the past on the French context. The Algerian press echoed the numerous debates in France intensely. Meanwhile the French press interpreted these public discussions as a 'return' or 'awakening' of memories or the 'burden of the past'.' Thus, on 4 December 2007, during the visit to Algeria by the newly elected President Nicolas Sarkozy, *Le Monde* carried the headline: 'France-Algeria: the Weight of Old Grudges', while *Libération* opted on December 5 for 'France-Algeria: the War of Memories'. Reading this daily's background piece, one finds a fairly good summary of the perceptions on bilateral relations, poisoned by the 'colonial legacy', and affected by the burden of 'a still painful past (…) which continues to be passed onto future generations as a frozen, even reinvented, memory'. Without introspectively revisiting colonial history, the editorial warns, 'the sick memory of the Franco-Algerian past will continue to distort the inevitable relations across the two shores of the Mediterranean'. Yet in a context where the instrumentalization of history for political purposes provides the core legitimacy of the Algerian leaders who are the heirs of the War of Independence, and where the same is also a key element in Sarkozy's power strategy, it will be a long time before it becomes possible to 'turn the page'.[2]

Still, whatever the Sarkozy case reveals regarding the persistent reluctance of certain segments of French society to acknowledge the repeated request for an apology by the Algerians, it appears that these tensions are also a sign that the relationship with the past is changing on both sides of the Mediterranean. During his state visit to Algeria in March 2003, President Jacques Chirac declared that the time had come 'to come to terms with our common past',[3] an initiative supposed to materialize into a solemn and definitive 'Franco-Algerian friendship'. This ultimately never came to pass.

These structural and interdependent changes in the French and Algerian societies, relating to the representations of the past, induce each state to join (or slow down) the tide, but also, in turn, to instrumentalize symbolic issues for legitimating power. There are many examples: the law of 23 February 2005 was initiated by a handful of parliamentarians who were elected, for the most part, from the right and from the south-east constituencies. They were all linked in one way or another to the *pied-noir* lobby or the veterans of the Algerian War. Other examples include the 'no-repentance' discourse of Sarkozy as a presidential candidate; the statements of President Abdelaziz Bouteflika about the 'mental blindness [of the French legislators] bordering on negationism and revisionism' or 'genocide perpetrated on Algerian identity [under colonial rule]'. It seems that politicians have seen it fit to return to the basics, namely to a discourse on the past which flatters the national ego. These political strategies and rhetorical postures may be enjoying some success, as suggested by polls showing a majority hostile to the idea that France should apologize to Algeria for the crimes of colonialism,[4] or by the relative consensus which appears to exist in Algeria regarding the expectation that French authorities should make a strong gesture of recognition. However, this does not mean that the policies of memory implemented at different levels directly correspond to the representations of the past by individuals as well as groups within the French and Algerian societies.

If one looks at Algerian society, it is clear that there are discourses which, if not fully contradictory, are in any case diverse. The discourse of power ranges from the controversial demand for recognition to the willingness to promote reconciliation, while the Algerian press, at least in part, reflects the diversity of stories on both the Algerian and French sides. Unlike French society, where the war in Algeria and, more generally, the nature of colonization are principally linked to thinking about diversity and therefore the relationship with the 'Other', in Algeria the interrogation of the past is at the heart of the question of the origins of power and the profound dichotomy between the state and society. After a civil war that claimed over 150,000 lives, and marked by countless atrocities (collective massacres, torture, attacks, rapes and disappearances) committed by both the armed Islamist groups and the forces of order, the question is 'how did it come to this?' Behind this fundamental question, three major themes cross each other at various levels which we should distinguish: there is the question of power and its acquisition; the question of national identity and its definition; and, finally, the question of violence and its origins.

We have to put independent Algeria's recent history into perspective. The political power acquired in the wake of the liberation war carried only very fragile legitimacy, and the nation-state was founded on problematic identity pillars (a policy of Arabization coupled with the growing centrality of Islam). The state sought to compensate for the gradual erosion of its basis through the rift between the realities of power and conspicuous forms of popular participation. These policies saw their limits in the period between 1988 and 1992, ending with the use of brutal force and the halting of the electoral process.[5] Islamism represented a competing legitimacy for the authorities: it contested their references and their claim to the monopoly of legitimate violence. If the 'war against terrorism' ended ten years in favour of the political-military rulers, a return to the status quo ante is no longer possible. The authorities see only one merit in the past, the ability to 'turn the page'. President Bouteflika's 'Charter for Peace and National Reconciliation', adopted by a referendum in August 2005, was the instrument needed to complete the process. However, the price already paid was heavy for the victims, and for the entire Algerian society, which had suffered the violence of these 'dark years'.

The credibility of the official discourse on the past is inevitably affected by this context. It can also be assumed that new conditions now exist for the evocation and formulation of past experiences lived and/or transmitted. Some have been able to register so-called 'awakening memories'. Benjamin Stora has pointed out the ways in which a constellation of several factors has encouraged a return to the past. Such factors include the crisis of ideologies, the passage of generations, the appearance in the public arena of people hailing from the Algerian diaspora, the new emphasis on the victims' narratives, the opening of the army archives, and the publication of innovative scholarly works in France. They also include the trauma of the 'Second Algerian War', which awakens memories of the 'first', or the end of the state's monopoly over the historical truth in Algeria.[6] These factors are certainly different in nature and, in the French case, are only in part specific to the question of Algeria. Nevertheless, the fact remains that the words of former victims as former perpetrators are released and circulated by the press, mainly in France but also in Algeria, and thus fuel widely publicized debates on torture, rape, on the repressions of 8 May 1945 or the massacre in Paris on 17 October 1961.[7] Algerians are rediscovering the pioneers of Algerian nationalism: though the reappearance of a forgotten figure such as Mohammed Boudiaf ended in tragedy with his assassination in 1992, those of Messali Hadj and Ferhat Abbas have been rehabilitated, an airport and a university are named after them, and they are mentioned in school textbooks. Traces of the absent, *Pieds-Noirs* or Jews, are also discernible, through the coverage of 'return journeys', the cancelled concert of Enrico Macias in 2000, the question of the maintenance of Christian and Jewish cemeteries, the preservation of property from the colonial period, or the controversy around the Algerian filmmaker Jean-Pierre Lledo's documentary *Algeria, Stories Not to Be Told*, censored in June 2007.

In these circumstances, the political uses of the First Algerian War and the demands for recognition addressed to France only underline the inability to read the new war in Algeria, and the Algerian leaders' refusal to recognize, in the former case as well as in the latter, any responsibility that could weaken their power. At the same time, however, a plurality of experiences and interpretations access the public sphere, as exemplified by social actors, activists of human rights, writers, filmmakers and historians.

Memories of groups in between:
the struggle for a 'just memory'

Reconciliation as desired by Bouteflika's Charter, which requires victims to forgive their tormentors, is not synonymous with justice, since those responsible for crimes, whether in the army or Islamists, are in practice amnestied. Nor is it synonymous with truth, as the fate of thousands of missing persons and many grey areas within this conflict are not established. Nor has there been a commission to shed light on these tragic events, unlike the recent implementation of 'transitional justice' in many countries in Latin America, Africa and elsewhere.

The Charter precludes any prosecution of the forces of order and even states that 'anyone (...) who uses or takes advantage of the wounds of national tragedy (...) to damage the reputation of [the state's] officers, who have served with dignity, or tarnish the image of Algeria internationally' may be punished with imprisonment. However, associations of the families of disappeared persons have been established to demand at least the truth, if not justice.[8] Indeed, no process of transitional justice is possible without a genuine political transition, which is not on the agenda at this time in Algeria. There remains the quest for truth against all odds: these women and men, through associations or individually, play the role of real 'fighters for memory'. They seek to establish responsibility for this tragedy beyond the fate of the disappeared, shedding light on the past to make it intelligible. They join other 'memory fighters', whose reflection on certain aspects of Algeria's past focuses on the big issues, such as the (non-)representativeness of the ones in power, the (non-)recognition of the plural nature of identities, and the emergence of violence as a means of settling political differences. One sees a real convergence of views on and memories of the past amongst intellectuals, artists and writers who 'remember' Algeria 'as it was before', compared with what it has become. Countless novels turn the metaphor of the 'becoming' of contemporary Algeria into fiction, creating a literary genre in its own right.

One example is the recent book by Maïsa Bey, *Blue White Green*, a double-voiced narrative of a girl and a boy, later husband and wife, living in an old colonial-style building in central Algiers, from the end of the war of liberation to the beginning of the 'civil war', thirty years later.[9] All the pieces of the Algerian puzzle come together in this work of fiction, which, like so many other more or less recent Algerian novels, excavates the various strata of life and connects the present to a past of ideal-typical characters, in order to better dissect a nation mired in a deep identity crisis. 'When I started writing', Maïssa Bey said in a recent interview, 'I was on the surface of things, in the middle of daily violence and horrors. Writing was an act of survival... When the situation finally subsided, I felt the need to understand this in light of the past, to go deeper in order to reclaim my history. And thus situate myself.'[10] The trauma of the black 1990s seems to have intensified the move towards introspection among a number of intellectuals. Their approach is primarily a quest for meaning, for the present and for oneself. Whether it is through fiction or investigation, whether by writers, filmmakers or academics, history is always a subjective material, allowing each one to include their personal story, as opposed to the official narrative hammered through by the Algerian state.

Thus, when Jean-Pierre Lledo, an Algerian filmmaker born to a Jewish-Berber mother and a Spanish father, had to escape from the Islamist threat to France in 1993, his forced exile came as a shock and nourished his most recent films, in which he tried to understand why Algeria had failed to remain multiethnic and multicultural following independence. At the heart of his 'trilogy of exile'[11] is the omnipresent issue of violence at the point of birth, or more precisely, the denial of violence which then bears on the present. His latest film refers to episodes of violence committed by the National Liberation Front (FLN) during the Algerian war which are still largely a taboo. What is more, the film delivers the Algerians' own memories, bringing them out in blunt shapes, not to produce the truth but rather to question the origins of contemporary Algerian identity. In looking for these witnesses of colonial Algeria, where the experience of inter-communal relations also built cohesion and solidarity, Lledo is not trying to deny the fundamentally unfair and oppressive nature of the colonial system as he has been reproached. His aim is rather to restore a largely overlooked aspect of shared representations of the past, a multiculturalism which is certainly very partial but whose traces transpire in language as well as in architecture. The sense of loss which shrouds it is also transmitted to new generations: the last sequence involves a young director from the Oran theatre interviewing 'Tchitchi', whom everyone remembers perfectly dancing rock'n'roll with young European ladies in years gone by. At the same time, the references to the massacres committed during the glorious 'revolution' or the statements justifying terrorism by the *moudjahida* Louisette Ighilariz cannot fail to evoke other, more recent massacres and acts of terrorism.

The cinematographic work of Lledo proceeds with his main characters in the manner of an obstetrician, which itself is a piece of 'memory work'. This is done for the protagonists in the film who remember, but also for spectators who confront them. The director's project is therefore hard to dissociate from the ways in which it is received: from the Algerian authorities' refusal to endorse its screening, to its private showings in Algeria, and from the debates held in cinemas in France to those in the two countries' press. The question is what effects such products have on the public and on the production of collective representations of the past. Yet if this attempt seems only half successful, this is not solely because the authorities still have the means to prescribe limits, and thus retain control over issues relating to national identity within the public space. It is also because such projects are structurally disadvantaged by the fact that they come from the outside. Indeed this is the condition for their very existence and even their coverage in the media. Lledo's approach is quite instructive of the limits confronting such 'memory work' anywhere, when it explicitly seeks to push the limits, to modify representations of the past. In this case, the film tries to contribute to the emergence of a more democratic Algeria, one which is more open to diversity and better equipped to manage internal conflicts. Lledo establishes the bitter fact that the people of Jewish or European origin who 'chose' Algeria have not fully found their place in this country, whose Arab-Muslim identity was confirmed by the Nationality Code of 1962. At the same time, it is his exile in France and his multiple identities that have enabled him to carry out this project, both financially and intellectually. This project, even if directed at audiences in Algeria, had to make a detour through France in order to obtain the recognition and legitimacy which the director lacked in his 'own' country.

In Algeria, where only a small audience have access to the works of Algerian artists and writers expressing themselves in French, the question of the position and legitimacy of these intellectuals vis-à-vis society on the one hand, and the authorities, on the other, is at least ambiguous. This is all the more so since the early 1990s, as these intellectuals and artists have been a target of choice for the Islamists, who are themselves viewed with contempt by the Francophone *intelligentsia*. This ambiguity is nothing new insofar as the subversive memory of the war in Algeria, as opposed to the unanimous epic of the revolutionary genre, was already the heart of novels like *The King's Dance* (1968) by Mohammed Dib, *Renunciation* (1969) and *The Dismantling* (1982, written in Arabic) by Rachid Boudjedra, *The Bone Seekers* (1984) by Tahar Djaout, a writer murdered in 1993, and *Love, Fantasy* (1985) by Assia Djebar. In this last book and her others, the author skilfully expresses the ambiguity of the relationship with French, both as an adverse language and an emotional vector, and also as a memory.[12]

Thus, the early years of independence, the writer had to meet the expectations of a 'public disappointed by Independence, and [expected] to share his ill-being and his unfulfilled aspirations'. The 'semi-externality' singles out the writer publishing in French, especially when recognized by the international literary establishment. At the same time, he remains a sort of spokesperson of his own people; in effect, this allows him to escape the obligatory consensus which governs communication within the group. One expects from him the words that cannot be enunciated from inside the circle demanding it.'[13] Yet this role of the francophone literature transforms the classical postcolonial relationship between France and Algeria, reversing the opposition to the colonizing Centre by the colonized Periphery. As Charles Bonn points out, a *caesura* traverses the Periphery and the erstwhile colonial Centre, which represents a certain notion of modernity, and acts as a reference point in 'the formal rupture with internal conformism in the Periphery', now carrying out 'a role partially reversed compared to the one described by post-colonial theory'.[14]

However, the writers' role of symbolic counter-power is both a source of creativity, bringing recognition to Algerian literature, and a marginalizing factor at the socio-cultural and political levels. They are stuck between the authorities and the mass of Algerians. The authorities' efforts to build a homogeneous nation anchored in Arab-Muslim identity have never ceased to instrumentalize the language question and stress the guilt of the Francophones, who were always suspected of treason. Meanwhile, for the mass of Algerians, French is something customary, yet fluency is synonymous with elitism and success in society. Caught between these two, the liberal elite cannot find any other legitimacy but that of the 'Republic of Letters', whose heart is in... Paris! Meanwhile the only worthwhile question on this side of the Mediterranean, and which the Algerian *intelligentsia* is summoned to answer, is what meaning to ascribe to the 'common past' and the 'shared memory' of the colonial period. From this point of view, rather than trying to understand how the past still weighs upon the emergence of post-colonial Algeria, it continues to seek, through the repetition of certain phenomena, the 'hidden truths' of the colonial past. This shift in perspective is a source of misunderstanding in the relations between France and Algeria. It worsens the imbalance in the debates on the memory of the Algerian war and colonization. These debates have their sources in France without the Algerians' being involved in defining what is at stake, and then have tremendous repercussions for the few spaces for debate that certain 'cultural intermediaries' manage to open up in Algeria.

The historian Mohammed Harbi has noted that '[p]aradoxically, it is Algeria, which emerged victorious from the war [of independence], which is haunted by France'. He is quoted by *El Watan*, a flagship of the francophone press, and principal resonating point for Franco-Algerian debates. 'How can we overcome this obsession?' asks the journalist. Can there be a 'just memory' between weight and choice in this common past that binds Algeria and France? Is a common historical treatment of French colonization in Algeria as well as decolonisation possible?'[15] It is quite telling that academic institutions have not been amongst the venues proposed for public conferences dealing with these issues. Instead, *El Watan* has organized debates like the one entitled 'France-Algeria: the War of Memories' (2 March 2006), bringing together Daho Djerbal, Mohammed Harbi, Gilles Manceron and Hassan Remaoun, at the Mercure Hotel. A lack of resources and academic autonomy forces the Algerian researchers to seek symbolic recognition outside or at the margins of scholarly institutions. In this sense, the situation of the three aforementioned Algerian academics is quite revealing: to be able to work on a history of the 'war of liberation', alternative to the one expounded by the official *doxa*, or on the colonial system, but also to focus on the memory and representations of the past as a legitimate subject of study, these historians have had to carve out their own autonomous space for free research. Mohammed Harbi was a former operative of the FLN during the war of independence, imprisoned after Boumediene's *coup d'état* and then exiled to France: this force detachment made possible to reinvent himself as an historian. His work, long banned in Algeria, is an authoritative account of the history of the FLN and the national liberation movement in Algeria.[16] Daho Djerbal, who has a position at the University of Algiers-Bouzaréah, is known primarily as the editor of *Naqd* magazine. Founded in 1991, it quickly became one of the main sites of intellectual discussion, exploring, without taboos, novel issues related to contemporary Algerian society. For his part, Hassan Remaoun, together with his wife Nouria Benghabrit, created the Centre for Research in Social and Cultural Anthropology (CRASC) in Oran, loosely affiliated with the local university. It is a humanities research body worthy of its name for Algerian researchers, and a genuine link to the international scholarly community.[17]

Yet these are but few building blocks for the development of critical knowledge: they can hardly create momentum, profoundly change the approach to history in the educational system, nor provide a wider audience with its insights into the past. Moreover, academic knowledge is validated outside the Algerian territory, at foreign and particularly French academic institutions, thus perpetuating an unequal relationship of a colonial type based on symbolic power. As Daho Djerbal has pointed out:

The malaise has to do with the fact that there is too much difference in the accumulation of knowledge: (...) we are in the position of the subordinate or the minor; always asking to be recognized by our peers and admitted into the top league. We take more time to reach the appropriate level, to speak the same language or at least use the same vocabulary and show that we have the same references. Our performance is measured by how much we speak compared with the others. We are continually expecting a formal acceptance notice to acknowledge that we mastered two types of knowledge: the knowledge that might allow us to give meaning to our own history, and the knowledge that might allow us to interact with the Other and provide him with meaning of his own story.[18]

Under these conditions, the project to build a common history for both French and Algerian societies appears, for now, illusory. While it is true that 'memory work', in the sense that Paul Ricoeur gives to the term, is most often a requirement blind to social and political conditions, the memories of experiences of individuals and groups are marginalized and cannot take part in the construction of common legacies linking France and Algeria. The paradox is easy to see. One can underscore the resistance of memory to the political uses of the past which contradict lived experiences. Similarly, the drive to influence 'memory', in order to build peace in situations where conflicts are inherited from the past, and to introduce new, socially-shared representations, amounts to decreeing or thinking about memory from a top-down rather than a bottom-up perspective.

Returning to Djerbal's argument, one encounters a double problem. There is a disconnect between Algerian society and the state on the one hand, and, on the other, a gap between France and Algeria regarding the relationship each has with the economy of knowledge and the construction of a national narrative of the other party. These are structural obstacles to the emergence of a shared memory. Shared memory is at the crossroads of 'historical memory', i.e. the reconstruction of the past, the prescription of meaning and interpretation at the level of the nation, and 'living memory', that is representations and memories of the 'experience carriers' in each of the societies concerned. Indeed, the political uses of the past that make up a nation, a party, or a group defined by reference to this or that origin do not necessarily match the representations of the past carried by individuals who make up the group, whichever level one analyzes, including the level of the nation.[19]

It is therefore all the more necessary in the case of Algeria, to make a detour towards the individual level, to measure the gap between official memory and living memory. This provides an undeniable indicator of the failure of the national project of the FLN state. If a person like Daho Djerbal today gives equal importance to oral history and to the testimonies of the principal actors in this history of Algeria, it means that the exchange of representations does not really function between the national narrative produced by state institutions on the one hand, and the individuals' memories on the other.

Individual memories: the confusion of time

One can conceive of collective memory not as the memory of a group but as a process and interaction between a public narrative of the past, and lived and/or transmitted experiences. In this case, the change of level of analysis and a qualitative survey through interviews are a means to assess the impact of policies on the representations of the shared past. They also are indispensable in crafting a dynamic concept of a social phenomenon such as memory.[20] Collecting life stories at the micro-social level helps one measure how far the effort to homogenize representations of the past leads to coherence between the resulting discourse and, at a macro-social level, national policies on memory. In the Algerian case, the task is not simply to ascertain whether individual representations of the past explicitly define themselves by rejecting the official discourse, but to analyze how each of these visions is structured by the other.

A series of interviews was conducted in February 2008 at Miliana, a small town in the mountains south-west of Algiers, with a sample of a dozen people.[21] Benefiting from a favourable summer climate, and located away from the plain and the main highway linking Algiers to the west, this large rural settlement offers an image of a micro-society whose surroundings were already very popular during the colonial era. The city centre is still characterized by architecture reminiscent of the French presence, even if high population growth and the slow rehabilitation of the downtown area have changed the outside appearance of the city significantly, much like in the rest of the country. Obviously, the survey does not claim to be representative, in the statistical sense of the term, while the limited number of interviews on the one hand, and the social respondents on the other hand, are not sufficient to establish a typology. However, despite its limitations, solely by changing the level of analysis, the investigation can launch hypotheses about the efficiency of memory policies discussed previously. It aims at sketching out convergences and divergences between public and private narratives about the past, thus avoiding a purely descriptive approach. We can distinguish two main groups of respondents, unequal in size. On the one hand, people who have experienced, whether as children or adults, pre-1962 Algeria, and on the other, those who grew up in independent Algeria and have only indirect knowledge of colonial Algeria. In some cases it was possible to conduct interviews over two generations.[22]

During these open-ended interviews, several themes were used as guidelines. Regarding the pre-independence generation, the issue of the French presence and the various communities of the city before 1962 allows one to see how the witnesses today reconstruct narratives of experiences under colonialism, including memories of the war of liberation. Their reconstructions also extend to the present day, with respect to the ways in which the authorities offer recognition to former *moudjahidin*, especially where women are concerned. Regarding the post-independence generation, there are questions of how memories are transmitted, how they resonate with the memory of the actors themselves but also with the official discourse on the history transmitted by the school and state media. If the focus on independent Algeria and the 'distortion' of the revolution is sometimes less analytical among younger generations, the relationship to political Islam and the rupture emerging during the years of terrorism is a fundamental dimension for their comprehension of the sense (or nonsense) in Algeria's recent history, but also its future since the relative 'normalcy' of the 2000s. At the end, the interviewer invited the respondents, through both images and words, to react to some 'clichés' related to the 'national imaginary', or, in contrast, to revisit some marginal dimensions, hidden issues or even taboos in the national narrative.

Addressing the past through historical 'icons' is justified by the fact that the Algerian regime has abused this revolutionary imagery, inspired by the Soviet model. It has been convenient to promote this 'faceless revolution', whose main leaders have been removed or eliminated, and where the people are the 'only heroes'.[23] This depersonalization of history fosters confusion. When the young Mohammed A. gives the researcher a tour of the town and passes through the 8 May Square, where the statue of a *moudjahid* with a machine gun is enthroned, he does not know if the name refers to the events of 8 May 1945, or rather the beginning of the insurrection of 1954 as he had always believed. This ignorance, he says, embarrasses him.

This sense of being dispossessed of one's own past is expressed in different registers but seems widely shared. The rejection of taught history is unanimous, and the generation born after independence makes a clear distinction between the 'real history of Algeria' and that transmitted by the school. There, everything is reduced to a binary opposition between the black of colonialism and the white of the 'national liberation struggle' (according to Hamida B., b. 1972). This does not help develop any critical reading of the past nor an understanding of the return of history, as Mohammed A stated. This judgement on official history is also shared by those involved in the war of independence themselves, for whom the use of history for political purposes and the emergence of a privileged caste are closely related. The FLN/state identifies itself with the former *moudjahidin* and grants privileges, such as pensions, to former combatants, and even to their children and grandchildren. As Aicha M. (b. 1929) says, when televized meetings commemorating the old *chouhada* (martyrs for the cause) urge Nicolas Sarkozy to offer an apology for the crimes of colonialism, the next thing they do is beseech Bouteflika to agree to a third term. There is a confusion of genres that makes Aicha smile. She had to wait forty years, and for the intervention of one of her daughters, to be recognized as a *moudjahada* – and be given the pension which goes with it. It is true that no claim had any chance of success without recourse to one or several networks within the administration, and that her case was delayed because the first commission in charge had been dissolved following revelations about certificates issued to false *moudjahidin*. However, as several respondents including Mohammed A. suggest, who can tell which *moudjahidin* are real?

It is also true that for Aicha M. as well as Youssef B. (b. 1934), always speaking with a great deal of modesty and discretion when discussing 'their' war, the involvement in the struggle was the natural thing to do, and necessitated no recognition apart from that of God. ('If I fought,' said the grandmother of Mohammed A., 'it is for Allah!'). The constant instrumentalization of the past by the authorities contradicts the ideals and values for which they fought. This observation is largely implicit but it transpires in the way they now refer to their experience of the Algerian war and its traumas. How can one take interest in history when it is used to justify so many injustices, says Aicha M.? Official and lived history exist side-by-side without mixing, because they are in two different registers, where the assessment criteria are hard to see.

However, looking at stories and evocations of experience within the family, and the question of what memory is passed to the next generation, we find that the first register obstructs the second. The attention given to the older generations' narratives is blunted by the connotations lent to them by all references to the glorious 'liberation war'. According to Karima B. (b. 1970), the younger generation does not have this culture, this curiosity vis-à-vis its ancestors, which would help it take ownership of its 'grand history' through the story of family. In the case of the two sisters B., this generational gap has been reinforced by their father's silence, and worsened after the family's move in the late 1980s from Algiers to Miliana, a city with which they do not identify and which was abandoned by its 'real' local families. In the case of the sisters B. as well as for Mohammed A., it is, in a fairly conventional way, the grandmother who passes on her memories, but for the young man, her stories refer to a mental universe that is not his own. Mohammed is unable to distinguish between the levels and place the personal memories of the grandmother in larger narratives. He is well aware of his superficial knowledge of national history, which has been transmitted to him mainly through the lens of official ceremonies and frozen images. This does not allow access to a much deeper historical reality, which, moreover, is not really reflected in the state discourse. However, he sees this deficit in the history of Algeria and ever more so in the Algerians' family memories as highly political: if the Algerian has no history, he says, then he has no identity and, therefore, he is also deprived of his citizenship.

For the young Mohammed A., just like the old Mohammed B. (b. 1928, father of Karima and Hamida), the question of the French language (in which these discussions were conducted by necessity) represents this identity crisis, following from the objectives once adopted by the Algerian authorities. The language stands for a legacy which the Algerian leaders insist has not existed since 1962. For Mohammed B., the figure of Ferhat Abbas, still appreciated by a nearly extinct elite, troubles the authorities. They do not know what to do with this complex character and his multiple identities, someone whose political career illustrates the ambiguity of Algerianness as constructed in the colonial era.[24] In Mohammed's view, French is still the language passed on from his father, and remains, more so than Arabic, a means through which to think and write. Yet if the use of French is indeed a legacy of the colonial period, as all interlocutors are well aware, the perception of this period is often fuzzy in the interviews of the post-independence generations.

While Hamida B. 'would have liked to live in that era', the nostalgia she has internalized is not that of 'French Algeria'. Rather it is the youth of her parents hailing from middle class backgrounds, who obviously had much easier and happier lives in comparison to their children who reached adulthood in the early 1990s. Karima and Hamida B. have some knowledge of both their family history (they go back to the grandfather, a city notable, landowner and a shopkeeper, and a veteran of the First World War) and of what life was like before 1954. There was family solidarity that would gradually disintegrate, one often hears, after independence and especially in the 1980s, but also good inter-community relations, ridden by ambiguities yet real. They mention the French school their parents attended, neighbourhood relations, particularly between Muslim and Jewish women who were considered culturally closer than the 'French' but were still called *gaouira* (foreign), and who had access to public spaces and even had stores of their own. This narrative of social harmony and relative acculturation has been passed on by parents who refer to the colonial era with a varying degree of nostalgia depending on their social position. Even if the meaning was not the same depending whether the school was mixed or indigenous-only, the passage through the French education system is a long-term identity marker. This is exemplified by Baya YD. (b. 1924), who even nowadays cannot read Arabic but only French, or Youssef B. (b. 1934), who received technical training in his college to become an instructor himself later, and whose colleagues and friends of his generation are more at ease with French than Arabic.

It is worth recalling here the social specificity of this group of respondents. However, social position, proximity to the colonial administrator, the spatial context, and therefore lifestyle are key elements in appreciating these men and women's judgments not on the legacy of colonization, as some like Youssef B. fought with exemplary courage, but on the French presence in Algeria. Indeed there is a great distance between, on one side, Mohammed B., Baya YD. or Youssef B., proud of their Turkish, Iraqi and Tunisian family roots, and descendants of the Oran *beys*, and Aicha M., on the other. The first group had landowner ancestors who 'lived like the French' in downtown areas, and were on good terms with their European neighbours, whom they resembled in terms of lifestyle as a consequence. Meanwhile, Aicha was a native of the countryside: her family's farm was destroyed by the French Army in 1957 and she moved into the poor quarter Annassers on the outskirts of Miliana, which was never inhabited by many Europeans apart from the marginal Spanish families in the neighbourhood. Aicha – coming from a very nationalist family whose father had strong memories of torture by the French at the time of conquest – insists on the difference between urban dwellers and the rural inhabitants who suffered much of the war. By contrast, Youssef B. notes that life in Miliana continued as before until March 1962, when the early attacks occurred and the 'Arab hunt' was organized by the OAS[25] in the city centre. The young Mohammed A.'s grandmother does not have bad memories from the time when she worked for the *gaouri*. The image of the French is still very much shaped by the war period. So much so that, according to her grandson, she cried when, during the visit of President Sarkozy in December 2007, she saw on television French flags adorn the streets of Algiers. She was also concerned about whether 'the professor' whom her grandson had met might have been afraid to come to Algeria!

One understands better therefore why Mohammed A. has a much more superficial knowledge of this period. While he knows that his grandparents were working as janitors at Swedish and Spanish homes, he is not aware of the meaning of the term *pied-noir*. 'Jew' is a taboo word – absent and eliciting a refusal to comment by the interviewee. He is very surprised to discover nineteenth century photographs of Jewish women who resemble 'Algerian' women. Yet, all the elderly respondents remember the presence of Jews, who, together with the Europeans, had businesses in the downtown area (Aicha M.), were present in the school and college classrooms (Youssef B.), suffered from exclusion and persecution under the anti-Semitic decrees promulgated by the Vichy regime in 1940 (Mohammed B.), and were targeted by the French administration as well as by refugees from Alsace. As for other communities, Karima and Hamida B. do not know that the European population was partly of Spanish origin. This is confirmed by Aicha M., who lived in Annassers, near the Zaccar mines, where families of Muslim and Spanish miners lived. The sisters know that their father went to France and received a veteran's pension, but confuse these two pieces of information. They do not know very well why he went there (between 1947 and 1953 as an accountant working in the public works) nor how he performed his military service (between 1958 and 1961 in the Aures and the north of Constantine). They know, by contrast, that he lived with a European concubine in the 1960s before marrying their mother, who was born in 1945. They also mention that life during the war was very difficult for their maternal grandmother as her husband disappeared after being arrested by the French Army. She had to live with her children in a camp.

More generally, passing through the very rich story of the father, Mohammed B., to that of the daughters, Karima and Hamida B., the socio-political and historical context of the time seems to disappear. Yet this dimension is very present in the story of these men and women, who, whatever their social background and level of proximity to the Europeans, have always had a very clear understanding of the nature of the French presence and its implications. While Mohammed B. was, according to his daughters, a *bon vivant*, more interested in going out with friends and playing football than in politics, he still offered a sophisticated analysis of Algerian political developments, and said he supported, at the time, the ideas of Ferhat Abbas. For his part, Youssef B.'s political awareness is linked with the death of his father in 1952. While he was dying of internal bleeding, his son was desperately seeking a physician when a café owner shouted 'leave the *bicot*[26] to die!' Youssef also remembers his passage through the Algerian Muslim Scouts movement, whose founder Mohammed Bouras was executed by the French in 1941. He remembers 8 May 1945 and unfulfilled promises after the Second World War, the feeling of marginalization created by exclusion from certain segments of the labour market, the persistence of discrimination policies (while his wife, Dalida YD., was included in the first electoral college, he was in the second college due to his parents' social backgrounds) and the daily racism of some *Pieds-Noirs* in the St Paul Street of the downtown area. The images of humiliation suffered during the war returned to him. In the *douars* (villages), people were rounded up in the square and forced to undress, men and women together (Youssef B); Aicha remembers the detention of parents, the frequent body searches, and her daughter's childhood memory of a *moudjahid* trampled by an army truck. Aicha also remembers very well 11 December 1960, when, after the major demonstration in Algiers by the FLN during a visit by General de Gaulle, women in the Annassers district secretly prepared Algerian flags, playing cat and mouse with the armed forces and avoiding soldiers' bullets.

The move to illegal struggle therefore appears to many respondents the result of a clear political consciousness. During these interviews, one discovers that each family had its own martyrs and anonymous resistance fighters, all marked by a great diversity. Without quoting all the stories, we will mention for the sake of illustration the story of Youssef B. His uncle was a guerilla and an ALN liaison officer in Miliana. Himself was arrested four times, in 1956 and 1957 in Miliana and 1960 in Algiers, and endured six months of torture at the hands of the paratroopers of Colonel Marcel Bigeard. He was later tried and acquitted by a court in Blida thanks to an attorney acquaintance of the family, and managed to escape twice. Youssef also emphasizes the role of women in the struggle, as illustrated by the case of Aicha M., who took enormous risks in organizing the transport and logistics between Miliana and Medea and all the way to the camps, as well as Baya YD. who roamed through the mountains, participated in collecting money, hid pistols, sheltered *moudjahidin*, and so on. What do the children know about this struggle, courage and suffering? If Kheira D., Aicha's daughter, recalls the arrest of her father, the torture, the execution threats and humiliations suffered, it seems that in any case, for Youssef B., these interviews were one of the very rare occasions where he could recount in detail the torture inflicted by the French.

While every family is unique, it is the political context of independent Algeria that can provide a broader sense and a collective dimension to words uttered in the tight framework of the family or close friends and relatives. Here, as in other cases and studies of intergenerational transmission, individual memories acquire a meaning only insofar as they are related to socially shared interpretations and reinterpretations, public narratives of lived experience.[27] However, it goes without saying that there are obvious misunderstandings between the generations which go in both directions. The disappointment of the generation which grew up under colonialism is commensurate with the expectations fed by a struggle supported directly or indirectly by all interviewed who belong to that generation. Mohammed B. has a fairly elitist view of the events. To him, the race for power by peasant leaders promotes the development of a culture of violence and the *coups d'etat* by Ahmed Ben Bella and Houari Boumediene. For him, this was an anti-democratic development which could not end except in the disconnect between the authorities and the people that characterizes contemporary Algeria. For Baya YD., the assassination of Abane Ramdane symbolizes the will of the FLN to eliminate from power intellectuals and 'good families' capable of giving another face to the new Algeria.[28] For Youssef B. as well as Mohammed B., the policy of Arabization and the nationalization of land were measures reflecting the inferiority complex of people like Boumediene, who sought to eliminate the francophone elite. These are views certainly held by people from more privileged social groups than the average Algerians. Yet even for women as different as Baya YD. and Aicha M., independence did not bring the progress that the Algerians were awaiting. This point of view is clearly shared by our young respondents and perhaps more significantly by a generation who feels marginalized and rejected by the system, who cannot rely on their studies to advance in the near or distant future, and for whom emigration is the main ray of hope.[29] For Mohammed A., the education system, totally disregarded by youth, illustrates the failure of the authorities, who lack a clear vision of the country's direction. The men who took power in 1962 were not prepared to run the country and are therefore responsible for a huge mess.

If for Karima and Hamida B. the 1970s and 1980s represent, regardless of the dictatorship and the military security power, the golden age of an easy-going and happy childhood in Algeria, their perspective on the developments following October 1988 mirrors that of Mohammed A. and a the generation caught in the maelstrom of the 'dark years'. For the latter, it boils down to one formula: 'we do not understand!' And indeed, it is striking that reference points blur when discussing the upheavals linking the suppression of riots in October 1988, the liberalization of the regime and the electoral victories of the Islamic Salvation Front (FIS) in 1990-1991, finally leading to the suspension of the January 1992 elections and the civil war that pit the armed forces against the Islamist groups in a conflict in which civilians were the main victims. Karima and Hamida B. amalgamate the events preceding the elections' interruption and those that followed. They clearly remember the events of October 1988: one refers to the gunfire and tear gas in Algiers, the other remembers the riots spreading to Miliana. They seem to be entering a tunnel where their existence is marked by emotional instability in the family or the workplace amidst a tense security environment. This is confused in their minds with the atmosphere of fear which was installed in Algeria when the FIS began to use religion as a way to seize power. This sequence is therefore perceived as a single bloc of seamless continuity, where the period of multiparty politics has no significance whatsoever. The two women have basically borne the concrete effects that the events have had on them, such as the need to wear a veil so as not to be conspicuous – although Karima claims to wear one now by choice and not by obligation. In 1990 and 1991, they voted (for the secular Union for Culture and Democracy (RCD) led by Said Saadi, as did their father), but would never do it again as 'whether you vote or not, it's the same thing'.

Condemnation of power tinged with fatalism – this is what Mohammed A. (born in 1986) feels. With him, the acronym 'FIS' does not provoke any comment. He believes that the foremost stake in this conflict is the *goursi,* literally 'the chair' of power, which led the 'terrorists' to steal and hide behind the words *'jihad'* and *'moudjahid'.* He remembers that at that time, parents forbade their children to talk about the subject and that, even today, they do not discuss it much. Nobody knows the truth about who committed the massacres – the Islamists or the army – but everyone tries to forget now because life continues. We must 'stand upright', he says, justifying his words, and continues that even with the truth, there would be no alternative but to move forward. 'God gives me the power of patience,' he says in conclusion, translating an Arabic saying. When discussing Bouteflika's 'Charter for Peace and National Reconciliation', Karima and Hamida B. make many observations similar to those of Mohammed. While they were initially shocked and saw the charter as a manoeuvre by the authorities to hide their responsibility for the violence, they now believe that it may be better to forgive, and not to speak out, because the truth – not least if hidden by the authorities – will probably never be revealed. This impression of confusion is not really dispelled by the older and more politicized generations. Mohammed B., the father of Karima and Hamida, and the erstwhile president of the RCD's local section in Miliana, once approved the interruption of the electoral process which, he said, prevented a general slaughter planned by the Islamists. He would no longer vote for the RCD because according to him, it recycles old politicians. He considers that the evil of the FIS has been exaggerated and that it is now necessary to forget.

Finally, for Mohammed A., the 'black decade' led Algerians to turn their backs even further on their recent and distant past. For him, terrorism has erased the old generation's memory of the colonial time, and given birth to a new generation, which he represents, that knows nothing about its history. The circle is closed. For Mohammed, Islam is the only link between people, the only source of solace in a world where *hogra* has become 'too big a word'. All generations grow up with Islam, and it shapes their daily life. However, for Mohammed, that Islam has nothing to do with the inauthentic religious education which he received at school, and which he compares with his courses in history and geography. The Islam he considers a solace is the one inherited from his father, a very old heritage which has the power of evidence, and which the young man shares with his friends even though they do not go to the mosque or pray five times a day.

Although less obvious then in Egypt for example, one can find among the lower class in Algeria a different relationship to time, not strictly historical: since there are no clear chronological markers, historical facts are in a way more abstract than for instance the life of the Prophet. Therefore, the debates over the interpretation of the struggles for power in contemporary Algeria, even if the official narrative is starting to be contested, is largely meaningless for the great mass of the Algerians born after 1962.

Conclusion

This chapter demonstrates that shifting the focus from collective memory, understood as the political uses of the past at the level of the nation, to memories which are shared by individuals – activists or ordinary citizens – allows us to define 'memory' in more complex ways as well as ground it in the 'real world'. [30] We believe that it is more interesting to study the divergences between the macro- and the micro-level than to examine each separately. At first sight, this move rejects all concepts of 'collective memory' as encapsulating what can be considered as the memory of the nation. It bolsters the cleavages exemplified by the people examined above, or those who remain silent, to the extent that fieldwork helps us capture their memories. These socially shared memories are not mere reflections of state propaganda. It is necessary to push this logic even further and view social or 'collective' memory as emanating from 'facts of communication among individuals',[31] or the 'interpenetration of consciences'.[32] This proposition stresses that 'individual' memories – whether transmitted or lived and therefore resistant – express themselves only in certain social frameworks, such as the family or intermediary groups located between the individual and the nation. In that sense, the micro-sociological level of analysis is no more authentic than the macro-sociological one. The two interact, converge or diverge, just as the activists who advocate the 'just memory' claim. That is why it is necessary to interrogate the Algerian context further. The distance between the official narrative and individual perceptions calls for prudence when seeking to capture 'memory'. However, these elements also constitute a situation where the past – or even history – cannot be reconstructed as a 'good' history, let alone a history where one might recognize oneself.

CHAPTER VI

'THAT MOST BEAUTIFUL PART OF ITALY': MEMORIES OF FASCIST EMPIRE-BUILDING IN THE ADRIATIC

BOJAN BASKAR

With Italy's unification and its eventual territorial rounding off with the acquisition of Rome and Venice, the country's international borders remained uncertain and often contradictory, despite Ugo Foscolo's authoritative claim that the Alps were Italy's natural frontiers. This vagueness was most obvious in the northeast, where Italy's expansion was blocked by the Habsburg Empire, which nevertheless contained at its borderland a substantial population who spoke various Romance dialects and increasingly identified themselves with the Italian cultural nation. Although the majority of the population, peoples from the Habsburg Adriatic borderland, were identified generically as Slavs by the Italians, they were generally not seen as an obstacle to expansion.[1] Due to the perceived imminent demise of the Austria-Hungary and the presumed inferiority of their own culture, the Slavs were expected to smoothly assimilate to the superior Italian culture. Historian Nicholas Doumanis has maintained that with regard to the 'Italianness' of the borderland, Italian nationalists tended to be as inclusive as possible, 'if only to claim more territories for the nation', and that it was irrelevant for them that the peoples of Alto Adige might have identified more with German than Italian culture.[2] Apart from ardent nationalists, however, there were others participating in the debate about borders in the northeast, and they were invoking different criteria for defining borders.

This chapter looks at contested memories of circum-Adriatic nationalisms, from the perspective of a failed experience of Italian empire-building in South East Europe. As a rule, the abundant literature on western Balkan (or eastern Adriatic) nationalisms has avoided considering the role of Italian imperialism, fascist as well as pre-fascist, in the eastern Adriatic developments. The Italian and Yugoslav nation-building experiments had some parallels with each other, but this has seldom been recognized by students of both.[3] This is mostly due to the regional compartmentalization of scholarship (southern Europe as distinct from South East Europe specialists). Yet this compartmentalization has itself been based on the assumption of an important civilizational and political divide between two Europes running along the Adriatic Sea. Scholars (Italians included) have not always been immune to Balkanist assumptions. When commenting for instance on the bloody demise of Yugoslavia, and searching for clues in the revived memories of the interethnic massacres during the Second World War, they seem unaware that the abominable *Ustaša* regime was the work of the Italian fascist state. While the *Ustaša* movement emerged as a Croat right-wing nationalist resistance to the Serb-dominated Yugoslav kingdom, it was soon appropriated by Benito Mussolini, who offered it refuge in Italy. There, over the 1930s, the militia was secretly trained and equipped, before being launched into Yugoslavia with a view to dismantling the unwanted state on the other side of the Adriatic.

There has only been a very weak awareness in the Italian national memory of how the imperialist projects of the Italian state ended in the humiliating debacle of the fascist New Order. This is now well-known among students of Italy. I argue in this chapter that the 'lack of will' in Italy to come to terms with the nation's imperialist and fascist past has wider repercussions that reach well beyond the national borders in the Adriatic. This is particularly evident in the recent trend in Italy towards commemorating all kinds of events related to fascism and its aftermath. This trend followed a nationalist turn of 'rejuvenated' communists now displaying a new sensitivity to the 'historical injustices and humiliations' suffered by Italy. Their eagerness to search for national reconciliation with those who fought on the opposite side and to construct a 'shared memory' was instrumental in upgrading local tragedies from the borderland to pan-national parables. In this chapter, I focus on this new politics of memory, and its culmination in the institution of the national *Day of Remembrance for the Victims of the Foibe and Esodo from Istria and Dalmatia,* whose defiant celebrations regularly complicate cross-Adriatic international relations.

Where does Italy end in the northeast?

The Italian imperialist expansion in the northeast was initially inextricable from the territorial rounding off of the new national state and therefore from the nation-building process. Territorial claims regarding the northeast steadily increased during the latter phase of Italian unification. In the 1860s, there was hardly an Italian statesman who thought that Trieste ought to be snatched from Austria. Prime Minister Alfonso La Marmora, who in 1866 followed Prussia in declaring war on Austria with the intention of taking possession of Trentino and Veneto, held that the port of Trieste was of such importance to the Germans that it would only be worthwhile to seize it from Austria in the event that Italy intended to rule over the whole Adriatic.[4] The tendency to progressively push the imagined eastern border further east can also be discerned in the evolution of individual opinions of the border. These reveal a typically inconsistent and superficial geographical knowledge of the Italian northeast.

Irredentists began to develop their views of Istria as an unredeemed Italian region during the 1860s and especially the 1870s. At the turn of the century, their demands still remained surprisingly modest, as they did not even claim the whole of Istria. They continued to take as a criterion the historical border of the Roman province of Histria, as well as that of the medieval Croatian state, thus recognizing the southeastern Istrian coast as legitimate Croatian territory.[5] The discourse on Dalmatia as *terra irredenta* took off only in the late 1900s, when Italian Adriatic irredentism was integrated into a wider imperialist design. Laments about unredeemed lands were then overshadowed by new arguments asserting the geopolitical necessities of Italian expansion and domination over the whole Adriatic. After a decade of somewhat silenced imperial aspirations following the debacle in Ethiopia, Italian imperialism was focusing again on the Mediterranean.

New territories were granted to Italy at the Paris Peace Conference in 1919 as a reward for joining the Allies: these included, besides Southern Tyrol, the provinces of Gorizia (the greater part of today's western Slovenia) and Trieste, and the whole Istrian peninsula. Meanwhile the promised Dalmatia went to Yugoslavia, with the exception of Zadar (Zara), the only local town with an Italian majority. Ideas about the northeastern border remained seriously divergent even among members of the Italian delegation to the Paris peace conference.[6] Prime Minister Vittorio Emmanuele Orlando and Foreign Minister Sidney Sonnino could not agree on whether to firmly insist on Dalmatia as Sonnino argued, or to ask instead for the now Yugoslav port of Rijeka (Fiume), as Orlando proposed. Since the two men disagreed on which one to demand, they decided to ask for both Dalmatia and Rijeka. The arguments used by the Italian delegation to underpin their territorial claims were primarily geographical and geopolitical. One of the auxiliary arguments was the Roman presence in these territories. During the Paris conference, the Italian army, archaeologists and alpinists hastily worked together on producing a map of Roman frontier barriers in the Julian Alps (*claustra Alpium Juliarum*). This map was used by Prime Minister Orlando in his response to US President Woodrow Wilson, to justify the tracing of the border of the new Italian march in a region where Italians did not live at all.[7] In the cacophony of discordant arguments, that of the superiority of Italian *civiltà* over the culturally inferior Slavs was invoked with great conviction.

Under Mussolini's rule, the principle of nationality finally became irrelevant: ethnically and linguistically 'alien' populations from the newly acquired provinces were called upon either to assimilate or to emigrate across the border. While on his tour of the Julian March in September 1920 (two years before he acceded to power), Mussolini delivered a speech in Pola (Pula), stating that the border of Italy in the east ran from Brenner to the Dinaric Alps, and added that 500,000 barbarian Slavs could be sacrificed for 50,000 Italians.[8] In the early period of fascism, the notion of natural frontiers as barriers protecting the nation gained importance, and the impact of civilizational discourse was still tangible. The irredentist tumult instigated by the perception of a 'mutilated victory' was silenced during the first years of the regime, because Mussolini, aiming at the annexation of Rijeka, did not wish to erode the treaty of Rapallo with Yugoslavia.

After 1927, when relations with Yugoslavia deteriorated, irredentism was promoted once again. Political, cultural and educational activities by irredentist organizations were now widely encouraged by the regime. Typically aimed at raising the consciousness of 'Italianness' in the eastern Adriatic, they included such endeavours as bringing the region into school textbooks and curricula, scientifically investigating the vestiges of Roman presence in Dalmatia, organizing excursions there, or encouraging research on shared Adriatic culture. Yet the resurrected 'Adriatic question' was no longer limited to Dalmatia and the Adriatic. In a 1929 speech, Dino Grandi, who was to become foreign minister, brings up race as a key argument for the expansion in the interior of the western Balkans, where 'ancient' cultural frontiers and civilizational fault lines are rediscovered:

The Adriatic no longer suffices to defend our independence as a Mediterranean race from the Slav races. There must be, beyond the Adriatic and its banks, a chain of states […] that virtually serves as a trench dividing the Orient from the Occident–bridgeheads commanded by Italy. We have made Albania; now we must make Croatia. […]Destiny decrees that the boundaries between the Occident and Orient lie on the Save, which Diocletian marked as the frontier between the empire of the Occident and the empire of the Orient.[9]

While foreign scholars largely refer to the northeastern border, a usage consistent with the contemporary notion of the Italian North-East used in Italy itself, Italian scholars as a rule refer to the eastern border, *il confine orientale*. Although, in most cases, this term seems to denote the northeastern border, it originates in the context of Italy's imperialist ambitions to expand to the opposite shore of the Adriatic, where the border of Italy would be the eastern border in the strict sense of the term. Italy has never had such an eastern border, at least not on the mainland, with the exception of a short-lived fascist occupation of Albania and invasion of Greece in 1940 and Yugoslavia in 1941. When Italian armies invaded countries on the eastern shore, the period of appealing to natural frontiers and strategic defensive barriers of the nation was largely over. Now it was the right of the stronger party – of the Italians – to their *spazio vitale* which counted.

The occupation of Yugoslavia provided the occupying force with a new and entirely unanticipated experience of the 'eastern border'. The latter actually proved to be the demarcation line between the Italian and German occupation zone extending from Italy to Yugoslavia and the Adriatic along a northwest-southeast axis. On the Yugoslav coast, and even more in its mountainous hinterland, the poorly prepared Italian occupying force was immediately faced with insurgency and the growing force of Josip Broz Tito's multiethnic communist resistance. The army became entangled in a vicious circle of repression, provoking ever fiercer counterblows by Titoist partisans. This experience of losing control over the Adriatic Balkan empire was further frustrated by increasing subordination to the German army, a growing dependence on its logistical means and material equipment, and Germany's economic domination in the Italian zone. These factors were aggravated by the Germans' barely concealed scorn for Italians and their permanent policy of *fait accompli,* including their failure to pay due attention to the demarcating line.

In short, the imperialist army's experience of the 'eastern border' amounted to coming up against a line traced capriciously by a cultural 'other' who turned out to be the admired and respected Teutonic ally rather than the Oriental 'Slavo-Communist'. No wonder that in memoranda released by the commander of the occupying army, Mario Roatta, one can discern 'a desire to flee the Balkan mess'.[10] Perhaps the 'messiest' thing for General Roatta was that he could not cope with the enemy nor with the ally, and that neither showed any sign of respect towards the Italian occupational force and fascism. Lacking the manpower, resources, knowledge and motivation necessary for the pacification of the 'third zone' (the outer tier of the occupation that had never before been contemplated by Italian imperialism), commanders of the army began to take measures aimed at withdrawal to the 'second zone'. In the remaining time (the whole of 1942 and up to Italian capitulation in September 1943), the army was trying to pull back closer to the Adriatic shore and to fortify the 'natural frontier' of Dalmatia running along the crest of the Dinaric Mountains. The Italians were being hindered in this endeavour by adverse circumstances, in the first place by the Germans, who would not allow them to disengage and who were imposing their own agenda on the Italians. This yearning of an imperial army to withdraw to the already 'imaginatively' appropriated Dalmatian *patria*, protected within its natural frontiers, epitomises the change back from the late ideology of 'living space' to the earlier ideology of cultural identity.

With the demise of Yugoslavia half a century later, the imperial dream of rule over the Adriatic – which had never died among parts of the Italian political class – was brought to life once again. Now the object of desire was largely Istria and Dalmatia, coastal regions of Croatia now shrinking under the expansion of the Serb secret ally. In contrast, the interior of the Balkan Peninsula did not generate any territorial fantasies. This is because the only fantasies that survived were those that were not recognized as imperial: fantasies bound to the ideology of cultural identity. This in turn was rooted in an obsessive notion that there is a cultural boundary between the Latin and 'Slav' worlds running along the eastern coast, a boundary coterminous with the boundary between the coastal plain and the Dinaric mountains above the coast.

From the 'Balkan Mess' to the 'Foibe Zone'

In a military report to the commander of the Second Army, Taddeo Orlando, commander of the ill-famed *Granatieri di Sardegna* division, described the extent of the insurgency, as well as measures being taken against it in the 'Province of Ljubljana'. In the same report, he also expanded on the theme of Slovene national character. According to him, the benefits of German civilization that had arduously brought this fistful of Slavs to the European level had been destroyed by twenty years of Serbian rule. This, he maintained, was strikingly visible in the mentality of Slovene youths, unstoppable in their anti-Italian hostility, which they displayed in all kinds of Balkan savagery, from the trivial spit to the bestial ambush and banditry activities.[11] Similar Balkanist imagery which seems to have been familiar to Italian rank officers included such phrases as 'Balkan megalomania', 'Balkan mentality', 'Balkan feverishness', 'Balkan Orient', 'Balkan mess', 'Balkan hell', 'Balkan manoeuvre', 'Balkan lava', 'Balkan impulse toward hate and vendetta', 'Slav swamp', 'primitive Croat psychology', 'atavistic impulses of the Serbs', etc.[12] These terms were already present in the idiom of earlier, especially frontier fascism. In the beginning of the twentieth century, Italy was clearly participating in the shaping of the image of the Balkans.[13]

Yet Maria Todorova has maintained that, 'maybe because of its physical proximity or because it did not become organically afflicted with a *mission civilisatrice*, Italy on the whole did not develop an abstract and hectoring pose toward the Balkans and never lost sight of their concreteness.'[14] It would be rather unusual if precisely the imperialist state which was most deeply involved empire-building in the Balkans, and which had tried to violently subjugate a string of local peoples, did not develop its own variety of Balkanist discourse. The idea that the Italian state had not been afflicted with a *mission civilisatrice*, however, is an unsubstantiated claim. On the contrary, the 'bringing of civilization' arguably played a more central role in the ideology legitimizing Italian colonialism than in the case of more successful colonial powers. There were two fundamental reasons for this centrality: 1) with its 'superior civilization' complex, Italy was compensating for its relative lack of economic power and efficiency; 2) indigenous discourses of civilization or *civiltà*, as opposed to barbarism or inferior culture, played a crucial role in the shaping of Italian local and national identities. Anthropologists working in Italy (and in the Mediterranean, more generally) have often observed a preoccupation with this privileged notion and the ubiquitous opposition of the urban and rural derived from it. Sydel Silverman, expounding on the notion of *civiltà* in a Central Italian town,[15] claims that *civiltà* does not have an exact equivalent in English. It primarily means civilization, but is also close to 'civility', yet broader in meaning. It refers to ideas about a civilized way of life, and always implies an *urban* way of life. As such, *civiltà* is an ideology about civilization.[16]

Italian Balkanist discourse is characterized by the abhorrence of Adriatic Slavs but also by its sharp delineating of the Balkans from the Mediterranean. The Balkans are often depicted as the anti-Mediterranean, a negation of everything Mediterranean – and *eo ipso* Italian. Italian attitudes toward the Balkans often lack the self-assured distance of northwest European attitudes: defining the Balkans as a negation of the Mediterranean may also mean anxiously dissociating Italy from the Balkans. This applies especially in the northeast, where the non-Balkan identity of a town such as Trieste, for example, is far from self-evident. Unlike in British, American or German Balkanist discourse, in the Italian variety, the civilizational fault line between the Mediterranean and the Balkans, between the Latins and Slavs, closely coincides with the boundary between the urban and rural. The exaltation of urban ways of life and the contempt for the rural, imagined as outside *civiltà*, had been contrasted by social anthropologists of past decades with northern European attitudes toward the countryside, and depicted as a Mediterranean cultural trait. In Italian Balkanist discourse, this veneration of the urban and contempt for the rural has become an unconscious criterion for judging the Balkans.

Within this framework, the dichotomy of urban and rural coincides with the contrast between the plain (or coast) and the mountain, i.e. with the 'close interpenetration of mountain and sea'[17] which has been seen as a prominent characteristic of the Mediterranean geography. This characteristic is conspicuous on the eastern Adriatic shore, where several generations of Western travellers, political commentators and scholars have pointed to it. Two opposed landscapes – plain and mountain – were often 'ethnicized' by being connected to the cultural contrast between the Italians and Slavs, or the 'Mediterraneans' and 'Balkanites'. Within the mindset of popular geographical determinism, the landscape and the people dwelling in it were imagined as homogeneous and mutually determined. Adriatic Slavs were thus pictured as warlike pastoralists of sterile mind and culture. Their desolate life, organised by their collective epic traditions and a ferocious defence of space, bore the imprint of arid, barren and isolated Dinaric expanses. Italians, by contrast, were pictured as cultured, docile and creative Mediterranean horticulturalists and fishermen, and as heirs and bearers of an ancient and superior Italic civilization. This discourse implied that the coastal regions of Istria and Dalmatia had nothing in common with the Balkans. Postulating the Mediterranean identity of these regions, and their separateness from the Balkans, was common during the Fascist period, and again in the early 1990s, during the Yugoslav wars.

Post-1945 Italian Balkanist discourse revolves around two main themes related to the tragic events of the interwar and postwar periods. The reprisals in 1943 and 1945 against local fascists and other alleged 'enemies of the people' are known as *infoibamenti* (throwing of dead or even victims still alive into *foibe*, i.e. Karstic crevasses) and *esodo* (the postwar exodus) of

Istrian and Dalmatian Italians from regions now under Yugoslav rule. The memories of those events were silenced, for various reasons, in both Italy and Yugoslavia. The only exception occurred among the Istrian-Dalmatian Italian diaspora, in good part settled in Trieste, just across the Yugoslav border. There, the issue of the *foibe* and *esodo* had a huge impact on local politics, as well as on postwar Italian-Yugoslav relations in the borderland. With the beginning of war in Croatia and Bosnia-Herzegovina – which launched the new term ethnic cleansing – Istro-Dalmatian exiles in Trieste immediately picked up the term and put it to use. They claimed that 'what the Slavs are now doing to one another they first did to us' or that the *esodo* was the first case of ethnic cleansing in the eastern Adriatic. Another claim, which emerged at the same time, was that the Italians had been thrown in the *foibe* for the sole crime of being Italian.

Over the 1990s, the *foibe* and *esodo* became national stories, especially during the second half of the decade, when the politically dominant part of the transformed Italian left chose the path of 'national reconciliation', through the forging of a 'shared memory'. This implied a revision of their view of the fascist period, and even more of the tragedy of the northeast borderland, as well as the role of both parties in these events. The search for reconciliation has been epitomized by the meeting in 1998 between Luciano Violante (then president of the Chamber of Deputies and an influential figure of the postcommunist PDS) and Gianfranco Fini (head of *Alleanza Nazionale*) in Trieste, where they stated, among other things, that the antifascist partisans and the militants of Mussolini's Social Republic were equally Italians. The Balkanist and anti-Slav discourse, previously characteristic only of the far right, was now embraced, to a certain extent, by the 'rejuvenated' left, which had at that time discovered a so-called 'new patriotism', and began developing empathy for those who opted for Mussolini's Italian Social Republic after the capitulation of 1943. The thesis that the Italians were ethnically cleansed, exposed to genocide or thrown in the *foibe* by the Slovenes and Croats for the sole crime of being Italian, was eagerly appropriated by some leaders of the party. Among these were Piero Fassino (secretary of the PDS at the national level) and Stelio Spadaro (secretary of the PDS in Trieste and one of the leading proponents of this 'new patriotism' in the region).[18]

Most academic historians, however, did not accept the ethnic cleansing thesis. Instead, they tended to underline the ruthless policy of the new communist regime, determined to eliminate all political opponents, real or potential, regardless of their nationality. In public discourse and among politicians, by contrast, the popular view prevailed that ethnic cleansing had been

committed by the barbarian Slavs (or Slovenes and Croats), and that their
acts had been fuelled by ancient and atavistic rancour towards everything
Italian. The view of the *foibe* massacres as 'anthropologically' springing
from the Balkan mentality of southern Slavs has been most widespread in
the borderland region of Friuli-Venezia Giulia (also known as Julian March)
where the imagery of the barbarian has drawn on the cultural repertoire
of 'frontier Balkanism.' This theme was developed at length in the novel
La foiba grande ('The Big Foiba'), published in 1992 by the Friulian writer
Carlo Sgorlon. In his novel, Titoist Partisans are depicted as 'an army of the
wood', who, in their 'archaic atrocity', 'subconsciously' follow an 'appeal of
the wood and forest.' Meanwhile, *infoibamenti* are ultimately explained by a
genetically inherited Balkan-type ethnic hatred and culture of war.

There are serious scholars, however, who do contribute to the construction of an eastern Adriatic *foibe* culture area. Thus the Triestine historian
Raoul Pupo, one of the leading authorities on the *foibe* and *esodo*, recently
characterized *foibe* as 'a technique of killing diffused in the whole Yugoslav
area'[19] – a rather vague statement indicative of an essentialist view of the
former Yugoslavia. Several historians also have a habit of using the term
foibe not in the literal but 'symbolic' sense, thus including not only those victims who were thrown (dead or alive) in crevasses, but all the Italians, civilians as well as fascist militiamen, who were executed after being sentenced
to death, or who perished in the post-war reprisals or during internments,
or even dispersed soldiers.[20] The overall number of *infoibati* is thus substan-
tially increased. In the same move, it is suggested that all of the victims
– fascist, non-fascist or anti-fascist – of communist reprisal and repression
were exposed to an especially barbarian, i.e. Balkan method of killing. The
notion that Italy borders a kind of a *foibe* culture area in the east has also
gained ground in the Italian political establishment: during a session of the
senate debating the proposal of the law on linguistic minorities in Italy,
senator Novi opposed the inclusion of a Slovene minority by arguing that
cultures such as that of the Slovene were 'infoibatory' and therefore unwor-
thy 'of our solidarity'.[21]

Divided memories: in Italy...

A decisive step towards recognizing the *foibe* and *esodo* as events of national
importance has been the institution of the national Day of Remembrance
for the victims of the *foibe* and *esodo* from Istria and Dalmatia. The initiative
for this memorial day came from the Triestine branch of *Alleanza Nazionale*
and its deputy Roberto Menia, a militantly anti-Slovene frontier politician
and a former street *squadrista*.

The first celebration of the Memorial Day in 2005 proved to be divisive. For this occasion, a highly controversial television film named 'Heart in the Pit' (*Cuore nel pozzo*) was broadcast on state television (RAI) at prime time and was seen by ten million Italians. It was the cause of much uproar, polarization and bitter polemics, both in Italy and across the Adriatic, even more so because it obviously represented a postfascist-inspired attempt at revising the postwar history of the northeast border, with a government propaganda feel. The film was actually produced on the initiative of the minister of telecommunications, Maurizio Gasparri, from *Alleanza Nazionale*. Its director, Alberto Negrin, already had a reputation due to his earlier sentimental and nostalgic films on fascism, such as *Me and Mussolini* and especially his film on the 'righteous gentile' fascist Giorgio Perlasca, featured as an Italian Schindler (*Perlasca, un eroe italiano*). In Slovenia, the film generated tension and indignation weeks and months before its broadcasting, especially among Partisan veterans and 'Italophobe' nationalists. An additional reason for the tense reception of the film was the fact that the freshly installed right-wing government of Janez Janša did not voice any protest, and even seemed to tacitly agree with much of the message expected to be conveyed by the film. The broadcast finally brought a relief and caused much hilarity among former Yugoslav audiences, who could not overlook its fascinating resemblance to Yugoslav films on 'good Partisans' and 'bad Germans' from the 1960s.

Two years later, in 2007, Memorial Day celebrations resulted in a cross-Adriatic dispute caused by a controversial address by President Giorgio Napolitano to a delegation of Dalmatian exiles. This time, it was Croats who were most offended, for they perceived the presidential address as an anti-Croatian statement with racist overtones, and as an anticipation of Italian pressure on Croatia, which had just started negotiations with the EU. In his address to the exiles from Zadar, former communist Napolitano adopted the rhetoric of the far right wholeheartedly. After briefly mentioning fascism, he spoke of the inevitable 'conspiracy of silence' and went on to describe Yugoslav vengeance as 'the barbarism of the past century', a 'bloodthirsty rage' and a 'Slavic annexation plan which prevailed particularly in the [Paris] Peace Treaty of 1947 and assumed the sinister contours of ethnic cleansing'. He also said that liberated Italy 'was humiliated and mutilated in its Oriental region'.[22] The Croatian president Stipe Mesić, another former communist with a Partisan background, blasted his counterpart by stating that his speech was an attempt to question the Paris Peace Treaty, and that it smacked of 'open racism, historical revisionism, and political revanchism'.[23] These words prompted a brief diplomatic spat between the two countries, with leading Italian politicians unanimously expressing their indignation at Mesić's words. Some even hinted that Croatia had yet to come to terms with its fascist past, thus implying that Italy had already done its part. Disapproving voices were also heard from the European Commission, though the Croats were hoping in vain for a comment on the *content* of President Napolitano's words. Some remarked that had a German president levelled similar accusations against Poland the international reaction would have been immense.

The proposed date for the Memorial Day, chosen by the deputy Menia, was 10 February. On that day in 1947, the Paris Peace Treaty between Italy and the Allies was signed, and Italy thereby had to cede part of the Julian March to Yugoslavia. Neofascists have always considered this treaty a *Diktat* by the Allied powers and therefore void. Some commentators, however, believe that 10 February was also chosen in the hope that, due to its proximity to another recently established memorial day – that of the memory of the Holocaust on 27 January – the *foibe* would attract some of the aura of cosmopolitanism of the former. The proximity of the two memorial days was undoubtedly seen as a resource by *Alleanza Nazionale*, whose president Fini courted Israel by renouncing fascism and Mussolini, and expressing his wish to visit Jerusalem as a foreign minister. All this has also been consistent with the wish of the right-wing exiles and postfascists to represent their tragedy – after having successfully imposed it on the national level – as an event symbolically comparable, if not equivalent, to the Holocaust. By struggling to establish an inherent relationship between these two otherwise incomparable tragedies, the exiles and their political supporters have been hoping to represent a relatively marginal event as something of European, even universal importance. This was for instance implied by the minister Gasparri, when he asserted the need to produce a fiction film on the *foibe*:

> If we make a documentary, even with the exhumation of bones, we only provoke repulsion. I think a fiction telling the story of one of these poor families would be more efficient. These are huge tragedies. Like that of the Holocaust or Anne Frank.[24]

Several other episodes from the Second World War have been represented as part of an 'Italian Holocaust': for instance, the massacre of the Ardeatine caves or the Porzûs massacre by communist Partisans of a twenty-strong unit of non-communist resistance fighters.[25]

...and in the eastern Adriatic

From the perspective of the Adriatic former Yugoslav nations, such as Croatia and Slovenia, the postwar tragedy of the Italian population from the eastern shore is part of a much larger and more complex tragedy. The overall number of people killed without trial at the end of the war on the whole territory of Yugoslavia is still fairly uncertain, yet assessments of this 'Jacobin' terror go up to 250,000 killings.[26] This overall number includes victims of all nationalities that existed within the country and of all political opinions (including those without them) – anticommunists, non-communists and 'inappropriate' communists. It included members of collaborationist militias as well as often reluctant regular soldiers of the Croat *Ustaša* puppet state. According to the growing consensus of moderate Italian and Slovene historians, the share of the Italian victims in this overall number has been 4000 to 6000 (up to 1000 of them perished in the pits). Considering the nationality of the victims, the Croats (at least 100,000 out of the total number) were by far the most numerous. Their disproportionate share is explained by the enormity of war crimes that the *Ustaša* puppet state committed against civilian Serb, antifascist Croat, Jewish and Gypsy populations. The bulk of the Croats massacred in the postwar reprisals consisted of regular Croat soldiers fleeing from the army and civilians of all ages, not of the *Ustaša* militiamen.

Two key symbols of this extremely brutal retaliation have since become embedded in the Croat collective memory: *Bleiburg* (a town on the Austrian-Slovenian border where refugees were handed over by the British to Tito's divisions and where the first massive massacre took place) and *Via crucis* (a forced march of death throughout Yugoslavia during which almost all perished). During the Titoist period, knowledge of postwar retaliations was strictly silenced. Only the Croat diaspora could commemorate killings and cultivate symbols like *Bleiburg* and *Via crucis*. After Tito's death in 1980, however, narratives of Croat martyrdom, together with martyrological narratives of other national groups, began to circulate within Yugoslavia itself and were soon efficiently fed into the fomenting hatreds and political conflicts among Yugoslav nations. It became clear that horrifying revelations about tens or hundreds of thousands of killed compatriots did not only relate to the reprisals at the end of the war. They also formed part of an array of interethnic and intra-ethnic massacres in the vicious civil war embedded within the Yugoslav antifascist resistance, knowledge of which was equally suppressed during the Titoist period.

One can easily imagine that Yugoslav nations, overwhelmed with these disturbing revelations and eventually pushed into a new cycle of violence after 1991, could not consider the tragedy of Italians of the eastern Adriatic a central event. Equally, they could not have been convinced by the claim that the Italians were killed for the sole crime of being Italian. All these peoples and national minorities, the Italians no less than others, were mourning and amplifying their own victims, while deaf to the suffering of others. This explains to some extent why both unofficial and official acts of acknowledgment of reprisals against the Italian population and of their criminal nature were late in coming.

In the case of Slovenia, by contrast to Croatia and Bosnia-Herzegovina, the interwar massacres and reprisals were largely intra-ethnic, and the number of Slovenes killed by other Slovenes reached several tens of thousands. Thus rituals of reconciliation among ethnic Slovenes themselves had to take precedence over official expressions of regret regarding the tragedy suffered by the Italians. National reconciliation had been proposed by the then reformed-communist president to the community of the 'defeated side', as well as to the Catholic Church (a key fomenter of collaborationism), and was officiated at the village of Teharje near Celje, a most notorious site of postwar mass killings. Various centre-left coalitions, heirs to antifascist traditions cultivated throughout the period of socialist Yugoslavia, have stayed in power in Slovenia virtually without interruption from the independence of 1991 to the mid-2000s. They have been reluctant to go too far with self-flagellation for the crimes of their predecessors, also due to the (not unfounded) fear that this would encourage the other side in its growing ambition to equate communism and Nazi-Fascism, and eventually to rehabilitate collaboration with the Nazi-Fascist occupiers as having been a legitimate tactic to fight the 'absolute evil' of communism.

In the newly-independent Croatia of the 1990s, which suffered the war under Franjo Tudjman's authoritarian rule, the official revisionism of the Second World War and related developments took a different turn. Communism was flatly anathemized, yet *ustaštvo* – a virulently anti-Serb and eventually also anti-Semite national ideology of the puppet fascist Croatian state set up by Mussolini and Hitler – was not unambiguously rehabilitated as has been widely believed. The reality is quite different, actually: what Tujdman (a former communist general under Tito) promoted was an odd blend of *ustaštvo* and partisan antifascism, a blend of antifascist resistance and anticommunist collaboration with the Axis powers. This was an attempt at reconciling the Croats on an anticommunist platform – those who fought on the side of the *Ustaša* state against communist partisans and those who fought on the side of the communist partisans against the *Ustaše*. This exercise in nationalist alchemy naturally necessitated diverse ideological operations, with two aims in particular. Firstly, it aimed to dissociate *ustaštvo* from its inherent fascism and its anti-Serb as well as anti-Semite racism, and to present it as a laudable patriotic struggle to liberate Croatdom from the Serbian yoke. Secondly, it aimed to purge antifascist resistance from communism (presented as a Serb or 'Byzantine' imposition) and to present it as an equally laudable form of Croat patriotism. Among other things, this implied a symbolic equation of key symbols, i.e. of Bleiburg (the central site of memory of *Ustaša* martyrology)[27] with Jasenovac (the *Ustaša* extermination camp where up to 100,000 Serbs, antifascist Croats, Jews and Gypsies perished).

Yet the lack of empathy for the suffering of eastern Adriatic Italians is also to be ascribed to other, perhaps more important reasons. Despite all the revisionism which followed the demise of Yugoslavia, in some regards, the view of the history of the Second World War has not really changed. Views on the Italians, Italian Fascism and the role of the Italians in the Second World War are a clear case in point. Not only do ancient ethnic and racist stereotypes on the part of Adriatic Slavs about short, dark, perfidious and land-grabbing Latins persist – but the one-dimensional view of their role in the war as framed by Tito's communist regime has efficiently survived until this day. From this perspective, former Yugoslav Slavs see themselves as clear winners of the Second World War who fully and unambiguously sided with the victorious Allies, whereas the Italians were all fascists and losers in the end. The status of Italy as a cobelligerent force fighting the same adversary as the Allied powers after 1943 has been unrecognized and the role of the Italian partisan resistance has largely been dismissed.

As fascists and the defeated party in the war, it has often been argued that the Italians deserved the punishment they received in the end for their misdeeds, and that this punishment was relatively light. However, opinions of this kind – which implicitly justify postwar violent reprisals as a reaction to the previous (undoubtedly bloodier) fascist violence – have disappeared from the public discourse and are largely considered unacceptable now. Many people – especially those originating from regions that were already suffering Italian frontier fascism between the two wars – may perhaps continue to believe that 'the Italians got what they deserved', but do not disclose this. Negationism of the *foibe* and mass killings is similarly characteristic of veteran partisan associations. Again, their negationism is mostly dormant and very few individuals actively follow the agenda of publicly countering 'the *foibe* myth'. Its public outbursts are largely defensive, as in the case of the nervous tension generated on the Slovene side of the border by the RAI propagandist telefilm *The Heart in the Pit*, as discussed above.

The perception among the above-mentioned Italian politicians that Croatia, contrary to Italy, did not come to terms with its fascist past seems to be both accurate and mistaken. It is accurate in the sense that Croat scholars, journalists and politicians have not found it necessary to encourage a serious, scholarly and informed confrontation with the roots of home-grown Croat totalitarianism, fascism, virulent racism and Catholic fundamentalism as interwoven in the *Ustaša* state. The study of the latter, both in domestic and international scholarship, has been seriously neglected. Compared to this, Italian scholarship on Italian fascism and imperialism has fared far better. Its quality in this regard is superior to its Croat (or Slovene, for that matter) counterpart. The lagging behind of the latter, predominantly nationalist historiography can also be discerned from the crudeness of its anticommunist stream. Its lack of sophistication is probably best exemplified by the fact that nothing comparable to the Italian school of *anti-antifascism* exists in the eastern Adriatic.[28]

On the other hand, since Italy is widely renowned for having avoided defascistization and the former Yugoslavs have very good reasons to resent this (not one Italian officer from a lengthy list denounced by the Yugoslavs as war criminals ever faced trial), the Croats may well find this perception among Italian politicians preposterous. Still, such injustice certainly cannot be an excuse for sweeping one's own misdeeds under the carpet. The perception of Italian politicians is, in a sense, also fundamentally mistaken since defascistization (or 'de-ustašization') was fully – and radically – implemented in Croatia, namely as an implacable physical annihilation of the *Ustaše*, followed by the long decades of severe punishment administered to survivors and their homelands.[29] This radically Manichean notion of defascistization, as adopted by the early Yugoslav communist regime, implied that the Croat (or any other) national 'body', after having been purged of its treacherous scum, was essentially innocent. The 'surviving' Croats were accordingly absolved of their guilt as a virtuous antifascist nation, which made a huge contribution to the liberation of the country (one third of the rank-and-file of the Yugoslav Army at the end of the war were actually Croats). Meanwhile, the 'non-Croat' *Ustaše* and their sympathizers represented only a minuscule minority of the population. The kernel of such national self-perception has survived the demise of the federal order and is part of the Yugoslav legacy for today's new nations.

Conclusion: towards a shared Adriatic memory?

To include the memory of the victims of the *foibe* and exile in the Italian memorial repertoire, and to symbolically relate these victims to the Holocaust might create an impression of belonging to the 'new European culture of apologies, mourning and collective guilt for national crimes such as the Holocaust and acts of violence against minorities';[30] or, for that matter, of being involved in the European memorial process characterized by the shift from triumphant to traumatic memories. A prerequisite of this shift is the democratization and pluralization of national memory. Yet, while this process has undoubtedly reached Italy, the commemoration of the *foibe* and exile proceeds via the repression of many other memories of other victims and other crimes, including victims of many of those who were thrown in the pits. The obsessive indignation at the fact that the *foibe* were concealed from the Italians for such a long time has become an unavoidable part of Italian political rituals during the last decade. Historical simplification and journalistic 'truths about the *foibe*' are extracted from the context of fascist imperialism in the Adriatic and adopted by a good part of Italian politicians. Thus they reproduce, and even generate, 'black holes' or 'gaps in Italian popular memory'.[31]

One might infer that *victims* (of 'Slav expansionism') are being commemorated and celebrated because Italian fascism and imperialism were not *victors* in the end, or for some other reason such as a turn to the European 'cosmopolitan' memory. However, I would argue that, above all, the memorial culture of the Italian neofascist and postfascist right is simply part of a nostalgia for the fascist empire. It memorializes eminent figures of fascism, in particular Mussolini, and venerates masculine and martial virtues, as well as the will to power which, due to various adversities, could not triumph. Flattering the Jews and shedding crocodile tears for their terrible plight is particularly hypocritical in a context where this goes hand in hand with demonizing the anti-fascist resistance and constructing alternative visions of archenemy. Meanwhile, instead of proposing a serious debate on Italian anti-Semitism, it offers a sugary history, produced in film and RAI studios, with the Italians playing the role of good people, saviours of Jews, and innocent victims of Slav or Nazi barbarity.[32]

Although the Adriatic Euro-region, encompassing all the municipalities around the Adriatic, was established in 2006 under the auspices of the Council of Europe, the emergence of a shared Adriatic memory seems as remote as ever. Meanwhile, the current Italian centre-left is clearly in favour of building a shared memory (*memoria condivisa*) at home, but also of exporting its project to former imperial lands. The president of the borderland region, Friuli-Venezia Giulia, has been trying for years to persuade the presidents of Italy, Slovenia and Croatia to perform a reconciliation ritual. However, the prevailing reality in Italy and around the Adriatic is one of the persistence, even proliferation, of divided memories. The parliamentary group of the 'Party of the Italian Communists' (PdCI) reacted to the institution of the *foibe* Memorial Day by proposing the institution of several new memorial days such as a day of remembrance for the African victims of the Italian colonial occupation, and a day remembering the crimes of Italian Fascism and its victims. Slovenia reacted to it with the institution of a national holiday devoted to the unification of the coastal region with the homeland. This is celebrated on 15 September, the day when the Peace Treaty of 1947 came into effect.

The proliferation of circum-Adriatic nationalisms is often interpreted as a reaction to European integration (and globalization). However, it is important to note that in the core of the former Adriatic empire, the process of commemorating the various victims from the days of the empire's demise displays unusual characteristics. Italian nationalist victimization, blaming everything on the 'Slav' or some other enemy, may easily coexist with a regionalist questioning of Italian unity and its Risorgimento tradition; the two may even form an inextricable knot. Italian Unity and the Risorgimento are themselves questioned because of their 'incompleteness', seen by their censurers as the flipside of Italy's inability to build a coherent empire. Post-colonial Italy is perceived as fundamentally flawed because it did not properly fulfil its historical mission. Nation-building and empire-building have been expected to coincide: with the failure of the latter, the former is also flawed.

These idiosyncratic imperialist, nationalist and localist-regionalist strands of Italian identity apparently point not only to the absence of *Vergangenheits-bewältigung* (coming to terms with the past), but also to the lack of public reflection about the demise of the Italian empire.[33] Not only is the memory (and the awareness of the extent) of fascist atrocities committed abroad submerged in countless ways, but the memory of Italy's empire itself has been erased to a remarkable extent. It is precisely for this reason that in current Italian discourse, both right-wing and left-wing, the eastern Adriatic and the whole Danubian basin can continue to be advertised as a space waiting for Italian 'penetration'. This time only economic and cultural sorts are meant, but nevertheless...

The Italian 'victim-oriented' commemoration process – which has provided the Adriatic face of Italy with a new centrality in the national consciousness (while, in economic and cultural terms, the Adriatic remains a backwater sea of Italy) – is simultaneously the key process of memory-making in the circum-Adriatic. Most countries from the eastern shore face analogous problems, with divided memories of tragedies generated in the context of Adriatic fascist and Nazi imperialism, since they all experienced a combination of anti-fascist resistance and the civil war. In all of these nations, the memory of atrocities committed by the Italian fascist occupation is being perpetuated by one part of the society and questioned by its other part. Inasmuch as the Italian state remains the leading actor in the region, it also holds the key to a reconciliation and dialogue of these trans-Adriatic memories.

CHAPTER VII

MEMORY, CONFLICT AND GENDER: *WOMEN IN BLACK* IN ISRAEL/PALESTINE AND FORMER YUGOSLAVIA

FRANZISKA BRANTNER

The production of collective memory reflects social arguments around the interpretation of the past. However, it is in the 'compression' process, which links individual remembrances and political uses of the past, that mainstream interpretations become generally accepted. These often neglect and exclude minorities with their trans-national aspects, including women's experiences and interpretations, as women often speak from the margins and the borders. Pierre Nora's concept *lieux de mémoire*,[1] for example, is not gender neutral, as the identified *lieux* mostly represent male-determined spaces of action.[2] Similarly, oral history projects embody subjective and (often) political decisions regarding whose testimonies are worth collecting, with women's stories often excluded in the process. Thus war-related projects tend to focus on the male side of war: battlefields and soldiers.[3] When women are remembered, they are often made to fit the paradigm of women as mothers.[4] This chapter seeks to redress this imbalance and argues that a closer examination of women's ways of remembering and forgetting, during and after conflicts, reveals fascinating new perspectives on conflict management in the Mediterranean and indeed beyond.

Official narratives of the past reflect the public classification, relevance assignment, evaluation and interpretation of events, through which the political and cultural self-image of a community manifest itself historically. Collective memories, independent of their degree of conscious constructedness, confer power and legitimacy on some and not others.[5] The place of women, and female action, is often marginalized within these webs of meanings. This poses the risk of limiting women's actual relevance and options for exercising influence in the reality thereby created. Hence not only are women's actions not remembered, but a 'women-free' or 'women as mothers history also limits women's role in the present. This has especially negative consequences in times of conflict and post-war transformations, when women should be empowered as they play a crucial role in successful transitions towards peace.

Recent UN studies on post-conflict transformation have highlighted the many ways in which women can contribute to a successful transition towards peace. Firstly, women tend to engage more than men in trans-ethnic or trans-national peace activism in times of turmoil as testified by the case of *Women in Black*, both in the Israeli-Palestinian conflict and the Yugoslav wars. Furthermore, women's efforts in the reconstruction of local health and education infrastructure are crucial in transformation processes.[6] Women's involvement in the development of legal, judicial and constitutional structures that promote gender equality has helped ensure that the entire population is confident that redress for grievances can be obtained through legitimate structures for the peaceful settlement of disputes and the fair administration of justice.[7] However, one aspect is often missing from these studies: the way women engage in and challenge official discourses on the distant and recent past. Memory survives even when people are denied a voice. Thus the memory of marginalized members of society is particularly salient, since this is in a way their tool of last resort, a means of passive resistance which can literally keep them alive. Are women capable of changing the collective memories of nations and at the same time the story of their borders, thereby transforming conflicts with neighbours themselves? If so, how and at what level do women's rights activists and feminists challenge master narratives of conflict, to create 'counter-memory'? [8]

Any such analysis must from the beginning grasp the limits of women's attempts at writing their history, especially with regards to the essentializing of 'womanliness', and to attributing typical 'female characteristics' to the narratives, such as that of women being more peaceful. Also, the plurality among women 'should warn us against any sweeping assertions on the relationships between gender and memory.'[9]

This chapter seeks to explore these questions based on two cases from the Mediterranean – the Yugoslav (particularly Kosovo) and the Israeli-Palestinian conflict. It is based on a comparative study of women's activism during and after conflict that directly and/or indirectly linked to the production of collective memories.[10] The chosen examples only serve to illustrate a few aspects of women's memory work in the region in times of conflict; they have no claim of comprehensive representativeness. My central argument is that trans-national and cross-ethnic feminist groups, while recognizing the power asymmetries among parties involved, tend to accept the Other more readily in his or her 'otherness', above all by critically reading the historical narratives of all sides. In doing so, these groups can provide precious new spaces to disturb mainstream constructions of national memories, identities and borders. The sections to follow will first present a framework for the analysis of such 'memory activism', and then analyze instances of activism through this lens.

As the objective is to assess to what extent and how women are capable agents of collective memories, while at the same time taking into account the social and political environment in which and upon which they act, it is necessary to look at the issue from a dynamic vantage point. It should shed light on the interactive articulation between the individual, on the one hand, and the social, political and cultural conditions of remembering, on the other.[11] Women's memory cannot only be understood in terms of concrete actions by individual strategic actors; any exploration must also look at social and interpretative frameworks which women, and especially feminist activists offer, and within which memories can be expressed.

Still, *how* do the dynamics of collective memory actually work?[12] A first step is to differentiate between the diverse levels of memory expression – for example between the public or private, national or local, spontaneous or purposefully provoked. In this context, the family is one important locus of transmission and framing of individual memories, a space where women traditionally play important roles. Andrea Pető has shown in her study of the conservative turn in historiography in Eastern Europe that this narrative was resurrected from the family domain into the public after 1989. She found that the resurgence of the conservative claim was possible because women had sustained it in the family during the years of the communist regime, under which this narrative was denied in public.[13]

Furthermore, independent of the level of memory expression, the available framework within which suppressed or denied personal and collective memories are resurrected should matter. These are the mental and social frames available at the moments when individual memories 're-enter' the public sphere. They enable the linking of personal memories to larger narratives, thus imbuing them with meanings. The feminist frame is one example, but there are others too: religious, nationalistic, etc.

This allows us to ask which specific (women or feminist) frameworks guide individual remembrance, or the selection of testimonies, and how. Furthermore, we can analyze gender activism, and ask what spaces – understood as conceptual frameworks but also practically as places – do women as strategic agents create for other women and men, in order to allow them to relate their individual remembrances back to the public. How do they frame such processes? Finally, we should investigate how women's activist and feminist spaces and memories relate to and/or challenge mainstream narratives, as well as who they empower or disempower.

Posing these questions does not mean that the women challenging collective memory in a bottom-up fashion, i.e. the individual influencing the collective, and not vice versa, are not influenced by their societies, or are 'free' in terms of their memories. Feminist narrative contestations do not come out of a vacuum, abstracted as it were from the context within which they originate. Yet, arguing that no memory process 'from the bottom up' is immune from contextual factors does not prevent one from studying projects seeking to challenge their context, and to assess the interplays between individual action and societal factors.

In the following section, I draw on Marie-Claire Lavabre and Sarah Gensburger's interpretation of Paul Ricoeur's concept of *'la juste mémoire'*[14] in order to structure the presentation of the cases. They argue that the concept of *juste mémoire* has three distinct meanings: a) in terms of traditional justice – allowing juridical justice to occur, b) in the sense of a just and correct equilibrium between 'ni trop, ni trop peu' of commemoration and memorization, and c) in terms of 'adjusting', or framing memories with a goal, mostly to pacify existing memories and allow for social coexistence.[15]

One final interrogation relates to the use of 'Self' and 'Other' in women's memory work. These are obviously fluid and relative constructs. Many cross-border or cross-conflict activities are based on shared experiences and identities, as well as common objectives that transcend ethnic and national identities. Common class identity and workers' rights struggles allow for solidarity across ethnic lines in the early twentieth century, albeit short of preventing war.[16] 'Mother' is another category often relied upon in order to facilitate such boundary-crossing activities. Emblematically, a women's group founded in 1989 in order to bring together Palestinian and Jewish women named itself 'Neled', which translates as 'we will give birth'.[17] Such approaches relying on shared identities risk however denying the 'other' woman her right to be other. Alternatively, activism based on feminist frameworks of identity deconstruction and the recognition of asymmetries is another way of encouraging cross-boundary cooperation. Such feminist peace movements base their work on the recognition that the 'Other' is and remains different, and that this entails responsibilities, such as balancing power differentials that underpin the existing relationship. The cases seek, thefore, to analyze how women and feminists perceive, interact with and treat 'the Other'. Activists can either acknowledge the absolute existence of the Other in a Levinassian sense,[18] and recognize the ethical obligations that it imposes, or deny the existence of such an Other, maintaining that in fact it shares the same human characteristics and ought to be treated as part of the 'Self'.

With this distinction in mind, the following section explores feminist activism's contribution to *'juste mémoire'* in terms of legal justice, activism (dealing with a 'trop' or a 'trop peu' situation) and memory adjustment.

Let justice be done

Justice during conflict

Memory activism on the part of women starts with the here and now, and the documentation, from a gender perspective, of aspects of ongoing conflicts that do not receive enough attention from the mainstream media. Thus, for instance, the Israeli *Machsom Watch* organization was founded in January 2001 in response to repeated reports about human rights abuses of Palestinians who were crossing army and border police checkpoints.[19] The group deploys women to monitor the behaviour of Israeli soldiers in the hope of reducing the level of abuse through their mere presence. Its members believe that the women's 'quiet but assertive presence at checkpoints is a direct challenge to the dominant militaristic discourse that prevails in Israeli society. It demands accountability on the part of the security forces towards the civilian estate, something hitherto almost unheard of.'[20] In addition, the women involved document and record their experiences. Their aim is to report the results to a wide audience; they keep for example a blog where they present the cases of violations they encounter. Furthermore, they make their material available to court cases initiated either by other human rights groups or themselves. An initiative on the part of three women – Ronnee Jaeger, a long time activist with experience of human rights work in Guatemala and Mexico, Adi Kuntsman, a feminist scholar who emigrated from the former Soviet Union in 1990, and veteran activist Yehudit Keshet, an orthodox Jewish woman – the group now involves 400 members. Membership is open exclusively to women for various reasons, including the fear that men might represent more direct threats to the soldiers. Another reason is the early experience of participating men attempting to explain to the women 'what was allowed and what was not at the barrier'.[21]

Memory activism during conflicts is thus often about transcending borders. The members of another group, *Yesh Din*, go to the territories, take testimonies and produce reports. Many of them are older women who have the courage to break the unspoken rule of not entering the occupied territories. One of their main motivations is to tell these stories to the larger Israeli public so that nobody can say afterwards 'I did not know'.[22]

Machsom Watch and *Yesh Din* try to affect the present as much as the future, as this is where we must start in order to affect tomorrow's memory. Theirs is a work of *memorization*, reflecting the idea of a *travail pour la mémoire* – an act in the present that affects the process by which today is transformed into tomorrow's past. As actors for change, highly aware of the continuous political manipulation of the past, their members attempt to limit *ex-ante* the range of future spaces for such manipulation. The testimonies they bring to the fore stem both from the political will to prevent human rights' violations, or at least to bring them to courts, and from the hope that such testimonies will make it more difficult for political contenders to exclude these dimensions of the present in the future. Maybe the *travail pour la mémoire* pushes the idea of manipulability of memories and history to the maximum and should be regarded as an additional way of contributing to a *juste mémoire*. Of course the actual influence of such work depends on future actors being interested in and willing to use the fruits of their work – this is their motivating hope.

Post-conflict justice

Perhaps the most visible impact of memory activism initiated by women has been the documentation of atrocities and witnessing in court in order to gain recognition and redress for violations of women's rights during conflict via the judicial system. The search for legal justice in such endeavors is closely linked to memory work. As Martha Minow has argued: 'both the public experience of witnessing the trials, or reports about them, and the products of such trials, may alter the way people remember and thus the way they deal with the tormenting past.'[23]

Women's participation in the International Criminal Tribunal for the Former Yugoslavia (ICTY) has been highly visible in the international arena and women have succeeded in gaining recognition for rape and sexual violence as a deliberate war strategy and as an ethnically targeted war crime. By recognizing these human rights violations as war crimes, the ICTY has significantly advanced international law. A report prepared by the international organization *Women Waging Peace* has documented the major efforts by local Bosnian women's groups in finding and preparing witnesses, collecting testimonies, and counseling those who give evidence at the ICTY.[24] Without Bosnian women human rights advocates and their push for the inclusion of gender expertise at all stages and levels of the ICTY's organization, the story of the Yugoslav wars would have been told differently.

Yet despite the international recognition of their grievances and the inclusion of these stories into the official *international* tale of the war crimes committed, there has not been a comparable spill-over to memories held at the local level.[25] According to the *Women Waging Peace* report, 'despite international attention and funding for the ICTY, little effort has been made to establish links between the Tribunal and local communities.'[26] Consistent with a pattern shared by other social movements around the world, it seems as if women's rights activists have been more successful at gaining recognition and justice internationally, where they received support from global activists, than in their home towns or countries.

Even in Yugoslavia, this pattern has not been limited to women's experiences. Pierre Hazan has more generally critiqued the ICTY for not sufficiently integrating its work at the local level,[27] and Martha Minow argues that there is 'too little resistance to hatred on the ground-level – where fears and aggression are stocked.'[28] One concern related to the translation of the international recognition to local communities is that of the legitimacy of the tribunal 'at home'. For example, an individual who generally mistrusts the tribunal will also mistrust its judgment about women's rights violations. Hence the challenge for women and other activists to identify avenues and frameworks of legitimacy that allow their stories to be translated to the local and regional levels, without necessarily having to prove the legitimacy of the international tribunal. Women's rights activists do attempt to build bridges by establishing individual stories, especially about women victims of rape, and initiating reconciliation projects within communities.[29]

It remains to be seen how the success of memory activism might eventually trickle down from the international to the local level. Unfortunately, funding from the international community – once international recognition had been obtained from the international tribunal – was then channeled towards often unsuccessful 'reconciliation' projects between men from diverse ethnic groups, instead of supporting women's local efforts at building bridges between international juridical recognition and local stories of the war.[30] This turn away from women's issues has forced the women's movement to limit its local activism.

In light of this, it is interesting to study how the Belgrade-based group *Women in Black* attend and support cases in the national Special Court for War Crimes and Organized Crime[31] and support the victims or witnesses and their families. As the mainstream media only marginally reports about the special courts, *Women in Black* journalists also try to cover and document the cases and the stories behind them in the public sphere outside the court rooms. According to Staša Zajović, co-founder of *Women in Black* Belgrade, the women go to the Special Court 'as activists, feminists, citizens, to make clear that the question is not only a legal one.'[32] These visits also enable participating women to voice their opposition to the claim that crimes have been committed in their name. To address this feeling of guilt, *Women in*

Black activists use and develop feminist concepts of care and transversal politics. In *Gender and Nation* Nira Yuval-Davis describes feminist transversal politics as follows:

> Transversal politics aims to be an alternative to the universalism/ relativism dichotomy which is at the heart of the modernist/postmodernist feminist debate. It aims at providing answers to the crucial theoretical/political questions of how and with whom we should work if/when we accept that we are all different as deconstructionist theories argue.[33]

Yuval-Davis continues:

> In "transversal politics", perceived unity and homogeneity are replaced by dialogues which give recognition to the specific positionings of those who participate in them as well as to the ´unfinished knowledge´ that each such situated positioning can offer.[34]

Staša Zajović contends that such feminist concepts of deconstructing identities, and the conscious decision 'I take care of who I want to take care of – not just because it is my brother or cousin', are important steps in liberating women, enhancing their ability to think across ethnic boundaries, and to accept and live with guilt. By contributing to the just appreciation of feelings in the administration of justice, *Women in Black* activists combine a search for legal justice with the broader goal of reconciling societies.[35]

In the end, bringing cases to court, and seeking justice for past wrongs is not only about gaining recognition and possibly compensation in the present, but also, and importantly, it is about avoiding the future denial of these atrocities. Women's groups have contributed to the search for a *juste mémoire*, especially for the female victims of the Yugoslav wars. But if the level at which justice is delivered does not coincide with that of the construction of memory, the contribution to *juste mémoire* understood in a national or local way is less explicit and less immediate. In that sense, obtaining justice on the international level is but one step towards a *juste mémoire*.

Ni trop, ni trop peu

Fighting against denial, visiting 'lieux de mémoire'

In the French discussions of the need to balance the respective risks of 'trop' and 'trop peu', the point of departure is generally the former. However, the reverse is certainly true for women's peace activists in the Mediterranean fighting against denial or *l'abus de l'oubli*. In Serbia today, one of the central struggles of women's memory activism is to fight against the ongoing denial of crimes, to remember the war, and to mourn the victims of all sides. History itself is a vital field in this struggle. In 2007, a press release by *Women in Black* Belgrade responded to an attack against Vesna Pešić, member of Serbia's National Assembly, who is also a prominent antiwar activist and human rights defender:

> On this occasion, we express our deepest respect and solidarity for women with whom, for the last 15 years, we have actively resisted war. Together, we were the most active in changing the dictatorial regime; today we are the most active against the denial of the criminal past. Going forward, we will support one another as we have thus far.[36]

This quote shows that these women consciously engage with the way in which the past is related in the present, and see their fight against the denial of past crimes on an equal footing with their activism to change the dictatorial regime.

One symbolically powerful method of protest adopted by *Women in Black* is mourning as a public spectacle. Women, all dressed in black, commemorate the war victims in public. In their black robes and silence they are 'visible, unavoidable, inescapably political'.[37] Mourning is traditionally associated with women, as they are often assigned the task to display grief for dead member of the community. However, *Women in Black* also mourn the enemy's victims, which turns the performance into a thoroughly subversive act. According to Nina Ulasowksi, the latter 'is made more potent by the extension of mourning for the enemy, recognizing the bereavement of the "other".... The public subversion of women's mourning is a refusal to align with notions of a political constituency deemed natural and pre-eminent by the demands of nationalism.'[38] As with the distinction made in the introduction, in this case women activists allow 'the Other' to remain distinct, while at the same time embracing him or her.

The *Women in Black* also occupy public spaces in Belgrade to remember overtly the crimes committed in their name. Such activities include standing at crossroads with signs that only say 'Srebrenica' for example, referring to the massacres committed by Serbs in Srebrenica. They expose in the public sphere the current pact to deny crimes on the part of the governing elites. Perhaps most radically, they visit places of past Serbian crimes in order to create new images of 'who are Serbs, who are Bosnians'. One of the first places the activists went to was Srebrenica, and now the list also includes Kosovo and Albania. The simple fact of entering the public sphere so brazenly is in itself an act of subversion by these women.

Similarly, feminist organizations in Israel are at the forefront of efforts to directly challenge the denial of the past. One such organization is *Zochrot*, which means 'We remember', but in the feminine form. It is not a women-only organization, but the fact of using the feminine form is an interesting reference to the role of women in the process of remembrance. *Zochrot* is a group of Israeli citizens working to raise awareness of the Palestinian experience of forced uprooting during and after the war of 1948.[39] According to *Zochrot*:

> The Zionist collective memory exists in both our cultural and physical landscape, yet the heavy price paid by the Palestinians – in lives, in the destruction of hundreds of villages, and in the continuing plight of the Palestinian refugees – receives little public recognition. Zochrot works to make the history of the Nakba accessible to the Israeli public so as to engage Jews and Palestinians in an open recounting of our painful common history.[40]

The *Nakba* day is marked with street events in major Israeli cities whose aim is to remind fellow citizens that Arab villages once existed in these places. The signs, some of which are posted on message boards in Jerusalem, Tel Aviv, Haifa and Ramat Hasharon, display messages like: 'Tzabar – until '48 there was a village here'. Zochrot has organized these activities together with feminist organizations *Bat Shalom* and *New Profile*. *Bat Shalom* (Daughter of Peace) also organizes a 'Women's Land Day' referring to the Palestinian 'Land Day'[41] which is meant to remember the expropriation of land – and to make audible the voices of Palestinian women who have taken part in the struggle and the suffering. In addition, *Bat Shalom* runs a 'Dealing With Past-Testimonies' project that also brings together today's activists and victims, often from recent past events. Limiting official Israeli control over the memory of the *Nakba* has relied mainly on the memories of Palestinians, whose recollection and sense of truth is contradicted by these official lines. Feminist groups bring these limits and contradictions back into the consciousness of Jewish Israelis.

In both cases, women and feminist activists contribute to the search for a *juste mémoire* by fighting against the denial of the past, the 'trop peu' of memory work that is governed by dominant political actors. However, campaigns of fear and intimidation, both in Serbia and Israel, continue to target those who openly refuse to accept national identity constructions based on a denial of the past. Women activists have reported aggressions against them throughout the Yugoslav wars.[42] Nearly all the Serbian activists I spoke to pointed to the demonization of feminists in Serbia for their disloyalty to the Serbian mainstream historical narrative. Especially now that the war is over, the nationalist ideology produces a new enemy, namely all those who threaten the nationalist interpretation of the past. The same can be said about *Women in Black* participants in Israel.[43] Such campaigns serve as means of 'othering' activists, delegitimizing their work and keeping more women from joining such movements. It is important to note the manner in which women's groups themselves are becoming defined as an Other, as a response to their work in destabilizing identity categories. As they work on behalf of memory *(travail pour la mémoire)*, they engage in shaping a future already being coined in the present, and thus alleviate the task of the generations to come. These generations will continue to contest the likely future denial of today's crimes by their very perpetrators.

Adjusting memories for pacification?

Whereas the question of denial often relates to the recognition of the 'Other', the 'adjustment' element of *juste mémoire* also refers to improving social coexistence within a society, via the 'adjustment of memories'. One potential complication on the way towards coexistence is the discrepancy between the roles assigned to members of society in the official, taught narrative of the past, and their self-perception or their actual roles. Such a discrepancy is the target for many women, attempting to 'right' or to 'adjust' the mainstream discourse.

Women often find the roles assigned to them in Yugoslav war histories limited to either victims or motherhood or the 'womb of the nation'.[44] The idea of 'women and children' as victims in need of protection is defined in opposition to 'male' roles in the masculine normative narratives of war.[45] Feminists have increasingly been active in challenging these descriptions that limit their agency in times of conflict and afterwards. Furthermore, women activists often see official, taught history as a very effective instrument, not only to perpetuate war mentalities but also traditionalist, patriarchal visions of society.

One mechanism at work is the stylization of traditional women's roles in order to (re)create a national mythos. Nita Luci and Vjollca Krasniqi, who compiled 'Life histories of Albanian Women in Kosova',[46] explained that Kosovar nationalists partly invoked traditions which did not necessarily exist before, but were more likely imagined traditions, often based on conservative images of womanhood.[47] Both authors described efforts at strengthening those aspects of communities that justify the exclusivity of national identity. They expressed fears that these efforts go hand in hand with the re-traditionalization of society, with women shouldering a disproportionate burden via their relegation to traditional roles. This reflects earlier research, which had shown that women share a 'particular symbolic weight... as keepers of national identity, purity and longevity that often becomes more pronounced, as do other gendered divisions of labour, during conflict.'[48]

Partly in reaction, Luci and Krasniqi's study attempts to portray the roles women played before, throughout and after the conflict in more balanced ways. Another example is the project of the Kosovar Gender Studies Center (KGSC), which documents the history of women in Kosovo politics from the 1980s onwards. Their objective is to challenge newly invented traditions, the 'women and children' assumption of many of the recent dominant historical narratives, and to tell the stories of women that were actors in the process, be it peace activists, democracy promoters, or members of the guerilla forces. The KGSC project documents the lives and stories of important women and, according to its project director, Luljeta Vuniqi, aims at 'complementing the official history', the idea being 'to add to our common knowledge and awareness of our past'.[49] Discussing the representations of the pre-war peaceful demonstrations, she emphasizes that the 'pictures in school books today only show the students' resistance, even though the women's movement was much stronger and much more vocal.'[50] The project is based on extensive interviews with the actors themselves. As in other cases, such reminiscence work has led to 'conflicting and sometimes divisive memories and experiences'.[51] The project's leaders had to tackle this challenge and decided not to settle on one 'correct' story but to allow the different versions to become visible in parallel.

These women's projects and feminist groups attempt to confront 'new traditions and rituals [that] are "invented" in the sense of being deliberately designed and produced with a view to creating new political realities, defining nations and sustaining national communities'[52] with the life stories of women. Interestingly, the issue at stake is not about 'representing the world from the standpoint of women',[53] nor is the claim that women saw the conflict or the war differently than men. Rather it is about describing what women actually did before, during and after conflict and war.

While such projects challenge those who control or impose social memories and historical narratives, they risk creating a unified 'women's' story, focusing on some (in their worldview, positive) and excluding other (normatively more negative) examples. Indeed, work seeking to include women in history often tends to invoke their 'positive' role, as if justification for their inclusion into history was really necessary. There is also a high risk of forgetting to contextuaize the women's stories thoroughly, in terms of 'who is speaking, what their personal and social agenda is',[54] or what class, ethnic community or race they belong to.

Nonetheless, such work is not only seen to fill important gaps of knowledge and purposes of contestation, but also to encourage other women to participate in politics, by demonstrating what women have actually been able to do. The goal is to open up spaces for women to enter public life by presenting models from the recent past. Furthermore, Nita Luci and Vjollca Krasniqi have insisted that documenting women's war stories is inherently important in terms of allowing women to speak. They argue that the mere act of interviewing these women, thereby rendering the interviewees' stories relevant and interesting, started a healing process. What is elsewhere qualified as reminiscence work,[55] is described by the two authors as having helped many women to work through their trauma and to re-assess their life stories, to feel valued and 'remembered'. These projects create conditions at the local level that allow women to (re)connect and interact with their individual memories in public within a framework that values their work and does not solely judge it based on its contribution to a national project.

Similarly, Isabelle Humphries and Laleh Khalili have documented women's memories of the *Nakba* discussed above and excavated the role of gender in *Nakba* memories. Using interviews with women in the Galilee – Palestinians living as Israeli citizens – and Palestinian refugees in Lebanon, they argue that, in prioritizing the voice of the male educated elite, the written history of the *Nakba* has excluded the female experience, an experience which has played an essential role in maintaining communal memory of life and loss. Humphries posits that in certain cases gendered social roles prevent women from being in a position to speak publicly at all – whether to a researcher or at public commemorations. Their project allowed women to tell their part of the story, and to work through the past in a context that valued their versions of this past.

Humphries' interviews in the Galilee, as well as those conducted by Khalili in Lebanese refugee camps, show that when women feel comfortable enough to speak they tend to discuss only certain aspects of the *Nakba*, and also in very specific terms, such as the recurring themes of rape and the loss of women's marital gold jewellery. Furthermore, they suggest that Palestinian women have different personal stories due to gendered division of labour, family reproduction roles and their general situation in public and private spheres of society at the moment of the tragedy. They find that many of these individual stories are framed according to the predominant value system:

> Listening to women's narrative of the Nakba draws attention to the details of women's everyday experience of the catastrophe often marginalized by dominant narratives centering around male activi-

ties and memories. Nonetheless, our findings do not take us to some autonomous cultural space beyond patriarchy. On the contrary, this study shows that women's experience and reproduction of memory are shaped by the values and discourses of patriarchy—the association of women's sexual exclusivity with family honor, the differentials of property ownership, the norms and customs of marriage, and the gendered division of labor. Marked silences surrounding rape heavily underline memory-making through the lens of patriarchy. Nationalist discourses and practices further construct remembering, through silencing some narratives and authorizing others.[56]

In this context it is interesting to note that this study was framed as an academic undertaking, and at least not a *prima facie* feminist activist initiative. By contrast, the above mentioned organization *Zochrot* has developed projects to similarly document women's testimonies of the *Nakba* in a film, where they interviewed survivors.[57] Given that the design of oral history and memory projects, or better their conceptual and political framing, has an impact on what and how stories are told and memories related to the larger, recognized narrative, can we find a difference between an activist, Israeli citizen-led project and an academic study? How do the frameworks, the cultural symbols, discourses around a project resonate with the individual?[58] At a first glance, the stories told in both cases resemble each other; a more in-depth comparison would require direct examination of all the primary material and interviews used.

Similarly, an ongoing project located in the Women's Centre for Legal Aid and Counseling in East Jerusalem documents the way women have experienced the Second Intifada. It will be interesting to compare the results of this study with earlier memories of occupation, not only in terms of the content of the stories related, but also in terms of the second one being a project clearly inscribed in the women's rights movement. This would allow an assessment of whether an openly feminist framework makes a difference to how individual remembrances are related back to the larger society.

Other women's activists have themselves started to tell their war stories, documenting crimes committed against them but also describing how they acted in these situations. Igballe Rugova, for example, one of the leading Kosovar women's rights activists and Executive Director of the Kosova Women's Network, narrates in the memoir *Blace Story* her effort to address the situation when Kosovo refugees were trapped at the Macedonian border in 1999. She describes how women and children suffered as refugees, but at the same time relates how they also successfully managed to bring attention to their plight.[59] Similarly, a year later she documented her work in the refugee camps in Macedonia, where women had organized support networks to improve living conditions.[60]

As we have seen, women's rights activists create and offer a social context for memory work, and generate a group within which women can tell their stories. It is possible that this creates conflicts with the mainstream narrative in the medium term. But if the pacification of memories is understood as reconciliation between different narratives, all narratives must first be in the public domain. Such women's projects contribute to social coexistence and a pacification of memories understood in terms of the inclusion of so far neglected and excluded stories.

Women activists do not decide to reveal such stories only to see them 'forgotten', however, and thus they engage more actively in how history is taught in one of the key institutions of memory formation, namely schools. Under Serbian Prime Minister Zoran Djindjić, *Women in Black* was allowed to work within schools to reveal the fascist dimensions of recent (and ongoing) history writing. As one of the goals of *Women in Black* Belgrade is to challenge the 'ethnicization' of history, the group has been working with pupils and teachers to develop new approaches to reconstructing recent and more distant pasts in ways not based on ethnicity. According to the activists, one of the main problems of the region is a history written and taught based on ethnic grounds, distorting the perceptions and collective identities of members of the communities and erasing historical complexities and interdependencies. They argue that the ethnic framework for 'telling' history prevents pacification and must therefore be challenged and replaced. As a result, they have decided to take the initiative and not to accept any notion of 'Other' given or prescribed by the authorities. At the same time, it is important for them to highlight the responsibility that comes from the fact that 'the crimes had also been committed in their names' and to recognize structural power asymmetries between individuals and groups.

Staša Zajović has explained the importance of deconstructing given dichotomies of 'us' and 'them' in the teaching of history. A reflective and critical engagement with ethnic and national identities requires first a process of raising awareness about one's own identity, in order to then confront the equally constructed 'Other'. Such deconstruction processes are at the heart of feminist theory and activism. The frameworks these activists offer are based on feminist concepts linking war, power structures, domination, militarism and nationalism. In order to allow for and create solidarity across borders of ethnicity and nationality, feminist authors like Chandra Mohanty or Bell Hooks 'analyzed the possibilities of alliances, and the impact of subjectivities and boundaries in creating and restricting relationships of principled solidarity within imagined communities'.[61] This brings us back to the above mentioned concept of transversal feminism, which centres on the 'multiple loci of oppression and the interplay of these with gendered experience'.[62]

What allows feminists to challenge ethnically based history writing is the recognition of the 'constructedness' of their own identities and, importantly, the power of existing dominance mechanisms that encourage co-operation among feminists across boundaries of conflict. Nina Ulasowski notes that 'contemporary feminism and its search for neo-solidarities are concerned with women interrogating their own positions of privilege and power in reference to interaction with others across race/class/age/ability/sexuality'.[63] What practically allows for such 'neo-solidarities' is an approach that has been described as 'reflective solidarity',[64] a 'feminist solidarity model based in common differences'[65] or 'rooting and shifting'. Nira Yuval-Davis describes 'rooting' as speaking consciously from one's subject position while 'shifting' attempts to sympathise with 'others' by listening empathetically, enabling exchange while recognizing different values and goals.[66] Importantly this 'sympathy' does not rely on 'the Other' being the same, but on a recognition of difference.

This work aims to 'appease' not necessarily the Serbian society, but the societies living in the region. Unfortunately the work was halted once Zoran Djindjić was assassinated and his successors decided that it was not in their interest to sustain it. Despite this setback, *Women in Black* continue their work in more informal ways. Staša Zajović has emphasized that their fight against ethnic loyalty in memorizing is one of the most difficult.

Many of the lessons and much of the wisdom encapsulated in these stories of 'adjusting memories' can be gleaned from one of the most outstanding projects of 'reconciliation of memories' across societies: the women's caravan of 2002. Some fifty women activists from former Yugoslavia and Albania travelled together for two weeks in a bus in various post-Yugoslav republics and Albania, crossing the borders that had been established – real or imaginary – between their countries and communities. According to the concluding report on this endeavour, 'their objectives were to engage with one another's reality, to bring to light the truth about the recent wars and the question of responsibility, and to assist one another in their respective struggles against community pressures of every kind; against compartmentalization.'[67] There is much to relate about this caravan, not only with regard to memory work, but also to reconciliation, peace and democracy. Suffice it to mention that it brought up the difficulty of accepting conflicting individual memories and having them confronted in one space. Glasson Deschaumes explains that the group managed to overcome difficult moments of disagreement and contradictory experiences partially by using the 'main methodological findings of Royaumont2'.[68] Importantly, each woman there had agreed to put '[her]self forward as a political subject; saying "I" rather than "we"; not confining one's interlocutor to a collective designation-assignation; and abjuring any hierarchization of victims'. These guidelines or rules are surely not limited to women's activism, but might reflect a general willingness to deconstruct experiences and re-assemble them in new formats of women's activism.

Conclusion

Often marginalized in society, women are rarely in a position to produce and invent traditions and memories top-down. Their task is rather one of challenging and often undermining the official management of collective memory, even if their counter-memory has the potential to become dominant. As a result, women's and feminist memory work in (post-)conflict situations revolves around engaging with 'socially organized forgetting and socially organized celebrations'[69] by the dominant actors of the conflict. In doing so, it seeks to contribute to the creation of a 'juste mémoire' in terms of juridical justice, the fight against denial and exclusionary history writing.

Women and feminists engage in diverse ways with the mainstream narratives and history of their – or other – nations, as well as with more global narratives. They do so through political and social activism or through academia. As we have seen, one strategy is to fight against the denial of unpleasant aspects of history, to constantly knock on closed doors. Another is to gather documentation and testimony, to document and process aspects of the present that are relevant to women's work and lives, and to do it professionally, so as to serve future generations of 'history writers'. The documentation in question can involve the work and activities of women's movements, of important female politicians, writers etc. Its inherent value lies in making – and keeping available for the next generations – the knowledge about these women and their lives, which would otherwise be lost and forgotten. Others collect testimonies of victims (and perpetrators), which can be used in courts. This process often involves moments of catharsis and healing. Feminist processes of documentation and testifying offer spaces and frames for linking up the personal with the collective. This has inherent value – especially if it helps to avoid such personal memories being immediately linked to frames that contribute to, or aggravate the conflict or tensions. Also, feminist spaces are not necessarily located at the national level, but allow for local or transnational frames for memory collections – thereby often destabilizing national master narratives that attempt to perpetuate exclusionary nationalist accounts of history.

Ultimately, feminist frameworks address one of the major dilemmas surrounding the 'memories' debate: the tension between the need for one (if possible true) story and respect for the many diverse individual remembrances. Feminist approaches as outlined in this chapter offer conceptual tools for addressing this tension – just as much as these feminist concepts are informed and influenced by activism on the ground.

Much of the memory work described in this chapter relies in its approaches on what feminist writer Chandra Mohanty called a 'feminist solidarity model',[70] within which women share the 'multiple, fluid structures of domination that intersect to locate women differently at particular historical conjunctures.'[71] The idea behind this concept, that each woman is individually situated on a historical chess board of diverse power asymmetries, facilitates an exchange about diverging or even conflicting individual remembrances in public. It allows for solidarity that is not necessarily based on turning 'the Other' into oneself. What many of the feminist activist women and men have achieved is to elaborate and develop a model of 'reflective solidarity',[72] which corresponds to the 'notion that we can engage cross-culturally, while being cognisant of differences and the historical contexts informing them'.[73] At the same time, such concepts have in common their search for middle ways in the 'immobilizing dichotomy between universalism and relativism', by recognizing and respecting difference, while aspiring to common goals of human rights and peace.

Such feminist solidarity that embodies reflective reckoning with power asymmetries and deals critically with historical contexts clearly has the potential of exposing the perennial and disastrous patriarchal and nationalist formations of collective memories. Nonetheless, such work runs the risk of finding its limits in the creation of a new 'women's' or 'feminist' identity. Memory is limited by group identity, and if feminist memories or women groups' memories are to impact upon wider society, they have to enlarge, or at least constantly deconstruct and open up their identity.

Overall, the crossroads of history and politics are just another domain of women's rights struggles. Be they about providing frameworks for recollection, documenting crimes, or fighting against denial, all such engagements entail a power struggle – whether with the male academic, the male politician or the male judge. The intertwining of power and memory is subtle and reflects the position of women and men in each particular area where it is played out. Yet it can also be a precursor for a new style of gender relations.

PART III:

CROSSING BORDERS, CONFRONTING MEMORIES

CHAPTER VIII

BORDERLANDS: THE MIDDLE EAST AND NORTH AFRICA AS THE EU'S SOUTHERN BUFFER ZONE

RAFFAELLA A. DEL SARTO

Introduction[1]

Once upon a time after the peace of Westphalia (1648), states had physical borders that concomitantly marked their territorial frontiers, circumscribed the limits of government authority, and defined the identity of the 'nation' as a bounded political community.[2] Reality always differed from the theoretical construct of the Westphalian model of sovereignty and borders,[3] and the concept of territorially defined 'nations' has also remained problematic in practice.[4] However, the idea of a triple function of borders—demarcating state territory, public authority, and the 'nation'—has continued to influence international law to the present. In our times, the spread of supranational and trans-national patterns of governance, trade and globalization, along with technological innovations, has considerably transformed the nature of state borders. Reflecting these developments, the social sciences operate with the notion of a 'multi-dimensional function of boundaries',[5] whereby the different tasks performed by borders are no longer necessarily congruent.

This departure from the 'classical' triple function of borders is most visible in Europe, where the integration project resulted in supranational areas of sovereignty, the creation of an internal market, a common currency, and a zone of passport-free travel. The gradual elimination of borders among the member states of the European Community (EC), and later on European Union (EU), is often contrasted with the 'hardening' of its borders *vis-à-vis* the outside world. The buzzword of 'Fortress Europe' in particular resounds strongly in the case of the EU's policies on immigration. Although the EU is increasingly restrictive regarding the movement of one category of people, i.e. migrants, this chapter argues that the image of the EU as a clearly defined territorial entity with fortified territorial and functional borders as well as identity boundaries is nevertheless misleading. First, the EU and its member states belong *de facto* to different and overlapping border 'regimes': this variable border geometry decouples some of the distinctive dimensions of borders from each other. Second, instead of fortifying its external borders and identity boundaries towards third countries in a black-and-white fashion, the EU is in fact expanding its variable border geometry to its periphery. As this process also entails a differentiated extension of governance patterns and functional regimes from the EU to its immediate periphery, the latter is progressively transformed into 'EU borderlands', a peripheral and hybrid area of transition.

By focusing on EU policies towards North Africa and the Middle East, this chapter explores the transformation of the 'southern Mediterranean' into EU borderlands.[6] This process involves the 'untangling' of the various social and political functions fulfilled by borders, the EU's 'outsourcing' of border controls to its periphery on specific issues, and the differentiated integration of the southern periphery into the EU's legal frameworks and regimes. Hence, the chapter further advances the argument that EU policies in the Mediterranean, and particularly the recent European Neighbourhood Policy (ENP), are creating a buffer zone around the EU.[7] In the Euro-Mediterranean context, this development blurs out the external borders of the EU and therefore adds to the portrayal of that polity as a neo-medieval empire.[8] Thus, departing from Brussels' euphemistic notion of 'neighbourhood', this contribution also proposes to use the concept of borderland(s) for analyzing the particular patterns in which the EU and its member states link their immediate periphery to the core. Attempts to co-opt the political and economic elites of North Africa and the Middle East into EU governance patterns, while excluding them from European decision-making processes, is a crucial aspect of this process.

The argument is developed as follows: the first section briefly explores the concepts of borders and borderland. Looking at the EU as a whole, as well as at its member states, the second section discusses the distinct and overlapping border regimes that characterize both the Union and 'Europe' broadly defined. The third section explores the extension of the EU's variable border geometry southwards, and how this reshapes the periphery into

EU borderlands. This is demonstrated through examples drawn from two issue-areas: first, the EU's cooperation with the states of North Africa and the Middle East on migration and asylum decouples territorial from functional boundaries, and outsources EU border controls. Second, cooperation in the fields of trade, energy and infrastructure connects the periphery, in differentiated ways, with the European core, as the former absorbs EU rules and legal frameworks.[9] This process also enhances the EU's capacity to permeate and control the periphery. In conclusion, the chapter makes the case for the use of the borderland concept as a theoretical lens to study EU external policies.

Borders and borderlands

The notable surge in border studies across the social sciences over the past two decades attests to the changing nature of borders in our times. In spite of repeated attempts to foster inter-disciplinary research on borders, a variety of analytical frameworks persists, along with notable differences in defining what constitutes a *border*, a *frontier*, a *limit*, a *barrier*, or a *boundary*—to name but a few concepts prevalent in the literature.[10] However, most scholars agree that borders are not merely fixed physical areas demarcating territory. Rather, borders and their meanings are historically contingent; borders are *institutions* which govern the extent of inclusion and exclusion, along with the degree of permeability and the modalities of trans-boundary movement. In other words, borders are complex political, social, and discursive constructs fulfilling a wide range of functions.[11] For instance, borders confine territory and hence regulate (or restrict) the movement of people and different types of goods. These *territorial* borders often also define an area in which specific laws and rules apply. Therefore, they usually coincide with at least some *functional* borders, for instance those defining the validity of a set of laws and of an authority's monopoly of power. However, other types of functional divisions may exceed the territorial borders of a polity. Membership in international trade regimes, patterns of economic integration or security alliances serve as examples here. Finally, borders also define political loyalties, communities, and identities. Emphasizing the symbolic nature of this type of borders, which are not necessarily congruent with territorial or functional borders, the literature tends to define them as *boundaries*.

Borders and boundaries certainly imply a distinction between 'in' and 'out', 'us' and 'them'. However, these binary differentiations may be far less clear-cut in practice, particularly if different types of borders co-exist and only partially overlap within a given space. Borderlands, defined as areas in closest geographic proximity to a border and directly affected by the existence of the latter, may be examples of precisely such hybrid spaces. A borderland may indeed represent 'a form of spatial or social transition from one core area to another',[12] particularly if the border is permeable—or if the area is shaped by multiple and disaggregated borders. In this case, a borderland becomes a zone of 'cross-over'[13], a zone of passage from one geographical area, functional regime, and even territorialized identity construct to another.

The nature of borderlands obviously depends on the type and configuration of the respective border(s). Hard borders performing multiple tasks, which characterize the ideal type of the Westphalian state, may create two separated social, economic, legal, and cultural spaces on each side of the border. Empires, on the other hand, had no fixed and clear borders: the Roman *limes* for instance created peripheral zones that served as a buffer for the imperial centre.[14] In between both extremes, we may conceive of permeable and flexible borders arrangements between modern states that enable the development of trans-boundary regions. These are hybrid spaces of exchange and differentiated integration, in which the difference between both sides is not necessarily enclosed in exclusive lines of separation.[15] As the borders of the European Union are becoming increasingly 'fuzzy' due to the integration process, it has been argued that the EU bears some resemblance to a post-modern empire.[16] Indeed, the EU's external borders are differentiated in scope and in tightness according to specific issue areas, such as trade, migration, or security.[17] Moreover, the distinction between inside and outside is disaggregated according to different functional areas and becomes blurred as a result. Yet the EU's variable border geometry also impacts on its immediate periphery by creating specific types of *borderlands*. In fact, the question of whether the EU is 'trying to harden and fix its border or [...] make them more open and fuzzy'[18] is not very helpful, since, as this chapter shows, both processes are simultaneously taking place for different types of borders. Before analyzing the particular features of the EU's borderlands in North Africa and the Middle East—which directly result from the Union's policies—the next section will therefore take a closer look at the flexible and differentiated border geometry of the EU itself.

The EU's variable border geometry

The European integration process had a conspicuous impact on the notion of borders in Europe.[19] Indeed, the completion of the internal market at the end of 1992 abolished the 'classical' border controls for the movement of goods, services, and capital among EU member states, as well as cemented the right of EU citizens to work and reside in any other member state.

The removal of borders among the member states saw the strengthening of the Union's external borders. These developments, together with the EU's increasingly restrictive migration and asylum policies, frequently conjure up the image of 'Fortress Europe'. This 'Europe' is described as ever more 'fortified' following the terrorist attacks of September 11th, resulting in tighter controls at the EU's external frontiers.[20]

However, the reality of border regimes in the context of European integration is far more complex than the image of an internally borderless and externally 'fortified' area allows for. In fact, a multiplicity of overlapping and cross-cutting border regimes, entailing disaggregated functions of borders, characterizes the EU and its member states. In this vein, we can conceive of different types of *territorial* borders confining the EU and its member states, which regulate the movement of people and goods and define areas of common jurisdiction. These territorial borders may or may not coincide with *functional* borders, which define membership in legal frameworks on specific issue-areas. Hence, different types of territorial borders overlap and cut across a variety of functional borders, both of which coexist with various layers of *identity boundaries* within the EU.

The example of the EU's internal market illustrates the multifaceted and disaggregated nature of territorial and functional borders in the EU and its members. As for the free movement of *goods* established with the completion of the internal market, the respective border controls moved to the EU's external frontiers. *In economic terms*, therefore, these borders became both territorial and functional limits of the Union, while also confining the legal space in which common EU law applies. Mainly regulating the process of economic integration, European Community law originally (and unsurprisingly) focused on trade, but it also gradually expanded to other areas, such as social and monetary policy. However, as member states may opt out of a number of these supranational regimes, a complex configuration of different functional borders is currently in place across the EU. The same observation applies to the movement of *people* within the Union. Indeed, the EU's internal market and its 'four freedoms' apply to all EU member states—at least *de jure*. Schengen, however, which created a zone for passport-free travel with a single external border, does not. The original Schengen Agreement was intergovernmental, and applied between five member states. It was incorporated into EU law with the 1997 Amsterdam Treaty, and currently comprises only 22 member states, as well as two non-EU members.[21] While new EU member states may eventually join the Schengen area, the United Kingdom and Ireland have voluntarily 'opted out'. Conversely, some non-EU members have 'opted in'. In this vein, members of the European Free Trade Area (EFTA) and the European Economic Area (EEA) such as Norway, Iceland, and Liechtenstein are part of the EU's internal market as well as of the Schengen area, and hence enjoy rights to the free movement of people. Yet the states that joined the EU in the last two rounds of enlargement did not automatically obtain the right to free movement of people upon accession.[22] Thus Schengen establishes both territorial and functional borders for the circulation of *people*, which only partly coincide with those defining the free movement of *goods*.

Particularly regarding the movement of people, the different 'lanes' for border controls within the same confined space in European airports clearly convey the complex web of border regimes within and around the EU. The variegated types of border controls (or the absence thereof) depend on diverse parameters, such as point of departure, routing, and destination ('domestic' versus 'international'; 'Schengen area' versus 'non-Schengen area'); they are also dependent on nationality ('EU, EEA, and Swiss passports' versus 'other passports'[23]). To complete the picture, we may also add the necessity (or not) of exchanging currency upon arrival, which in itself is a technical barrier to the free movement of people.[24] Indeed, the boundaries of the so-called Euro-zone, which define participation in the EU's common currency, are not congruent with EU membership, nor the 'Schengen area', for that matter.

Thus the variable border geometry that defines membership of the EU, the Schengen area, the internal market, and the 'Euro-zone', clearly implies a disassociation of different types of territorial and functional boundaries (which may also coincide, however). From this vantage point, the differentiated integration of EU members and EEA/EFTA states into different supranational rules and legal frameworks also entails the establishment of distinct territorial and functional borders. These coexist with *internal* borders among member states, which still define distinct political and legal orders, along with national identities.[25] However, in the absence of border controls for goods and people, these internal borders are no longer territorial in the strict sense.

The *identity boundaries* that bisect the EU are multiple, overlapping, and hybrid as well. Efforts to create an overarching European identity have been part and parcel of the integration process since its inception, and culminated with the introduction of EU citizenship with the 1992 Maastricht Treaty. Yet, while different national—and regional—identities are alive and kicking within the EU, the European identity construct has remained vague and in a permanent state of flux. Indeed, the hitherto six rounds of EC/EU enlargement have also expanded the definition of who belongs to the 'European club'. Current discussions about the EU's future extensions, which coincide with debates on the 'borders of Europe', are also indicative of the highly amorphous European identity dimension.[26] These discussions also involve the interchangeable use of the terms 'Europe' and 'EU', which, however, may entail quite distinct identity boundaries. To give examples, many non-EU members in Eastern Europe and the Balkans, along with EEA countries such as Liechtenstein, may define themselves as 'European', whereas for many British nationals, the term 'Europe' describes 'the continent' on the other side of the English Channel. Citizens of Scandinavian countries—whether EU members or not—are likely to sense a higher affinity with each other than with nationals of the EU's southern European (or 'Mediterranean') members, although they may all agree on the existence of an overarching European identity. Hence, multiple identity boundaries at the supranational, national, regional, and sub-regional level underpin the EU, its member states, and the wider European continent. These boundaries are clearly disaggregated from the web of territorial and functional borders defining the EU and its member states.

The variable geometry of borders in the EU—and in Europe at large—is also increasingly observable in the European Union's relations with its 'near abroad'. Indeed, looking at EU policies towards North Africa and the Middle East, one could clearly note the variable expansion, and therefore blurring, of the Union's borders. As a result, the southern periphery is gradually transformed into 'EU borderlands', as elaborated in the following sections.

Borderlands: The EU and its southern periphery

Migration, 'secure borders' and the outsourcing of border controls

The abolition of internal border controls in the Schengen area prompted a stronger cooperation in visa and immigration policies among the signatories as well as the adoption of common rules regarding third country nationals. With the incorporation of Schengen into EU law in 1997, and particularly following the Tampere European Council of October 1999,[27] however, some competences in the realm of EU external border controls were also conferred to the European Commission.[28] Thus, as Brussels expressed its new objective of 'strengthening the European Union as an area of freedom, security, and justice',[29] the adoption of common legal frameworks and procedures on a wide range of domestic and external issues intensified. These include the free movement of persons within the EU, judicial cooperation, police and customs cooperation, as well as visa, immigration, and asylum policies, along with the fight against terrorism, organized crime, and trafficking. More recently, the EU created a border agency, FRONTEX, and the Commission has recurrently been calling for the creation of a unified EU border patrol.[30]

While a growing cross-pillar linkage between the EU's Justice and Home Affairs and its External Relations is observable, migration and 'secure borders' have undoubtedly moved to the top of Brussels' agenda in its relations with third countries in recent years.[31] In this vein, the European Commission recommended in 2003:

> In order to be effective, the objectives of a Community policy on illegal migration need to be taken into account in the global framework of the EC's relations with third countries. The Seville European Council left no doubt that combating illegal immigration requires a greater effort by the European Union and a targeted approach to the problem, with the use of all appropriate instruments in the context of the EU's external relations [...].[32]

With regard to North Africa and the Middle East, reinforced cooperation on the issues of migration, drug trafficking, organized crime and terrorism reflects the 'externalization' of EU *internal* policies over the past decade. This process implies the gradual expansion of the Union's legal boundaries to third countries, which only have limited access to the EU's institutions, however, and are excluded from its decision-making process.[33] While seeking to co-opt the governments of the so-called southern Mediterranean states into the EU's external border management, Brussels is gradually '*transporting the actual border beyond the borderline*'.[34]

The objective of cooperating with the 'Mediterranean partners' on the management of the EU's external border—on migration, drug trafficking, organized crime and terrorism in particular—was already included in the 1995 Barcelona Declaration, which established the Euro-Mediterranean Partnership (EMP), or Barcelona Process. Over the past decade, Euro-Mediterranean cooperation in these fields has witnessed a growing degree of institutionalization. Thus the EU's Common Strategy on the Mediterranean, which was adopted at the 2000 Santa Maria de Feira European Council, envisaged the setting up of a legal, institutional, and judicial framework for combating and prosecuting cross-border crime.[35] During the 2002 EMP Valencia meeting, foreign ministers agreed to adopt a *regional* co-operation programme on border-related issues.[36] At the same juncture, the European Commission started to negotiate readmission agreements[37] pertaining to illegal migrants with Morocco (in September 2000), as well as with Turkey, Albania, and Algeria (in October 2002). It also declared its aim to conclude such agreements with Egypt and Tunisia.[38] In 2002, the European Council identified nine countries with which the EU should deepen its cooperation on migration and borders, including, *inter alia*, Morocco, Tunisia, Libya, and Turkey. In mid-November 2007, the EU and its 'Mediterranean partners' held their first meeting at the *ministerial level*, specifically to discuss migration in the framework of the Barcelona Process.

Migration also played a prominent role in the initial discussions on the emerging European Neighbourhood Policy (ENP)—back then termed 'Wider Europe'. Indeed, cooperation on borders as well as in justice and home affairs – two fields becoming ever more intertwined within the EU – is a cornerstone of the ENP, which rewards compliance with 'a stake in the EU's internal market'.[39] As a result, all ENP Action Plans concluded to date with the states in North Africa and the Middle East contain provisions on migration, trans-national crime, and border management, along with sections on cooperation in Justice and Home Affairs. The thread in all these initiatives consists of EU financial and technical assistance for the strengthening of the administrative and institutional capacity of border management by third countries. This includes the training of (border) police and judicial officials, the supply of sophisticated technical equipment, and the sharing of information on criminals—and illegal migrants. From the outset, the Commission adopted the principle of conditionality, by asserting for instance that 'co-operative countries' will be rewarded with a 'more generous visa policy [...] or increased quotas for migrant workers, closer economic co-operation, trade expansion, additional development assistance, better market access or WTO compatible tariff preferences'.[40] While adopting an explicitly bilateral and differentiated approach based on 'positive conditionality', the ENP in fact institutionalizes the principle of extending greater benefits to 'reform-willing' states, including the realm of the EU's external border management. As the ENP Action Plans concluded with the southern countries vary greatly in terms of benefits and concessions, and considering the great importance of migration and border controls for the EU and its member states, 'cooperative' governments undoubtedly obtained a better deal from Brussels. The differentiated allocation of EU funds to the 'neighbours' under the ENP, according to their degree of 'cooperation', further supports this observation, particularly as some governments in the south are discovering the value of migration as a bargaining chip in their relations with Brussels.

The ENP also offers the prospect of opening the EU's (hitherto internal) cross-border cooperation programmes to the 'neighbours', with the aim of fostering patterns of integration in the border region. While this entails a blurring of some functional borders between the EU and its southern periphery, borders pertaining to the specific issue of migration are growing stronger, and are partly also changing their configuration and physical location. Indeed, the EU's priorities in the field of migration are the conclusion of bilateral readmission agreements, which typically also apply to third-country nationals, along with EU support for reinforcing the external borders of the respective third country vis-à-vis its hinterland. In this vein, Brussels has been urging North African countries in particular to tighten controls at their southern borders in order to limit migration flows from Sub-Saharan Africa transiting through the Maghreb towards Europe.[41] The European Commission also recently proposed to utilize the financial instruments of the ENP to cover cooperation between North African countries and their Sub-Saharan 'neighbours' on 'issues of common concern, including migration'.[42] At the same time, the media reports on the creation of EU-financed detention centres for irregular migrants in Morocco, Tunisia, and Turkey have obviously raised serious human rights anxieties.[43] In the wake of an EU 'technical mission on illegal migration' to Libya in November 2004—a country with which the Union does not so far maintain any institutional ties—Brussels is also currently seeking to sign a cooperation agreement on border controls, organized crime and illegal migration with Tripoli.[44] In the meantime, EU-funded detention centres for illegal migrants have also been established in Libya, according to media reports.[45]

Cooperation at the EU level, however, co-exists with a web of *bilateral* agreements on border issues between single EU member states and specific countries of North Africa and the Middle East. Regarding migration, numerous bilateral readmission agreements or memoranda are in place, while others are currently being negotiated.[46] For instance, Italy and Libya have been formally—and rather secretly—cooperating on borders and migration since 2000.[47] The bilateral scheme entails the supply of equipment for 'effective' border management by Italy, as well as Rome's financing of at least one detention camp in Libya, which houses the illegal immigrants which the Italian government deports from its territory. Malta, which has become an important migration entry point to the EU since it joined the latter in 2004, has also been interested in cooperation with Tripoli on migration.

What emerges from the discussion so far are three significant patterns concerning territorial—and functional—borders in the Euro-Mediterranean area. First, EU policies do not follow the rationale of hermetically closing a physical border between the Union and its southern periphery. Rather, the states in North Africa and the Middle East are turned into a buffer zone, as Brussels co-opts their governments into the control of migration and organized crime by offering an array of incentives. Along with this, key aspects of the EU's external border management are physically transferred to the territory of the southern 'neighbours' and partially 'outsourced' in terms of personnel. In return, the states in the southern Mediterranean are bound to strengthen *their* external border with their respective hinterland countries, with financial and technical support from Brussels. The process of *closing* an EU external border, however, concerns only one specific category of people, namely illegal migrants, including third-country nationals in transit on their way to Europe. Indeed, EU member states are far less restrictive regarding skilled (or seasonal) labour migration from North Africa and the Middle East for Europe's labour market.[48] Thus, regarding the movement of unwanted migrants, the EU does not only externalize its policies to the south; by binding the southern governments to EU governance patterns through specific legal provisions, agreements, and incentives, the EU also exports the principle of exclusion to its borderlands.[49]

Second, the buffer zone around the EU should not be conceptualized as a homogenous, let alone congruent, area. In relation to the EU, there are differences among the states of North Africa and the Middle East regarding the permeability of borders. For instance, visas for both the Schengen area and the United Kingdom and Ireland are required by the citizens of most countries in North Africa and the Middle East, but Israeli citizens can enter both for a period of 90 days visa-free. At the same time, border regimes *among* the states of the so-called southern Mediterranean are underpinned by very different rules as well as degrees of permeability. For instance, one can draw an interesting distinction between the restrictive visa policies of Morocco and Algeria, or between the exceptionally hermetic border between Israel and Syria – two states that are officially still in a state of war – and the *comparatively* permeable border between Israel and Egypt.

Third, and related to the previous point, the strengthening of cross-border cooperation under the ENP further blurs the borders between the EU and its periphery. Indeed, Brussels prioritises the inclusion of its 'neighbours' into cross-border cooperation platforms such as Intereg, which already operate among EU members, to foster economic and social development in the 'border areas'. These programmes also aim at enhancing the cooperation by local authorities on both sides of the common border regarding the management of the latter, as well as on environmental and cultural issues.[50] The overall objective of creating comparatively integrated spaces across the border, that is, areas of transition, is certainly relevant for conceptualizing North Africa and the Middle East as EU borderlands.

Connecting the periphery to the European core

The outsourcing of the EU's external border management goes hand in hand with Brussels' efforts to connect the southern periphery to the 'core' in a number of key areas, such as trade, energy, and infrastructure. The result is an expansion of EU functional regimes to the EU's borderlands, linking the states of North Africa and the Middle East to the 'European core' in a differentiated manner. It is not by accident that these efforts involve issue-areas that are of vital (economic) importance to the EU. They are also geared at enhancing the ability of the European Union to 'expand' itself to, and control its periphery.

In the realm of *trade,* the EC/EU has been pursuing its main objective of establishing a regime of free exchange in industrial goods with the countries of the 'southern Mediterranean' from the outset of the European integration process.[51] Since the launching of the Euro-Mediterranean Partnership in 1995, Brussels has signed, or updated previously signed, free trade agreements with all the countries covered by the EMP.[52] Although the EU envisages the creation of a Euro-Mediterranean free trade area in industrial goods by 2010, for the time being its trade relations with the states of the southern periphery remain highly heterogeneous. Indeed, the level of trade liberalization varies according to the history of bilateral relations, the degree of economic development of the partner state, and the willingness of the respective government to embark on the path of trade liberalization. Thus Turkey is linked to the EU through a customs union, which was first envisaged in 1963 with the signing of the Ankara agreement, and which entered its implementation stage in 1995. Among the remaining southern Mediterranean 'partners', the EU's trade relations with Israel are certainly the most advanced—in fact, the first bilateral free trade agreement in industrial goods of 1975 was fully implemented by 1989; bilateral trade relations were updated with a new agreement in 1995. Implementation of the EU's free trade agreement with Morocco and Tunisia is relatively advanced, whereas Algeria and particularly Syria lag behind.

The offer of 'a stake' in the EU's internal market in exchange for reforms, as the ENP has it, will result in a further diversification of the EU's trade regimes in the south. While the Euro-Mediterranean free trade area remains a long-term objective, the ENP's principle of differentiation certainly permits taking economic relations with single 'neighbours' further. In addition to putting participation in various EU-internal programmes on offer, Brussels is currently discussing liberalizing trade in services and the right of establishment with the most 'advanced' southern EMP states. Again reflecting the principle of differentiation, the EU is currently negotiating the liberalization of its, traditionally protectionist, trade in agriculture and fisheries with Morocco, Egypt, and Israel—but not with the other southern signatories of free trade agreements. In addition, the EU has been creating a web of differentiated border regimes on the circulation of industrial goods across its Mediterranean periphery. At the same time, the softening of these borders across the Euro-Mediterranean inevitably creates new ones, for example between the 'southern partners' and those countries that do not have a free trade agreement with Brussels. Finally, it is worth emphasizing that the exclusion of agricultural products from the free trade regime—a sector that is economically far more important for most states of North Africa and the Middle East than trade in industrial products—undoubtedly reflects the unequal power relations between Brussels and its southern 'borderlands'.

The rationale of connecting the periphery to the core in a highly differentiated manner – according to the priorities and interests of the EU and its member states – is also visible in the field of *energy*, which was a strategic policy objective of the ENP since its inception. Energy cooperation with the states of North Africa and the Middle East obviously reflects the EU and its members' concern to increase, diversify, and secure the energy supply from the periphery. In 2007, the Council stressed once more the 'need to further strengthen cooperation'[53] on energy with the southern Mediterranean, aiming at the integration of energy markets, energy security, infrastructure projects, and sustainable development as far as renewable energy is concerned. Even more tellingly, the Commission declared that the 'completion of [an] electricity and gas ring in the Euro-Mediterranean region remains a priority.'[54] Accordingly, the Commission launched the 'Euro-Mediterranean Energy Partnership' in December 2007.

However, the EU's policy on energy is also based on differentiation through the establishment of different 'energy regimes' across the Euro-Mediterranean area. In 2007, Brussels signed an energy cooperation agreement with Algeria, a country that provides around 30 per cent of its gas imports. This agreement followed lengthy negotiations, as the EU insisted that Algeria's gas company Sonatrach dropped restrictions in natural gas supply contracts that prevented customers (i.e. European gas companies) reselling the gas within Europe.[55] In the same year, joint declarations on energy cooperation were also signed with Morocco and Jordan, both of which are, or are likely to become, transit conduits of gas to the EU.[56] Brussels is also currently conducting negotiations with Cairo on the planned Arab Gas Pipeline, which will bring additional energy resources from Egypt and potentially Iraq to Europe.[57] The EU is also committed to working for '[the] integration of Libya into Euro-Mediterranean energy cooperation'.[58] Brussels puts a premium on Turkey, which is of enormous strategic importance as a transit country of energy supplies from the Caucasus, the Caspian Sea, Russia, and Iran. The effort to persuade Turkey to join the Energy Community Treaty of 2005, which aims at creating an integrated energy market with potential EU accession states, however, has become entangled with Ankara's EU accession negotiations.[59]

Thus EU policies towards its southern periphery aim at expanding the Union's rules of market liberalization, trade, and competition to its borderlands in the energy sector, which goes hand in hand with the internal efforts to create an integrated energy market. While the Union's envisaged 'electricity and gas ring' across the Euro-Mediterranean conveys a conspicuous centre-periphery approach, Brussels follows the principle of differentiating its energy relations with the 'Mediterranean states' according to the interests and needs of the EU, its member states—and European energy companies. Thus, EU energy policy *vis-à-vis* the states of North Africa and the Middle East clearly aim at penetrating and controlling the periphery in a differentiated manner regarding a commodity that is of crucial importance to the 'core'.

The establishment of flexible regimes while connecting the periphery to the European centre is also visible in the fields of *transport and infrastructure*. By 2000, the Commission had called for enhanced cooperation in the transport (and energy) domain in order to 'reinvigorate the Barcelona Process'.[60] The objectives are to develop a 'trans-Mediterranean multimodal transport network' and to adopt common institutional, legislative, and regulatory frameworks. These also concern the 'interface' between transport services and the customs, police, and immigration authorities, as well as the banking and insurance sectors. The Commission's goals also involve beefing up aviation and shipping safety, as well as bringing the southern partners (to various degrees) into the European global navigation satellite system Galileo.[61] A Euro-Mediterranean Transport Forum has been set up to oversee cooperation in the fields in question. However, in a rather imposing manner, the Council of the European Union defined the aim of the forum as the 'extension of the trans-European transport network to [the] Mediterranean Region'.[62]

While the ENP reaffirmed the importance of the transport and infrastructure sector,[63] its principle of differentiating among 'neighbours' further entrenched some already well-established EU practices. As in the fields of trade and energy, the Union's transport policies aim at exporting a set of laws, regulations, and governance from the EU to the entirety of its southern 'borderlands' in the long term. At present, however, cooperation is more advanced with some countries than with others. To give an example, the Commission stated its aim of 'creating a Common Aviation Area bringing together the EC and all its partners located along its southern and eastern borders' by 2010'[64]. Thus far, however, only Morocco and Israel have benefited from this objective. The former signed a bilateral agreement providing for open markets as well as for extensive alignment of aviation legislation (according to Community rules and regulations) in December 2006.[65] Negotiations between Brussels and Israel started in 2007[66] and resulted in an 'open sky' agreement in February 2008. This will bring all existing bilateral air service agreements between the member states and Israel in line with EU law, while allowing EU and Israeli airlines to operate flights in the aerospace of the other party.[67]

As the establishment of these functional border regimes on transport and infrastructure are obviously not meant to facilitate the circulation of migrants, the rationale behind the EU's efforts to connect the periphery to the centre is mainly economic. Certainly, modern transport systems and infrastructure are relevant for the economic development of the 'Mediterranean states'; however, they also facilitate the circulation of goods—and tourists—while they are crucial for investment and business. At the same time, the process of connecting the periphery to the EU core is reminiscent of the expansion of territorial control of the modern state, which resulted from the establishment of railroads and transportation from the mid-nineteenth century onwards.[68] From this perspective, the expansion of the EU's infrastructure to the south reorganizes territorial and political space and further blurs the borders between 'inside' and 'outside', while increasing EU power over its borderlands.

Finally, the EU is currently contemplating the gradual integration of its southern periphery into its cooperation schemes, as well as funding programmes, in the field of *research and development*. The 2007 Cairo Declaration, adopted at the Euro-Mediterranean Ministerial Conference on Higher Education, envisages the build up of a 'Euro-Mediterranean Research Area', which would involve the approximation of higher education standards and the participation of the countries of North Africa and the Middle East in EU research and mobility programmes such as Erasmus Mundus and Tempus.[69] However, Israel has been participating as an equal partner in the EU's framework programmes for research and development since 1998, which, given Israel's highly advanced status in technology and research, also obviously benefits the EU. In other words, differentiated regimes in the area of research and development are slowly emerging between the EU and its southern periphery, reflecting mostly the priorities of Brussels institutions and the Union's member states.

To sum up, the EU's differentiated exportation of its rules and modalities in the fields of trade, energy, infrastructure, transportation, and research connects its borderlands to the core, while establishing different functional borders across the EU and its periphery. The functions of this web of borders are highly disaggregated. As a result, various border configurations co-exist and overlap in the EU's southern borderlands, blurring further the distinctions between 'inside' and 'outside' at different levels. At the same time, the EU's attempts to connect its southern periphery to the core in crucial fields permit for a greater capacity to permeate and control its borderlands, and to take advantage of it economically.

Conclusion

The analysis of the EU border regimes *vis-à-vis* its southern periphery considerably qualifies the image of 'Fortress Europe', where the latter is defined by the existence of hard and neat external borders. While EU member states continue to belong to different concentric border regimes, the Union's policies towards North Africa and the Middle East not only aim at expanding its own governance framework to its neighbourhood but also entail the export of the variable border geometry towards the periphery. In effect, this involves a disassociation of the classical functions of borders across the Euro-Mediterranean area. Indeed, as a result of its policies—whether in the framework of the Barcelona Process or the ENP—the EU increasingly emerges as an entity with fuzzy borders, where 'the neighbours' in its southern (and eastern) periphery act as a buffer area, or EU borderlands.

With regard to one specific category of people, i.e. illegal migrants, the EU is undoubtedly reinforcing its 'borders'. However, this objective is only partially achieved by reinforcing borders controls between EU territory and the immediate periphery. More importantly, the policies of the EU and its member states on illegal migration and cross-border crime turn the 'southern Mediterranean' into EU borderlands through a multiplicity of agreements, which also include the partial outsourcing of border controls. Concurrently, EU policies towards North Africa and the Middle East aim at connecting the periphery to the European core through the differentiated integration of the former into various sets of EU rules, laws, and practices, as the examples of cooperation in the field of trade, energy, and transport show. This process also enables the EU to permeate its periphery in a differentiated matter, exert control over the latter, and advance the economic and political interests of the Union and its members. As a consequence, the EU can be conceptualized as an entity with very different *functional* boundaries, which include or exclude the southern peripheries to varying degrees. The fallout of this process is the establishment and reinforcement of functional and territorial borders *between the EU's buffer zone and its respective hinterland,* such as sub-Saharan Africa as far as the Maghreb is concerned, or Asia and the Arab Peninsula for the countries of the Eastern Mediterranean.

Thus while, in theory, borders still divide between 'ins' and 'outs', the practice of EU policies towards North Africa and the Middle East corroborates the existence of a third category, which corresponds to the notion of borderland. Reflecting a hybrid area of transition, the EU's southern borderlands are characterized by a net of different boundaries according to different functional and territorial lines within which the Union's rules and regulations apply. To put it differently, the EU's differentiated expansion of its governance patterns to the borderlands blurs the distinction between insiders and outsiders. This process also involves the expansion of EU control over the periphery, along with the co-optation of the 'southern' elites into EU governance patterns, without conceding them any access to the decision-making process of the European Union.

While these features can sustain the conceptualization of the EU as a neo-medieval empire,[70] the concept of borderland, or indeed frontier in the premodern sense of the word, also has a number of advantages in the study of EU external relations. First, it permits the evaluation of EU policies towards its immediate periphery as a direct outcome of the Union's particular political nature,[71] characterized by concentric and overlapping circles of national and supranational governance patterns, enlargement (which is tantamount to territorial expansion by agreement), and, indeed, fuzzy borders. Second, the notion of borderland lends itself to considering different layers of 'cooperation' 'integration', and indeed co-option, which are characteristic of the transit area between the EU and the periphery's hinterland. In this context, attention can also be paid to the gradual expansion of different regimes and functional boundaries. Finally, and perhaps most importantly, the concept of borderland allows for an analysis of EU interests and unequal power relations in the external policies of the European Union—notions which the fashionable literature on 'Europeanization' and 'normative power' in EU studies tends to conceal.

CHAPTER IX

BORDERS BESIEGED: A VIEW ON MIGRATION FROM THE EUROPEAN-AFRICAN EDGE

HENK DRIESSEN

Introduction

During the last week of September and first week of October 2005, thousands of 'undocumented migrants' from West Africa stormed the barbed wire border fences that surround the two Spanish enclaves of Ceuta and Melilla on the Mediterranean coast of Morocco. They had previously been camped in the hillside pine forests on the Moroccan side of the European-African frontier. Although there had been many individual and small-scale attempts to break through the enclaves' fences since at least 1998, the incursions of autumn 2005 were unprecedented in scale and coordination. As a consequence, they became world news.[1]

Storming Ceuta and Melilla's three to six metre fences in groups of hundreds, with ladders made of branches and using stones and rocks against security forces, was a new strategy for African migrants to forcibly enter the European Union (EU) 'through its backdoor'. The dramatic events of autumn 2005 were later repeated, albeit on a much smaller scale. For instance, on Christmas Eve 2006, dozens of 'Subsaharans' (as African migrants are often called in the local press) who had been camping in the hills on the Moroccan side made an attempt to climb the Melilla fences. They knew that during the festivities, Spanish border surveillance would be low. Nonetheless, their attempt was thwarted by Moroccan border guards.[2]

The vast majority of undocumented migrants are young males from Sahelian[3] and West African countries: a case in point is that of Boubacar, a man of 24 years, born in Guinea-Bissau. He left his native village in March 2004 with 600 Euros of savings and travelled through Senegal, Malí, Burkina Faso, Niger and Algeria. By the time he arrived at the Algerian-Moroccan border, most of his savings had been spent on transport and bribes. He decided to walk, as many African migrants do, from the Algerian border to the pine forests just outside Melilla. He was arrested six times by the Moroccan police and border guards, beaten up and sent back to the Algerian border, where the rest of his savings were 'confiscated'. He finally managed to hide in Melilla's hinterland for several weeks until the massive border assault of 28 September 2005. That day, he climbed over two fences within a few minutes, sustaining wounds to his throat, fingers and leg, and was treated by the Spanish Red Cross. Boubacar hoped to be able to get to mainland Spain and travel to Barcelona where some of his relatives were living and working.[4]

At least eleven people died and dozens were injured on September 28, including some border guards, as Spanish and Moroccan security forces tried to block the passage of the African migrants into the enclaves. Hundreds of migrants who managed to enter Melilla and Ceuta were housed in temporary residence centres and makeshift camps. Hundreds more were detained in Morocco and dozens of those who made it to the enclaves were expelled on the basis of a revived 1992 bilateral agreement between Spain and Morocco. Both countries sent more troops to the enclaves to reinforce border control. Spain began to raise the height of the fences and announced the construction of a third fence as an extra barrier between its enclaves and Morocco.

The vice-president of the European Commission estimated at the time that 30,000 Africans were waiting their turn in Algeria and Morocco to enter the enclaves or cross the Mediterranean in small boats. In the weeks following the border incidents, the EU began urging Morocco to sign a repatriation agreement that would put Rabat under obligation to take back transit migrants from third countries. In the meantime, alarming reports were being published by *Médecins sans Frontières* as well as by other NGOs and United Nations officials about human rights violations against the undocumented migrants who rushed the fences. More than 500 people were transported to the deserts near the Moroccan-Algerian border and the Western Sahara, where the police and army abandoned them without food and water. Moroccan troops continued to clear the wooded hills near Melilla and Ceuta of sub-Saharan migrants, many of whom fled to the slums of Tangier where they went into hiding.[5]

These violent incidents at the border of the Spanish enclaves illustrate the contradictions inherent in EU policies regarding the crucial issue of immigration: there are tensions between political and economic interests, and a lack of uniform and consistent EU-wide border policy and practice. This chapter's aim is to place the recent events in Melilla and Ceuta in historical perspective, and to show how the nature of Melilla's border in particular has changed over the past centuries. This is therefore a case study in the historical ethnography of borders and cross-border movements with wider comparative implications.[6]

Betwixt and between Europe and Africa

The Spanish enclaves of Ceuta (76,000 inhabitants) and Melilla (67,000 inhabitants) are, together with a few islets off Morocco's Mediterranean coast, the last surviving relics of the once vast Spanish empire. They are the only two remaining European territories in mainland Africa. Together they cover about 35 square kilometres. Approximately one third of Ceuta and Melilla's population is of Muslim (Berber and Arab) origin and there are small yet influential communities of Jews and Hindus. These complex societies are unusual in a way that other anomalies in the modern political order, such as nearby Gibraltar, are not. The Spanish-Christian dominance over Ceuta and Melilla is contested both from within and from without. Since 1961, the enclaves and islets have been claimed by Morocco, while successive Spanish governments have defended the 'Spanishness' of these miniature territories for historical, geopolitical and symbolic reasons. They have argued that the enclaves belonged to Spain and formed an integral part of Spanish identity long before the emergence of the Moroccan state. In fact, Melilla was occupied in 1497 as the first in a string of strongholds along the North African coast. Isabel and Ferdinand, the *Reyes Católicos*, exported the Reconquest of Muslim al-Andalus across the Mediterranean. Ceuta fell into Portuguese hands in 1415 and became Spanish in 1668.

The enclaves are also free ports and complicate Morocco's historically sensitive relations with Spain and, more recently, with the EU. In 1995, the enclaves achieved autonomous status within the Spanish state and were granted a special tax and visa regime within the EU.[7] They are the only land borders of the EU with the developing world.

Ceuta and Melilla are multi-ethnic and plurireligious towns with characteristically frontier societies. They are in many respects schizoid: European and African, Spanish and Moroccan, Christian and Muslim (Jewish and Hindu), cosmopolitan and parochial, liberal and intolerant, affluent and poor. It is tempting to consider the enclaves together.[8] Yet, there are differences between the two which are determined to a large extent by their geographical position, in particular by their distance from the Iberian peninsula. One may well wonder whether this important geopolitical factor has a differential impact on the nature of intercommunal relations in the two enclaves.

In 1991, Spain acceded to the Schengen Agreement, leading to intensified Spanish border control. One of the consequences has been the mass arrival to Ceuta and Melilla of the so-called undocumented migrants from North and sub-Saharan Africa, who cannot cross over to the European side of the Mediterranean. Only very few still manage to hide in or underneath trucks ferried to Spain. Until the late 1990s, the vast majority was living under appalling conditions. Over the past ten years, there have been several racial clashes in Melilla and Ceuta between Spanish Christians and Moroccan Muslims, and between Spanish Christians and clandestine immigrants. From time to time, the immigrants would be relocated to refugee detention centres in mainland Spain in order to reduce local tensions. In 1996, migrants were still entering the enclaves at night by walking in from Morocco through the hills. Since then, the borders of the enclaves have been increasingly reinforced by high double fences, armed border guards, and sophisticated electronic detection systems. At the same time, new temporary residence centres with more decent living conditions were built for these immigrants. Soon, however, they too became overcrowded.

The demand for consumption and the lack of regular employment in both enclaves stimulate an uncontrolled proliferation of petty itinerant trades and services for the immigrants: peddling of cigarettes, newspapers, cannabis, fruits, chewing gum, second-hand clothes, and trinkets of all sorts; and occupations such as parking guards, guides, car washers, carriers, cleaners, beggars and prostitutes. There is a pecking order in this parallel economy, based on ethnicity, gender, age, 'cunning' and sometimes physical strength. Sub-Saharan Africans are mostly at the bottom of this fluid and informal underclass hierarchy. But they are strikingly entrepreneurial (in fact, some of the street vendors claimed to come from families, villages, and ethnicities involved in long-distance trading for generations) and inventive compared to the Moroccans, who dominate the local hashish traffic, and the Algerians, who are strong in car guarding. Black Africans have set up several improvized car-washing places along the coast roads, they sell newspapers in the streets and help to load cars at supermarkets. The Spanish-Christian inhabitants of the enclaves make frequent use of such cheap services. This was the local situation in the mid-1990s. There are striking parallels with the predicaments of clandestine immigrants from West Africa who began to arrive in New York City in the early 1990s. The migratory flows of West Africans to the Spanish enclaves and to New York City, and their involvement in informal economies as well as in newly emergent communities, are part of the same forces of global restructuring, albeit with differences in scale.[9]

All those living in Ceuta and Melilla are 'border people' *par excellence*, but the immigrants without official papers are much more so than the established citizens, regardless of the latter's ethnicity. From time to time, when the numbers of immigrants increase, small incidents and rumours heighten the tension, not only between immigrants and established citizens, but also among the immigrants themselves. As gateways for clandestine cross-Mediterranean migration, the enclaves have become a major problem for local and national Spanish authorities, as well as for the EU. The Spanish authorities increasingly depend upon the willingness of their Moroccan counterparts to enforce a stricter regime on the other side of the border. Over the last few years, Morocco has indeed been keeping closer watch on its coastline, in response to mounting political pressure from its northern neighbour and the EU, as well as the prospect of financial support. It has managed to reduce the out-pouring of migrants, cramped in small boats on their nocturnal passage across the Strait of Gibraltar to Spain.

In July 2002, Moroccan soldiers invaded the small uninhabited island of Perejil (Parsley Island in English, Leila in Arabic and Tura in Berber), 250 metres off the Moroccan coast and three kilometres from Ceuta, to set up a base on the islet. Spain reacted furiously: since 1668, it has regarded Perejil as part of its national territory. A military confrontation between the neighbouring countries seemed imminent. Spanish commandos dislodged the Moroccan navy cadets and Morocco retreated. The status quo ante was restored. This incident made it clear that Ceuta and Melilla are vulnerable defence outposts. This, together with the recent storming of the two enclaves' borders reveals the ironies, tensions and complexities in the relationships between Spain and Morocco, EU and non-EU countries.

Spain and the enclave governments complain that clandestine immigration to the enclaves has dramatically increased since 1998. They suspect that Morocco has not done its best to guard its borders with the enclaves, because it disputes Spain's sovereignty over them since its independence in 1956. Indeed, over the past fifteen years, Morocco has frequently used clandestine migration and border control for leverage in its negotiations with Spain and the EU. It is also becoming increasingly obvious that Morocco, as a country of transit migration from West Africa to Europe, is being confronted with rising numbers of migrants who either find themselves

stuck in Morocco, or who regard Africa's northernmost country as a sec-
ond-best destination. The West African migrants add to the thousands of
young Moroccans who want to flee the country illegally each year, or who
provide fertile terrain for recruitment by Islamic radicals. The *bidonvilles* of
Morocco's major towns are indeed boiling with the pent-up desperation of
the jobless.[10]

Shifting definitions of and practices at the Spanish-Moroccan frontier

The Spanish state was built upon the experience of *Reconquista* that lasted almost seven centuries. At the end of the fifteenth century the reconquest was carried across the Mediterranean to include a string of coastal
strongholds which became a defensive frontier of Christianity in Africa.
The expulsion of the Jews and Muslims from the Iberian Peninsula to the
sultanates of North Africa entailed, to some extent, a cultural closing of
the Spanish-African frontier and a fixation of the boundary between Christianity and Islam in the western Mediterranean. From the Spanish seizure
of Ceuta and Melilla to their development into ports of free trade and bases
for colonial penetration in the early 1860s, the enclaves largely functioned
as so-called *presidios*, military garrisons cum penal settlements. Along this
fluid line of strongholds on the so-called Barbary coast, two empires, the
Habsburg and Ottoman, and two enemy religions, Christianity and Islam,
confronted, grew accustomed to, and accommodated one another.

As the centre of European gravity gradually moved north and westwards,
the southern Mediterranean became more and more peripheral to the main
thrust of Western European interests, which focused increasingly on the
Atlantic. This shift in the world system was in a sense sealed by the Span-
ish-Ottoman truce of 1580. Piracy became, in the apt words of Fernand
Braudel, 'a substitute for declared war' between Islam and Christendom.[11]
The swing in international politics had a profound impact on Melilla, more
so than on Ceuta, given the latter's close proximity to the Peninsula. Melilla
found itself increasingly isolated from Spain, and was gradually forced to
rely on its own meagre resources. The eastern Rif, in which the enclave
was the major port and stronghold, was itself a frontier zone between the
sultanate of Morocco, of which it was only a nominal part, and the Ottoman empire to the east. Relations between Melilla and its Berber hinterland
consisted of raids and counter-raids for goods and slaves, which sometimes
aimed at the desecration of each other's religious shrines.

Although the Ibero-African frontier was mainly defined in religious
terms, it was anything but a closed religious barrier between Catholicism

and Islam. There are many cases of deserters or captives from Melilla who converted to Islam, and of Berbers, albeit to a lesser degree, who took refuge in the enclaves and apostatized to Catholicism. When studying cases of such religious barrier crossings, which by implication entailed naturalization, it becomes clear that religion was paramount in defining the core of personhood and society on both sides of the border, as well as the divide between civilization and barbarism. The first cases of naturalization without conversion I could find in the local archives dated back to the 1860s, when Muslims and Jews from Melilla's hinterland obtained Spanish passports to travel to Algeria (the Muslims planned to work in the wheat harvest in western Algeria) and to Melilla (the Jews wanted to trade in the enclave).[12]

Looking at the Spanish-African frontier from below, it is also a fact that there was not only a gap between frontier ideology and frontier practice, but also between the views and attitudes of the representatives of central authority and the people living at the border. For instance, trade between Melilla and its Berber hinterland was strictly forbidden by the central authorities of Morocco and Spain, yet it was going on almost continuously, in spite of endemic hostilities between the garrison and Berber tribesmen. Whereas in metropolitan Spain all Muslims were indiscriminately called *moros*, the inhabitants of Melilla distinguished several categories of Muslims, such as *moro fronterizo* (tribesman living in the frontier zone), as opposed to *moro del rey* (Muslim under the control of the Sultan), or between *moro de paz* (Muslim of peace) and *moro de guerra* (Muslim of war). To be sure, in daily life at this frontier, the boundaries between these categories were rather fluid.

Although the borders between the enclaves and Morocco were often violent (examples include piracy as maritime jihad by Barbary corsairs, mutual raids, the 'War of Africa' in 1860, the 'War of Melilla' in 1893, another 'War of Africa' in 1909 and the Spanish wars of pacification in northern Morocco from 1914 till 1927), there were also peaceful cross-border interactions. With the transformation of Ceuta and Melilla into free ports in 1863, and the enlargement of the enclaves' territories (their borders were fixed by the distance of a canon ball shot from the Spanish outer fortifications) following the 'War of Africa' three years earlier, their civilian populations increased, and the enclaves became more open and dynamic in terms of the movement of people, goods and ideas. They also served as bases for the Spanish colonial penetration of Morocco, though at a high cost in human life and material resources, due to fierce resistance by Berber tribesmen.

During the Spanish Protectorate (1912-1956), which was clothed in the ideological mantle of benign paternalism and the civilizing mission, the borders of the enclaves became almost fully permeable. Yet at the same time, the enclaves preserved a distinct status within the Spanish Protectorate over Morocco. When Morocco gained its independence in 1956, Ceuta and Melilla remained under Spanish sovereignty, but the vast majority of Berbers and Arabs who continued living in the enclaves were not granted Spanish nationality. The presence of large minorities of ambiguous, stateless inhabitants in the enclaves became an important source of friction, occasionally violent, between Spanish Christians and Moroccan Muslims in the 1980s, as enclave Muslims felt discriminated against, in spite of the fact that many of them had been born and raised in the enclaves. In the 1990s, there were some rather fierce conflicts between the established inhabitants on the one hand (many of whom were themselves descendants of immigrants, mainly from Andalusia), and the new immigrants from sub-Saharan Africa on the other.

Ceuta and Melilla as outposts of the EU

Spain's entry into the European Community in 1986 meant yet another profound change in the nature of the Spanish-Moroccan frontier. Both the sea and land borders between Spain and Morocco became external limits of the EU. Spain's entry into the Schengen area in 1991 further deepened the western Mediterranean divide. The Strait of Gibraltar marks not only a political, demographic and economic division, but is also increasingly perceived on the European side as an ideological and moral boundary between democracy and secularism, and authoritarianism and Muslim fundamentalism. Once again, the enclaves found themselves in an awkward predicament. As the only territories with land borders between the EU and Africa, Melilla and Ceuta function as a stepping stone to the EU for African migrants. Their economic survival depends to a large extent on daily crossborder flows of goods (contraband included) and people (thousands of workers and consumers) with the Moroccan Nador and Tetouan provinces. Tens of thousands of people living in these provinces profit from the open border exchange. A return of the enclaves to Morocco, and the consequent disappearance of the borders, would be economically disastrous for Moroccan border dwellers. As a minor exception from the EU visa regulations, inhabitants of Ceuta and Melilla, as well as a limited number of Moroccans living in the adjacent areas, have special permits for moving in and out of the enclaves, whereas for African migrants it has recently become impossible to enter the enclaves in legal ways. In other words, economic interests require that the enclave gates to Fortress Europe remain open in a highly selective way, while EU-wide politics of security and identity dictate that the gates remain closed to undocumented immigrants.[13] Only a limited quota of seasonal labourers and students from well-to-do families, businesspeople, professionals and other members of the elite are granted entry.

Since Spain joined Schengen, its sea and land borders with Morocco have become increasingly fortified and militarized. Previously, Europe had served as a safety valve for Morocco: since the early 1960s Europe had been an easy, accessible destination for Moroccans and other North Africans seeking jobs or greater freedom. Now, the sea border is electronically monitored by radars on, and helicopters above the Andalusian shore, whereas the perimeter of the enclaves has been reinforced by double metal fences from three to six metres high, equipped with thermal and infrared cameras and razor wire. Nonetheless, the external borders of the EU in Africa remain permeable, as the events of autumn 2005 have clearly shown, although the extent of permeability has decreased enormously since the turn of the millennium. The reshaping and reinforcement of the Spanish-Moroccan frontier not only represents an implementation of EU political and economic legislation but also a 're-demarcation' of the cultural boundaries of the Union.[14]

One of the effects of the clampdown on irregular migration on both sides of the Strait of Gibraltar has been a growing diversification of crossing points into the EU since the late 1990s. Migrants now increasingly cross the sea borders from more eastern points on Morocco's Mediterranean coast and Algeria to mainland Spain; from Libya to Malta and the island of Lampedusa south of Sicily; and from the western Sahara, Mauritania, Senegal, and other West African countries to the Canary Islands. Another effect has been that many sub-Saharan migrants who intended to cross the Mediterranean into Europe reconsider their plans and stay in Morocco, Algeria and Tunisia.[15]

In spite of the intensified militarization of the Spanish-Moroccan frontier, the sometimes violent repatriation of arrested border crossers and the death of hundreds, if not thousands of boatpeople, the Mohammeds, Osmans, Suleimans, Hadis and Horanos, young men in their teens and twenties from Mali, Senegal, Niger, Burkina Faso or Morocco, cannot be stopped from trying to reach 'paradise' across the Mediterranean. Murals in Moroccan towns, and other expressions of popular artistic imagination, such as human figures made from wire attached to a fence in Bamako, Mali, attest to the daily practice of cutting across Europe's external borders.[16]

Conclusion

This paper has shown that the recent storming of the border fences of Ceuta and Melilla by undocumented migrants from Sub-Saharan Africa, and the consequent reactions of the security forces of the Spanish and Moroccan states, fit into a long history of often violent encounters at this 'border of borders', as the enclaves may be described. Over the past five centuries, the divide marked by Ceuta and Melilla has never been stable and uniform, nor simple and uncontested. Its permeability has varied over time. As defensive outposts of Catholicism in North Africa, the enclaves represented the cultural frontier between Europe and Africa, in which religious affiliation defined (and to a certain extent continues to define) people dwelling on both sides of the border. Despite endemic reciprocal hostilities, there were also peaceful exchanges among people on both sides, such as trade, smuggling, crossings of the religious divide and even cross-border marriage.

In the second half of the nineteenth century the enclaves became bases for colonial penetration presented as 'civilizing' missions. Even during the relatively brief interlude of the Spanish Protectorate (1912-1956), in which the enclaves and Spanish Morocco were in many regards one single socio-political formation, the former kept their border-like *status aparte*. With the independence of Morocco in 1956, Ceuta and Melilla were in and part of a re-politicized border zone between two modern states, in which violent encounters and threats never completely disappeared. When Spain joined the EU in 1986, the two enclaves were integrated, although not fully, into the EU external border regime. The frontier was both politically and ideologically sensitive: those who found themselves on the wrong side faced mounting pressure to stay away from the external border. Mamadou, a young man from Dakar, Senegal, who had twice failed to make the night crossing to Spain, concluded a talk with me one late afternoon in Tangier, June 2002, with the following words: 'We'll keep arriving here to enter Europe. It is either swimming or drowning, as simple as that.'

CHAPTER X

HARDENING CLOSURE, SECURING DISORDER: THE ISRAELI CLOSURE POLICIES AND THE INFORMAL BORDER ECONOMY BETWEEN THE WEST BANK AND NORTHERN NEGEV (2000–2006)

CÉDRIC PARIZOT

Introduction

This chapter discusses the informal social and economic exchanges taking place since the beginning of the Second Intifada (September 2000) between Palestinians in Israel proper and those in the West Bank.[1] An analysis of the border economy in the region of the Northern Negev (Israel) and the Southern Hebron Hills (West Bank) allows us to better evaluate the impact of Israel's closure policies as well as the construction of the Separation Wall around the West Bank. Started in 2002, the Fence[2] was officially meant to separate the Israelis from the Palestinians and provide a degree of security on the Israeli side. I argue that while putting on stage state power and providing a sense of border, these policies also open up spaces for different forms of trafficking and crime. The tightening of Israeli closure policies over the West Bank has therefore had the paradoxical effect of promoting disorder and blurring borders.

Through this case study of the Israeli regime of separation imposed on Palestinians in the West Bank, this article addresses the broader question of the close connections between the hardening of border policies, on the one hand, and the rise of illegal trafficking and criminality on the other. Yet I do not conceptualize borders as solely the product of state policies. Rather, I regard them as ongoing processes structured by the practices of the multiple actors involved around them. Moreover, I do not consider that borders produce binary divisions between spaces and actors. Since they are ongoing processes, people constantly move between positions of resistance and of oppression.

The study of informal mobility and exchanges across the borderlands[3] between the Palestinian enclaves and Israel proper (inside 1967 borders), as well as Israeli controlled areas in the West Bank, sheds light on the mechanisms employed by Israel to control the Occupied Palestinian Territories (OPT). Palestinian movement into Israel or into Israeli controlled areas in the OPT has been both an instrument and a target within these control mechanisms. Between 1967 and the first Intifada in December 1987, the authorities encouraged Palestinians to cross into Israel and to integrate into its economy. Making Palestinians dependent on the Israeli economy was part of the 'carrot and stick' policy introduced by Moshe Dayan after the 1967 war.[4] Later, in the 1990s and throughout the second Intifada (2000-), the Israeli government often used the allocation of work permits as a means of inflicting collective punishment on the Palestinians or to put pressure on the Palestinian National Authority (PNA).[5]

Another likely motivation behind the system of checkpoints and barriers put in place by Israel during the Second Intifada was to channel and regulate the intensity of Palestinian flows in the West Bank, rather than stop them. By slowing and prolonging cross-border journeys, the army and the police were able to better monitor the movement of people, while enhancing their own capacity to intercept individuals or groups suspected of plotting attacks on Israeli targets, whether in the West Bank or on the other side of the border.[6] In fact, despite the increasingly robust Israeli closure policies since the start of the Second Intifada, a significant number of Palestinians still enter Israel. In the third quarter of 2005, there were still 65,000 Palestinian workers employed in Israel and in Israeli settlements.[7]

Observing informal mobility and exchanges also provides a unique perspective on the effects of the Israeli closure policies on the ground, both in the short and the long term. Economic relations between people in the borderlands have been profoundly affected by the Israeli system of checkpoints and curfews. The growing number of legal and physical obstacles imposed upon the Palestinians have made border crossers increasingly dependent on skilled individuals and networks, both Arab and Jewish, which have devised new strategies of bypassing barriers. Furthermore, the widening gap between the relatively prosperous Israeli economy and that of the Palestinians, which is rapidly deteriorating, has intensified trafficking and smuggling activities. In other words, the Israeli border policies have fostered the emergence of a new economy which reshapes the context in which these very policies were intended to establish a separation between Israelis and Palestinians. The shifts in the relations of economic interdependence between Israeli and West Bank Palestinians could have future security repercussions for the region as the Barrier nears completion. Over the last seven years, this 'economy', situated along the borderlands, has become a hotbed of illegal and criminal activities.

Finally, looking at Israeli closure policies through the lens of the border economy makes it possible to clearly assess their effects in terms of security on both the Palestinian and Israeli sides. This study of the connection between the tightening of borders on the one hand and criminal activity on the other is relevant to other areas of the world. I draw on the work of Peter Andreas and Jorge Santibañez-Romellon on the US-Mexican border, introducing the micro-analytical perspective of ethnography.[8] My research is based on data collected during successive periods of fieldwork that I have carried out between 1996 and 2006 in the region between the Northern Negev (Israel) and the Hebron Hills (southern West Bank). By listening to, following, and at times observing directly people's everyday efforts to circumvent the Israeli border-closing measures, I have tried to grasp the mechanisms through which this frontier economy has exacerbated power inequalities, multiplied antagonisms and conflicts, and altered perceptions on the ground.

'Smugglers need borders'

Before focusing on the issue of the border economy, the chapter briefly describes the region between the southern Hebron Hills and northern Negev, its inhabitants and their history over the past sixty years. From the point of view of observers located in the main population centres of the occupied West Bank and of Israel, such as Ramallah, Jerusalem or Tel Aviv, the Northern Negev and the Hebron Hills are seen as remote peripheries, marginal territories or even borderlands. Yet, at a closer glance, it appears that over the last six decades, movement and exchanges amongst the local populations has led to the emergence of robust socio-economic networks and interdependencies across various spatial divides. From 1948 to 1967, when the Green Line functioned as a *de facto* international border between Israel and Jordan, these exchanges took place through smuggling and clandestine travel. After 1967, when Israel invaded the West Bank and integrated it into its own economic space, these exchanges developed even more intensely – and legally. Smuggling intensified in the 1990s when Israeli authorities imposed systematic limitations on Palestinian movement. While these limitations did not completely stop Palestinian mobility, they criminalized exchanges between the Northern Negev and the West Bank and provided the basis for a parallel economy.

Nowadays, the Negev is inhabited by both Jews and Arabs, with the former accounting for around 75 per cent of the population. Jews reside in the main city of Beer-Sheva and its suburbs, in the poor development towns built in the 1950s, and in small *kibbutzim* and *moshavim*. The Arabs inhabiting the Negev live separately from the Jews, in suburbs and slums at the periphery of Beer-Sheva. They are the descendants of the 11,000 Bedouin who remained in the Beer-Sheva district after the creation of the State of Israel in 1948. Most Bedouin fled or were expelled *manu militari* to the West Bank, the Gaza Strip, Jordan and Egypt.[9] Those who stayed obtained Israeli citizenship at the beginning of the 1950s. Yet, in the same period, they were displaced to an enclosed zone in the north-eastern Negev, which was placed under military administration until 1966. Excluded from the urban infrastructure of Beer-Sheva and from the formal labour market, the Negev Bedouin had no choice but to revert to agriculture and livestock herding.[10] In the mid 1960s, after the military administration was abolished, the Israeli authorities decided to resettle the Bedouin into seven planned townships: Tell as-Saba', Rahat, 'Ar'ara, Ksîfa, Shgîb as-Salâm, Lagiyya and Hûra (Map 1). At the beginning of 2000, the 140,000 Bedouin living in the Negev area constituted a semi-urban, low-skilled proletariat, half of them living in these planned townships, and the other half residing in slums scattered around the main road axes.[11] The lack of productive and commercial activities in the townships and slums, coupled with the Bedouin's low level of qualifications, renders them highly vulnerable to economic crises.[12] The stagnation provoked by the second Intifada made their condition even more precarious.

From the point of view of Palestinians living in the central or northern areas of the West Bank, the south Hebron Hills (*Jebel al-Khalîl*), is a marginal territory marking the limit of the Bedouin-populated desert. Palestinians often consider these Bedouin groups 'traditional' and 'brutal', with little loyalty to the national cause.[13] Far from the main urban centres, the Jebel al-Khalîl area is hardly visited by people living north of the West Bank. In

2005, on the Palestinian side north of the Green Line, the four main towns Dhahriyya, Sammu', Yatta and Dûra, and the surrounding hamlets (*kharab*, singular, *khirbet*) had a population of 120,000. As with the Bedouin of the Negev, starting from the 1970s, the peasants of the Hebron Mountains went through a process of proletarianization, conditioned by the integration of the Palestinian economy into the Israeli one after 1967.

1949-1987: Integrated margins

Throughout the nineteenth and the beginning of the twentieth century, the Bedouin living in the plain of Beer-Sheva and the peasants of the Hebron Hills were connected by means of regular social and economic exchanges. Following the first Arab-Israeli conflict (1947-1949) and the establishment of the Green Line,[14] many people would illegally cross the new border on a regular basis in order to maintain contact with the southern Hebron Hills. Some of them imported goods originating from the neighbouring Arab countries into the Israeli market. In some instances, smuggling developed on a large scale and was in fact encouraged by the Israeli authorities.[15] The aim was to supply the then fragile Israeli economy.

In 1967, after Israel occupied the West Bank and Gaza, the Green Line ceased to function as an international border and the Israeli authorities promoted the flow of people and goods between Israel proper and the newly acquired territories.[16] Bedouin and Palestinian peasants could now trade openly. Responding to Israeli demands for labour in the construction and agriculture sectors, peasants from the southern Hebron Hills abandoned their fields to work as wage-earners in Israel proper, a general trend observed in the rest of the OPT at that time.[17] As with the entire Palestinian population, the residents of this region became dependent on the Israeli labour market. By the end of the 1980s, 30 per cent of the Palestinian workforce was employed in Israel and provided half of the earnings in the OPT; by the end of the 1990s, under conditions of relatively open but controlled borders, the corresponding figures were 20 per cent and one third.[18] The Bedouin started to frequent the markets of Hebron and the surrounding villages, where they could find products they needed, as well as a more socio-culturally amenable environment. Furthermore, the Bedouin and Palestinian peasants developed deeper social relations through intermarriage: during the 1970s and the 1980s, many Negev Bedouin contracted matrimonial alliances with Palestinian brides from the Hebron Hills, both of Bedouin and peasant origin.[19]

Social and economic ties underpinned the flow of goods, people and values that eventually also fostered the exchange of cultural practices and representations. There are multiple examples registered in the literature on the Negev Bedouin. The mutual influences between the Bedouin and the Palestinian peasant society were observed by scholars as early as the 1970s in marriage celebrations, religious beliefs, genealogical practices, models of authority, etc.[20] Over the 1970s and the 1980s, and to a certain extent until the 1990s as we shall see, cross-border relations extended the social, economic and political spaces of the Bedouin and their peasant neighbours and integrated these marginal territories. Between 1980 and 1985, the Hebron Hills were further incorporated into the Beer-Sheva region, with the creation of nine Jewish settlements on the Palestinian side of the Green line.[21] In 1992, the population of these settlements reached 1,923[22].

1987-2000: Back to smuggling

This process of integration came to an end with the outbreak of the First Intifada in December 1987. During the Palestinian uprising, a sense of border re-emerged. Jews living within the 1949 borders became reluctant to cross the Green Line into territories which they now regarded as increasingly hostile, and Palestinians from the West Bank and the Gaza Strip faced limitations of movement.[23] In the beginning, the Israeli army imposed curfews and closures in the Occupied Territories as ad hoc security measures. Over time, these measures developed into a more articulated project of separation from the Palestinians.[24] The latter became visible during the Gulf War in 1991, when the Israeli authorities revoked the general entrance permit giving Palestinians access to Israel proper, and imposed a system of individual permits.[25] Later, the authorities built up controls on Israeli employers and introduced new legislation allowing Asian and Eastern European immigrants into the labour market in order to replace Palestinians.

Yet, despite these measures, a significant number of Palestinian workers remained in Israel throughout the 1990s. The effect of the curbs was felt only after several years. In the initial period (1987-1992), the Israeli authorities faced the employers' resistance. Accustomed to their Palestinian employees, Israeli businesses continued to hire Palestinians on a massive scale. In fact, numbers continued growing, and it took some time for Israeli entrepreneurs to see the influx of Palestinian workers as a threat to their own safety and security. Attacks against Israelis stirred up anxiety amongst the businesses and the numbers of Palestinian employees started declining. As Adriana Kemp and Rebecca Raijman put it, 'This [changing] "mood" acquired highly tangible expression; in 1992, the number of workers from the territories in Israel peaked at 115,600, but in 1993, it plunged to 83,800. This drop was the result of government decisions on closure and on bringing in labour migrants [from Asia and Eastern Europe], but it also reflected decisions by Israeli employers not to engage Palestinian workers any longer.'[26]

Although the tightening of border controls between 1992 and 1996 halved the number of Palestinians in the Israeli labour market, after 1997 the number began to increase: by August 2000, on the eve of the Second Intifada, it had reached 145,110 Palestinian workers. 'Foreign workers' did not completely replace the Palestinians. Israel's rising levels of prosperity, a consequence of international investors' reaction to the Peace Process, fed demand for labour.[27] Moreover, the 'foreign workers' allowed in by the Ministry of Labour were mostly directed to the larger Israeli businesses, rather than to small and mid-size companies, which often preserved relations with their Palestinian employees.[28]

Limitations imposed on Palestinian workers resulted not so much in changes in absolute numbers, but rather altered the conditions of employment, the relative share in the total labour force in the OPT, the shifting directions of labour flows, and the decrease in working hours per employee.[29] The Gaza Strip suffered more than the West Bank. The percentage of Gaza workers entering Israel fell from 45.8 per cent of the local labour force in 1987 to 15.4 per cent in 2000, while the number of West Bank workers dwindled from 35.6 per cent in 1987 to 24.8 per cent in 2000. According to Leila Farsakh, the reorientation of the worker flows also bore witness to the readjustment of borders during the Oslo period (1994-2000): while Gaza was progressively separated economically from Israel, the West Bank remained integrated in the Israeli marketplace.[30]

In addition, the new set of border-tightening policies compelled Palestinian workers and small Israeli companies to turn to illegal trafficking. Before the first Intifada, many entrepreneurs used to employ 'undeclared' Palestinian workers. In 1987, 60 per cent of Palestinian labourers did not have work permits.[31] During the 1990s, Israeli employers and their workers breached the law again by illegally crossing the borders between the Palestinian enclaves and Israeli-controlled areas. Small Israeli companies still employed Palestinians, while Israeli Jews often entered the Hebron Hills region to pick up their workers in local towns such as Dhahriyya, Sammu', Yatta, and help them avoid police and army controls. The authorities were unable to stem the ongoing clandestine passages of Palestinians actively aided by Israeli Jewish and Israeli Arab employers.

In the mid-1990s, the building of a fence around Gaza and the delimitation of 'borders' between Palestinian Authority enclaves and Israeli-controlled areas fostered new forms of exchange and trafficking. The fencing in of the Gaza Strip reoriented the flows of Bedouin and Jewish clients towards the Hebron Hills, and boosted trade with the Negev. The markets of Hebron and, later, Dhahriyya, replaced Gaza City as the chief competitor of the Beer-Sheva market. Hence, the small border town of Dhahriyya saw incredible levels of prosperity in the second half of the 1990s. Its market grew beyond the needs of the immediate hinterland and became an important centre of exchange where Negev Bedouin, as well as Jews from Israel proper and from the settlements came to buy goods and services that were much cheaper than on the Israeli side of the Green Line.[32]

The creation of the PNA and the delimitation of the new administrative borders corresponding to Palestinian autonomous and semi-autonomous areas, respectively called Area A and Area B, resulted in new difficulties for the Israeli police, as it put smugglers and criminals outside their jurisdiction. In the mid 1990s, car theft within Israel increased significantly.[33] Cars which were stolen in Israel were subsequently brought into the West Bank and Gaza.[34] Dhahriyya and Yatta in the Hebron Hills became the main centres of trafficking. The Bedouin emerged as the key smugglers. By the end of the 1990s, the latter had established operations which were set to become even more profitable once the Second Intifada broke out.

The Second Intifada and the rise of the border economy

This traffic and the informal economy it created developed further during the Second Intifada, thanks to the tightening of Israeli closure policy. On the one hand, the growing number of legal restrictions and physical obstacles[35] imposed by the Israeli authorities between 2000 and 2005 dramatically limited the entry of Palestinian workers into Israeli-controlled areas. According to the Palestinian Central Bureau of Statistics, their overall numbers dropped from 145,110 in August 2000 to 65,000 during the third quarter of 2005. At the same time, the new obstacles boosted the demand for the services of suitably skilled individuals and networks which could assist workers to cross into Israel. These actors seized the opportunity to establish different forms of trafficking channels around the emerging 'borders'.

Tightening closure, motivating crossing

During the Second Intifada, Israel cut the number of work permits issued and progressively reinforced its closure system in the southern Hebron Hills.[36] Passing through police or army controls became more difficult in the spring of 2002. During 'Operation Defensive Shield', the Israeli army re-invaded the towns of Dhahriyya, Dûra, Sammu' and Yatta (Map 1). Palestin-

Map 1

NOTHERN NEGEV (ISRAEL)
and SOUTHERN HEBRON HILLS (WEST BANK)

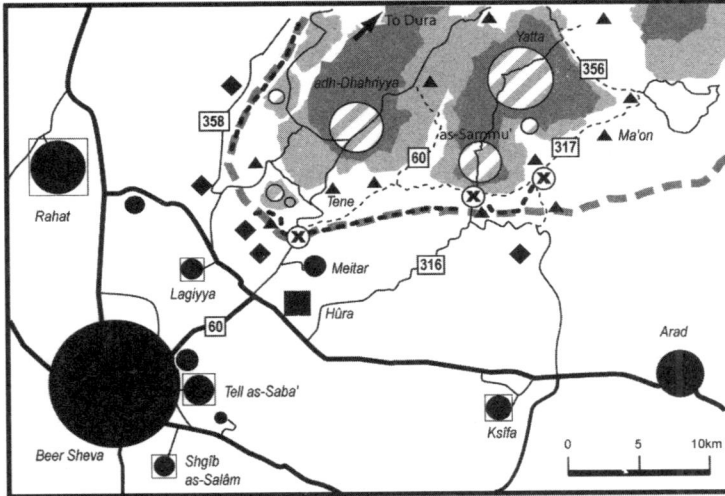

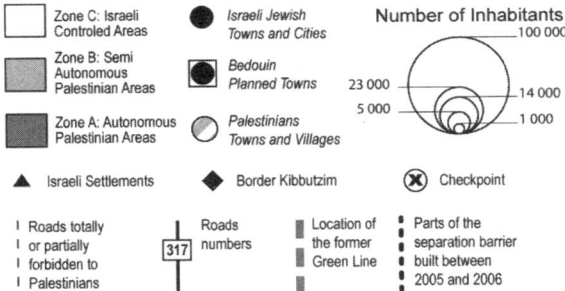

North

To Dura

Yatta

356

adh-Dhahriyya

358

as-Samu'

60

317

Ma'on

Rahat

Tene

Meitar

316

Lagiyya

60

Hûra

Arad

Tell as-Saba'

Ksîfa

0   5   10km

Beer Sheva   Shgîb
as-Salâm

Zone C: Israeli Controled Areas

Zone B: Semi Autonomous Palestinian Areas

Zone A: Autonomous Palestinian Areas

Israeli Settlements

Israeli Jewish Towns and Cities

Bedouin Planned Towns

Palestinians Towns and Villages

Border Kibbutzim

Number of Inhabitants

100 000

23 000

14 000

5 000

1 000

Checkpoint

Roads totally or partially forbidden to Palestinians

Roads numbers 317

Location of the former Green Line

Parts of the separation barrier built between 2005 and 2006

Golan

West Bank

Israel

Gaza

Negev

Shadrock ROBERTS, ©2006 - shadrock@oddpost.com. **Sources**: Central Bureau of Statistics State of Israel - http://www.cbs.gov.il/publications.local_authorities01/local_authorities_e.htm (visited on July 2006); Central Bureau of Statistics, Palestinian National Authority - http://www.pcbs.gov.ps/site/3354/DesktopDefault/aspx?tabid=3354(visited on July 2006). **Maps:** Survey of Israel, 2003. Israel, 1:250.000 South. B'Tselem, September 2005. The Separation Barrier in the West bank; UN OCHA, January 2006. West Bank, Access and Closure. **Notes:** Population Calibrated with Philcarto - http://perso.club-internet.fr/philgeo

ian police stations were partially destroyed or, as in Dûra, transformed into a base for the Israelis, while the towns were then placed under an extended curfew.[37] In order to stop car smuggling, the Israeli authorities imposed a severe regime on Dhahriyya and Yatta: even though the border towns were evacuated a few months after the operation, the army has continued to carry out targeted assassinations or arrests.

In 2004, closures entered a new stage. Until then, Israeli policy had relied on the surveillance of the checkpoint located close to the Green Line on the road linking ad-Dhahriyya to Beer-Sheva, and on random patrols (Map 1). Border guard patrols would stop Palestinians attempting to enter Area C (OPT under Israeli administration) or to use the by-pass roads reserved for Israeli settlers.[38] During the summer of 2004, the army built up earth mounds and established temporary checkpoints which cut off Dhahriyya, Yatta and Sammu' from Hebron and from the central areas in the West Bank.[39] Later, following a suicide bomb attack in the town of Beer-Sheva, the Israeli army created two new checkpoints on road 317: one south of Sammu' and another north of the Jewish settlement of Metzadot Yehuda. The Israeli authorities made it increasingly difficult for local Palestinians to enter both Israeli-controlled areas and Israel proper.

Between 2000 and 2005, these closure policies dealt a sharp blow to the Palestinian economy and exacerbated the economic gap with Israel. While GDP per capita remained relatively stable in Israel between 1999 and 2003 (at $16,940 and $16,240 respectively), in the Palestinian territories it fell from $1,850 to $1,110, dropping to $934 in 2004.[40] In the southern West Bank, the general crisis increased the impoverishment of a population which was already among the poorest in the West Bank.[41] Thus, paradoxically, Israeli closure policies reinforced the need to cross into Israel. The collapse of the Palestinian economy compelled the population to seek jobs elsewhere. Moreover, the growing economic inequalities between the Bedouin and their Palestinian neighbours became evident. Added to increasing difficulties in moving across what used to be the Green Line, these inequalities changed the terms of cross-border exchanges between the two populations.

Smuggling and extorting workers

During the 1990s, Bedouin and Palestinian drivers shared the market for transportation from the Hebron Hills to the region around Beer-Sheva. After the outbreak of the Second Intifada, the restrictions on movement prevented Palestinians from competing with the Bedouin. West Bank drivers remained only in the main towns of Dhahriyya, Dura, Yatta and Sammu' and their surroundings. As a result, the Bedouin progressively secured a monopoly over worker traffic and managed to impose much higher prices.

Under these conditions, the transportation of Palestinians quickly became a coveted source of increased income for Bedouin drivers, as workers from the Hebron Hills went on crossing the Green Line in search of work inside Israel. New Bedouin groups joined the fight for monopoly. For their part, Palestinians had little choice but to continue crossing the Green Line, as there were no jobs in the Palestinian territories, while work in Israel paid three times as much. Between 2005 and 2006, in the area controlled by the Palestinian Authority, an unqualified labourer was paid NIS 50 (€10) a day, compared with between NIS 100 and NIS 150 (€20–30) a day paid for undeclared work in Israel.[42] Consequently, Palestinians had no choice but to accept the high fees charged by the Bedouin, who claimed that the passage had become riskier and therefore more expensive. At the outset of the Second Intifada, workers came into Israel from Sammu', Dûra, Yatta, Dhahriyya and the surrounding villages. They would pay up to NIS 150 (€30) each for a one-way trip to the Bedouin towns of Hûra and Lagiyya, or the Jewish towns of Beer-Sheva and Qiryat Gat. Many would remain in Israel for a week or even a month in order to spread the cost of the journey. Between 2002 and 2005, the construction of the Separation Wall in the North of the West Bank drove migrants into the Hebron Hills. Some people from the regions of Nablus and Ramallah travelled all the way to the south in order to cross the Green Line. They would then take Bedouin or Jewish Israeli taxis to reach the regions of Hadera, Kufr Qara, and Baqqa al-Gharbiyya. The cost of such a journey would reach more than NIS 500 (€100), the equivalent of three to four days of work (Map 2).

The sharp rise in prices and the tightening of Israeli police controls drastically changed the circumstances under which one could stay in Israel. Palestinian workers travelled less frequently and remained in Israel proper for months. The wealthiest and the luckiest would rent places to sleep in the planned townships of the Bedouin. However, as increased controls by the police made local landlords fearful, most of the workers were forced to lodge in improvized hideouts to protect themselves from the night cold. In northern Israel, they gathered in public dumps; in Beer-Sheva, they slept in the sewers.[43]

According to my own estimate, between 2003 and 2005, an average of 40 Bedouin minibuses crossed through the border zone between the South of Sammu' and the West of the Ramadhîn daily. Each month, there would be 8,000 to 12,000 individual one-way trips between these two Palestinian towns across the Green Line.[44] This traffic was worth between NIS 800,000

Map 2

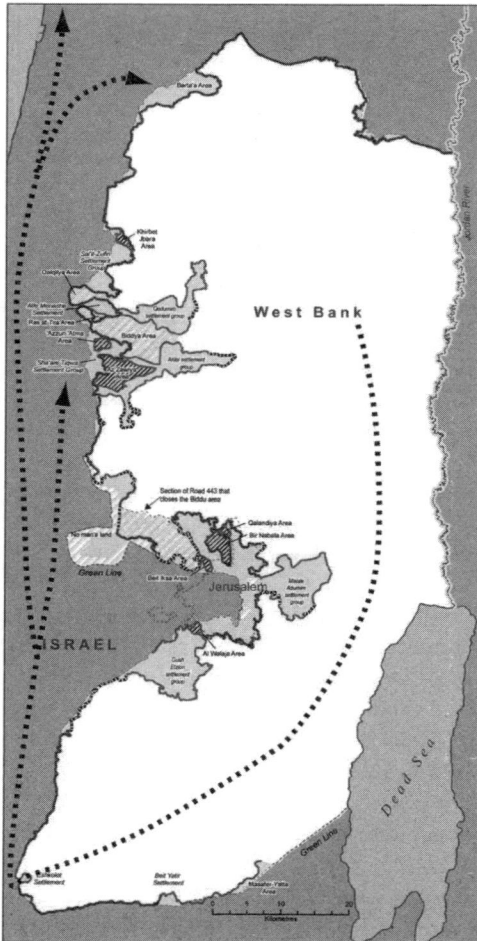

One of the routes taken by some
Palestinian workers in order to
circumvent the Wall in the
Northern West Bank and
to enter Israel between the end of
2005 and the beginning of 2006

Barrier Route in July 2006

— Completed - 362 km

···· Under construction - 88 km

— Planned - 253 km

Planned
36%

Completed
51%

Under
construction
13%

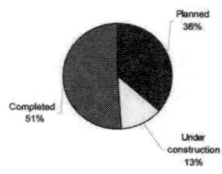

Cartography and Barrier Themes:
OCHA-oPt IMU
Map 5 July 2006
Base Data: MoPIC (2000)
updates OCHA (2005)

and NIS 1,200,000 (€160,000–240,000) per month. These figures exclude workers who crossed into Israel on foot or in private cars, as well as those who took Israeli Jewish private cars or taxis. The Bedouin's control over trafficking in people is only one example of their increasing power in the local economy. Bedouin individuals and groups also smuggle fuel in order to supply illegal petrol stations inside Israel. Livestock, clothes and furniture are also smuggled on both a small and a large scale. The resultant profits stand in sharp contrast to the dwindling incomes of households which have characterized the economic crisis in the OPT.

Paradoxical effects: consolidating or blurring borders?

The changes in worker trafficking currents reveal the profound shifts in power relations between the two populations: the Israeli Palestinians (the Bedouin) and the West Bank Palestinians. While the Bedouin have gradually assumed the position of helpers or patrons, the situation of the Palestinian workers has continuously deteriorated. The scarcity of work and the increasingly severe controls on clandestine workers entering Israel have made the Palestinian labourers even more vulnerable in relation to their smugglers. The picture is even grimmer when considering the ever more precarious position of Palestinian workers while they are inside Israel, in relation to both Jews and Arabs.

The deteriorating relationship between the Palestinian workers and their employers has had a direct impact on the mutual perceptions of the border populations, i.e. between the Israeli Palestinians and their kin and networks in the OPT. I have shown elsewhere[45] that, at the end of the 1990s and the beginning of the 2000s, their exchanges were increasingly marked by bitterness and even violence, with the result that there is now distrust and even fear on both sides. This has fostered a feeling of difference on the part of the cross-border partners. Practised on daily basis, and over a long period of time, these differences have been internalized. This is all the more true as people have been using such experiences to reconstruct dominant narratives that stress distinctions between them. Each individual experience is added to other stories that people have either heard or witnessed personally. Narratives about 'us' and 'the others' are often presented as facts: they are built upon such multiple layers of stories.[46] These cross-border encounters and the experiences people draw from them contribute to an Israeli discourse of a binary opposition of 'Bedouin against Palestinian', whether 'West Bank dweller' (*dhaffâwi*) or 'Gazan' (*Ghazzâwi*).

In a way, the tightening of the Israeli border policies during the Second Intifada, and the border economy emerging as a result, has created the impression of established boundaries, or at least some sort of a separation between Israeli and Palestinian spaces. This has led to a growing rift between the Palestinians on the two sides of the Green Line, and dissociation between these two groups. The Jewish population in Israel, too, has the sense that separation has occurred and, Palestinians have completely disappeared from the landscape of ordinary Israeli citizens.

Yet, acknowledging the growing sense of separation should not make one completely overlook the complex readjustment in the relations among local populations. Palestinian workers still enter Israel in order to work. Though diminishing, their numbers in Israel are still significant: between 2005 and 2006 they were still at the 1996 level. What is different is that Palestinians have moved into marginal areas and economic activities where, over the last six years, forms of unfettered, Dickensian capitalism prevail. The paradox is that on the one hand the Israeli State has ostensibly been seeking to reassert its authority at the 'border', while on the other, these very actions gave birth to networks and economic activities deep within Israel operating outside state control. Israeli border policies appear to have conditioned disorder and blurred borders, rather than securing clear-cut boundaries that separate communities.

Entrepreneurs without borders

The blurring of borders in the Israeli-Palestinian space becomes all the more apparent when considering the entrepreneurial networks operating within the border economy. Looking at the latter, it would be wrong to ascribe fixed positions to groups according to their administrative status (Israeli citizens, Palestinians, etc.) or ethnic background (Jews, Palestinians). The networks of border entrepreneurs are highly heterogeneous and involve complex cooperative arrangements between the different Palestinian populations in southern Israel, as well as including representatives of the state. Such arrangements have long existed but their new reconfiguration testifies to the effect of the Israeli closure policies. The networks in question provide one with an interesting perspective on the local power mechanisms during the Second Intifada, as well as the way in which the Israeli State maintains control over the borderlands.

Moving markets

In the northern Negev and the Hebron Hills, economic networks involve as many Bedouin as Israeli Jews, profiting from the opportunities in the cross-border marketplace. However, Israeli policies have, over time, redirected the influx of Palestinian workers into Israeli society. The import of

Palestinian labour by Israeli Jews has dropped significantly, while remaining stable with regard to the Bedouin. Palestinian workers now play a different role compared with that before the Second Intifada. In 1999, they still had a significant place in the construction and agriculture sectors, 27 per cent and 12 per cent respectively, but in 2004, they accounted for only 8 per cent and 4 per cent in these two areas. The Israeli economy now relies less on 'delocalization *in situ*',[47] i.e. the import of cheap Palestinian labour, to lower costs and improve productivity. With the new restrictions on Palestinian workers, it is as if the authorities have indirectly pushed for a policy of 'delocalization at the margin', i.e. the procurement of cheap labour for the benefit of specific marginal groups, such as the Bedouin or the Jews living in the development towns of the Negev (Sderot, Ofaqim, Yeroham, etc.).

It is also worth considering the extent to which the Bedouin economy has become dependent on the import of Palestinian labour and goods. During the Second Intifada, the Bedouin also suffered an economic downturn, exacerbated by child benefit cuts by the government. Instituting a separation barrier between the Negev and the Hebron Hills dealt an additional blow to the fragile Bedouin economy. Without cheap Palestinian labour and access to low-priced Palestinian building materials, the cost of house building doubled, putting pressure on local households' budgets. Moreover, the high rate of population growth (5.5 per cent per year) in the Bedouin communities creates a strong demand for housing, as there are serious shortages in the residential areas. Finally, household expenditures grow as daily consumption goods are purchased on the Israeli market, and not on the cheaper Palestinian market. The outbreak of the Second Intifada and the border controls imposed on Dhahriyya limited the access of Bedouin to the West Bank and Gaza, previously their chief source of consumer goods. However, Dhahriyya and Hebron traders adjusted well by opening new shops in the Bedouin town of Rahat in Israel, which boosted the local market's rapid growth. Over the next six years, it became the main shopping destination for the Bedouin, apart from Beer-Sheva. Merchants from Hebron and the West Bank, accounting for up to 60 per cent of the retail business in Rahat, have to register their shops under local names, which leads to joint ventures with local Bedouin.

Informal cooperation with the state

The Israeli authorities have instrumentalized cross-border entrepreneurial networks. The Israeli police, Border Guards and the General Security Services (*Shabak*) collaborate informally with the smugglers of Palestinian workers. The state agencies often pressure the Bedouin drivers into becoming informants. When they arrest a driver, the authority representatives threaten to confiscate the smuggler's vehicle, to impose a hefty fine, or even to send him to jail, unless he agrees to collaborate, in some cases even to identify suspects or wanted individuals. It is difficult to avoid this indirect form of surveillance. Furthermore, some drivers do not hesitate to report their competitors. The authorities are also indirectly involved in the distribution of work permits. Former Palestinian collaborators who settled in Israel proper sometimes use their position and their links with *Shabak* to obtain work permits for their family members and neighbours in the occupied territories. By interceding on behalf of their kin, they are able to maintain favour with them, while acting out their role as informant for the benefit of their Israeli patrons.

The tolerance shown towards the new border economy brings twofold benefits to the Israeli authorities. First, it facilitates the operation of cheap sub-contracting networks of information. Second, the privileges granted to the smugglers and to the clandestine workers allow *Shabak* and the police to build up *de facto* patron-client relations with a part of the local population. This practice creates a system of controls similar to the one described by Amira Hass concerning parts of the Palestinian elite during the Oslo period.[48] That system had worked through VIP cards allocated by the Israeli authorities to members of the PNA and NGO activists. The card would allow the holder to travel almost freely in the whole Israeli-Palestinian space. Hass claims that the beneficiaries would therefore refrain from public protest against measures taken by the Israeli authorities, for fear of losing their right of movement, source of income and, eventually, their social capital.

Conclusion

In sum, between 2000 and 2005, before the completion of the Wall in the southern West Bank, Israeli policies of closure have not succeeded in suppressing the exchanges between the inhabitants of the Negev and the Hebron Hills. While these policies have reduced the intensity in flows of people and goods, they have also given rise to new forms of exchanges. This is due to the fact that while the obstacles created by Israeli policies have indeed discouraged many Palestinians from entering Israel, on the other hand, these very obstacles and the damage they caused to the Palestinian economy made it even more necessary for the Palestinian labour force to search for employment and opportunities inside Israel. Furthermore, the growing number of legal and physical obstacles imposed upon the Palestinians has made border crossers increasingly dependent on skilled individuals and networks to help them pass.

Consequently, the tightening of Israeli closures has had the paradoxical effect of both rendering the crossing more difficult and yet even more necessary. In this context it has stimulated new forms of trafficking, as Palestinians from both sides of the Green Line set up well-organized networks to smuggle people and goods into Israel. They helped a highly organized border economy take root, which reshaped existing social and economic ties between the local regions.

The border economy has in turn produced ambivalent effects, as it has both reinforced and blurred borders between local actors. On the one hand, this border economy has helped reinforce the sense of a boundary between the Israeli Palestinians and their brethren and partners in the West Bank. This economy has brought about a shift in power relations between local populations and has led to the emergence of wild forms of capitalism affecting mutual perceptions among Palestinians. Yet, on the other hand, this new border economy has blurred boundaries between the people involved. It is structured around extremely heterogeneous networks of border entrepreneurs, where the place and the position of the actors are not necessarily defined according to ethnic origin or citizenship. Indeed, the identification of the oppressed and the oppressor depends on the perspective of the observer. To paraphrase Pablo Vila, the metaphor of resistance is not consistent with border situations. As he explains:

> [m]ost current mainstream border studies [in anthropology]... identify a subject who is clearly and undoubtedly "resisting", and a structure of power that, without contradictions, is always "oppressing". This makes us lose sight of the much more complicated picture of the actual border, where people constantly move from positions of "resistance" to positions of "oppression".[49]

Indeed, border economies such as that developing between the Northern Negev and the Southern West bank during the Second Intifada do not generate clear-cut binary worlds or divisions at the border.

This is all the more true as the instrumentalization of smuggling networks by the Israeli authorities further blurs the boundaries between the state and the smugglers, the formal and informal, the legal and illegal. While it might reinforce control over local borders at first, down the line, the instrumentalization of smuggling networks could render the whole mechanism of control dysfunctional. These heterogeneous networks enjoy a certain degree of autonomy, as has already has been seen in Israel in the past. It is not rare for soldiers to pass information to smugglers, or close their eyes to certain illegal practices. In the mid 1990s, on the border with the Gaza Strip, informal collaboration between Border Guards and local thieves allowed the development of significant trafficking in stolen cars that extended temporarily beyond the control of Israeli State authorities.[50] At the end of the 1990s, on the Egyptian border, young Bedouin with good connections with both the army and the police were able to exploit the poor coordination between the two agencies to manage a successful drug-running operation.

The completion of the Wall in the southern West Bank and the implementation of effective separation between Palestinian and Israeli spaces and populations will bring new challenges to Israeli authorities. First, the Wall will not merely deal a sharp blow to the Hebron Hills economy, it will also seriously weaken the neighbouring Bedouin economy, a process that might have later repercussions on the local Negev economy. The completion of the Wall will then lead to new frustrations among a population already involved with the state in a long-lasting conflict over land. The second challenge to the Israeli authorities, and to a certain extent to the PNA, lies in gaining control over the smuggling networks that have been structured around the economy of border. What if these entrepreneurs find themselves unable to trespass the border? If they do not find a way to circumvent the Wall, these entrepreneurs might go in search of alternative illegal sources of income inside Israeli and Palestinian spaces. This will not merely increase the rate of criminality in the Negev, it will also endanger security and the economic prosperity of neighbouring Israeli and Palestinian areas. All in all, in the Israeli-Palestinian context, as is often the case in many other regions in the world,[51] the tightening of border policies tends to increase the margin of criminal activities and disorder in the borderland space.

NOTES

Introduction

1 Walker, Rob B.J., *Inside/Outside: International Relations as Political Theory* (Cambridge: Cambridge University Press, 1992). See also the essays included in Albert, Mathias, David Jacobson and Yosef Lapid (eds), *Identities, Borders, Orders: Rethinking International Relations Theory* (Minneapolis: Minnesota University Press, 2001). For a detailed discussion of the notion and practices of territoriality in international politics, see the chapter by Raffaella A. Del Sarto in this volume, including the wide-ranging academic literature cited therein.

2 However, as we are reminded by Joel Migdal, there is always a 'tension between the actual borders of states and other virtual boundaries that frame human communities' which is exacerbated by the process of globalization. See Migdal, Joel (ed), *Boundaries and Belonging: States and Societies in the Struggle to Shape Identities and Local Practices* (Cambridge: Cambridge University Press, 2004).

3 Horden, Peregrine and Nicholas Purcell, *The Corrupting Sea: a Study of Mediterranean History* (Maiden MA: Blackwell Publishers, 2000).

4 See 'Investing in the Mediterranean: the Med's moment comes', *The Economist*, 10 July 2008.

5 The same notion of multiplicity is at the centre of Matvejević, Predrag, *Mediterranean: A Cultural Landscape* (Los Angeles: University of California Press, 1999).

6 See, for instance, the various case-study chapters in Brandell, Inga (ed), *State Frontiers: Borders and Boundaries in the Middle East* (London: I.B. Tauris, 2006).

7 Braudel, Fernand, *La Méditerranée et le monde méditerranéen à l'époque de Philippe II* (Paris: Armand Colin, 1949).

8 Herzfeld, Michael, 'Practical Mediterraneanism: excuses for everything, from epistemology to eating', in William V. Harris (ed), *Rethinking the Mediterranean* (Oxford: Oxford University Press, 2005).

9 See also Fabre, Thierry and Paul Sant Cassia (eds), *Between Europe and the Mediterranean: The Challenges and the Fears* (London Palgrave Macmillan, 2008).

10 Pirenne, Henri, *Mohammed and Charlemagne* (New York: Barnes and Noble, 1956 [1935]).

11 See Pace, Michelle, *The Politics of Regional Identity: Meddling with the Mediterranean* (London: Routledge, 2005), as well as Emmanuel Adler's idea of Mediterrane-

anism as a (potential) common identity bond between Israelis and Palestinians. See his chapter 'A Mediterranean canon and an Israeli prelude to a long peace', in Emmanuel Adler, *Communitarian International Relations: the Epistemic Foundations of International Relations* (London: Routledge, 2005), pp. 235–43.

12   See the essays included in Adler, Emanuel et al. (eds), *The Convergence of Civilizations: Constructing a Mediterranean Region* (Toronto: University of Toronto Press, 2006), especially Chapter 12 by Kalypso and Dimitri Nicolaidis, 'The EuroMed beyond civilizational paradigms'. See also Pace: *The Politics of Regional Identity*.

13   Youngs, Richard, *Europe and the Middle East. In the Shadow of September 11* (Boulder CO: Lynne Renner, 2006).

14   This theme, not unfamiliar in the context of southern Europe and the Balkans, was classically developed in Ayubi, Nazih N., *Overstating the Arab State: Politics and Society in the Middle East* (London: I.B. Tauris, 1995).

15   See Kalypso and Dimitri Nicolaidis: 'The EuroMed beyond civilizational paradigms'.

16   Albert, Jacobson and Lapid (eds): *Identities, Borders, Orders.*

Chapter I

1   Sarkozy's script-writer was referring to the split between the Byzantine Empire, the successor to Rome in the East, and the Holy Roman Empire of Charlemagne that challenged Constantinople's claims in the West in the year 800. Cf. Sarkozy, Nicholas, *Discours de Toulon* [Public speech, delivered on 7 February 2007]. [http://www.u-m-p.org/site/index.php/s_informer/discours/nicolas_sarkozy_a_toulon]

2   Aliboni, Roberto, Ahmed Driss, Tobias Schuhmacher and Alfred Tovias, *Putting the Mediterranean Union in Perspective* (Lisbon: Euromesco, 2008); Zorob, Anja, *Projekt 'Mittelmeerunion' – 'neuer Schub' für die EU-Mittelmeerpolitik?* (Hamburg: German Institute for Global and Area Studies, 2008).

3   The Habsburg Empire did control parts of the Adriatic Sea until the early twentieth century, yet to describe it as a power with a Mediterranean orientation would probably not be accurate. Another key actor in the politics of the region with a decided longing for the Mediterranean was the Russian Empire.

4   Yılmaz, Suhnaz and Ipek K. Yosmaoğlu, 'Fighting the Specters of the Past: Dilemmas of Ottoman Legacy in the Balkans and the Middle East', *Middle East Studies* xliv/5 (2008); Sundhaussen, Holm, 'Was ist Südosteuropa und warum beschäftigen wir uns (nicht) damit?' *Südosteuropa Mitteilungen* v (2002), p. 96; Brown, Carl (ed) *Imperial Legacy: the Ottoman Imprint on the Balkans and the Middle East* (New York: Columbia University Press, 1996), p. 1.

5   Kinglake, Alexander William, *Eothen* (London: 1898, republished in 2004 as e-book by the University of Adelaide), p. 1 [http://ebooks.adelaide.edu.au/k/kinglake/alexander_william/eothen].

6   Troebst, Stefan, 'What's in a historical region? A Teutonic perspective', *European Review of History* x/2 (2003), p. 176.

7   Scheffler, Thomas, '"Fertile Crescent", "Orient", "Middle East": the changing mental maps of southwest Asia', *European Review of History: Revue Européenne d'Histoire* x/2 (2003), p. 255.

8   Fromkin, David, *A Peace to End All Peace. The Fall of the Ottoman Empire and the Creation of the Modern Middle East* (London: Phoenix Press, 2000), p. 32.

9   *Ibid., p.* 16.

10 Patten, S. N., Review: 'The Nearer East. By D. G. Hogarth', *The Annals of the American Academy of Political and Social Science* xxii/115 (1903), p. 359.

11 King, Charles, 'The new Near East', *Survival* xliii/2 (2001), p. 49.

12 Imperial architecture has left many testaments to the dual nature of French colonialism as *mission civilisatrice and* Christian Mission. Before the completion of the Hassan II Mosque, the 1930s Sacré-Coeur Cathedral was Casablanca's most remarkable building. In Tunis, the office of the French Resident-General sits right opposite St Vincent de Paul Cathedral, both situated on the erstwhile 'Avenue de France', now renamed 'Avenue Habib Bourguiba'.

13 Silverstein, Paul, 'France's Mare Nostrum: colonial and post-colonial constructions of the French Mediterranean', *The Journal of North African Studies* vii/4 (2002), p. 4. One colonial writer, René Maunier, established the immediate relationship between colonialism and Mediterranean heritage succinctly: 'We have this many proofs that the Mediterranean has remained even today the Greco-Roman sea, and that the light (*lumière*) of classical civilizations has not been extinguished. It is up to our country to maintain [the light] on Algerian soil: it is up to France to use her force to confirm the grandeur of Rome, as she has perpetuated its wisdom through her genius.' (*Ibid.*, p. 4).

14 *Ibid., p.* 6.

15 Hartog, François and Jacques Revel, 'Historians and the present conjuncture', *Mediterranean Historical Review* xvi/1 (2001), p. 2.

16 Troebst: 'Historical region', p. 185.

17 Sundhaussen, 'Südost Europa', p. 93.

18 *Ibid., p*p. 96-97, 99.

19 Müller, Dietmar, 'Southeastern Europe as a historical meso-region: constructing space in twentieth-century German historiography', *European Review of History: Revue Européenne d'Histoire* x/2 (2003) p. 403.

20 Troebst: *Historical region*; Braudel, Fernand, *The Mediterranean and the Mediterranean World in the Age of Philip II* (London: HarperCollins, 1992).

21 King, Russell, 'Ants and frogs round a pond: interpretations of Mediterranean historical geography', *Journal of Historical Geography* xxvii/4 (2001), p. 590.

22 Horden, Peregrine, 'Mediterranean excuses: historical writing in the Mediterranean since Braudel', *History and Anthropology* xvi/1 (2005), p. 27.

23 Pirenne, Henri, *Mohammed and Charlemagne* (Mineola, New York: Courier Dover Publications: 2001).

24 Cooke, Miriam, 'Mediterranean thinking: from Netizen to Medizen', *Geographical Review* lxxxix/2 (1999), p. 293. Ibn Khaldun was probably less concerned with the Roman Empire's downfall and more inclined to redeem the loss of the Abbasid Caliphate and the glorious history of *Al-Andalus*.

25 Herzfeld, Michael, 'The horns of the Mediterraneanist dilemma', *American Ethnologist* xi/3 (1984), pp. 446.

26 Horden: 'Mediterranean excuses', p. 26.

27 Herzfeld, 'Practical Mediterraneanism: excuses for everything, from epistemology to eating, in William V. Harris (ed), *Rethinking the Mediterranean* (Oxford: Oxford University Press, 2005), p. 46.

28   Scheffler: 'Fertile Crescent', p. 271.
29   Nocke, Alexandra, 'Ex Occidente Lux?' *Mare. Die Zeitschrift der Meere* lxvii (2008), pp. 52-53; 'Israel and the emergence of Mediterranean identity: expressions of locality in music and literature', *Israel Studies* xi/1 (2006), pp. 143-173.
30   The Israeli version of Mediterraneanism has indeed been labelled as escapist by critics, and for good reason. The concept does not challenge hegemonic notions of modern Zionist identity, nor the fact that Israel 'continues to define itself in terms of a homogenous political and cultural identity'. Kemp, Adriana, David Newman, Uri Ram and Oren Yiftachel (eds), *Israelis in Conflict. Hegemonies, Identities and Challenges* (Brighton: Sussex University Press, 2004), p. viii.
31   A special issue of the journal *Cities*, based on a workshop on 'Cities in the Middle East' held at Ben Gurion University in 2004, criticizes the attempt to 'Mediterraneanize' Israel as a conscious effort to shift the gaze away from the contested relationship with its immediate neighbourhood. Cf. Öktem, Kerem, 'Faces of the city: Poetic, mediagenic and traumatic images of a multi-cultural city in Southeast Turkey', *Cities* xxii/3 (2005), pp. 241-253.
32   The writers around Cevat Şakir Kabaağaçlı and Azra Erhat sought to synthesize modern Turkish and ancient Greek legacies into an Anatolian-Mediterranean identity. This well-meaning yet intellectually unassuming project they propagated during boat trips along the Turkish Mediterranean shores. Christened as *Mavi Yolculuk* (the Blue Voyage), it has survived well into the days of mass tourism as a semi-spiritual voyage into nature.
33   Eksi Sözlük, *Akdenizlilik* [Mediterraneanism] (2004) [http://sozluk.sourtimes.org/show.asp?t=akdenizlilik].
34   Interestingly, liberal and liberal-Muslim elites have recently turned to a neo-Ottomanist identity that selectively celebrates the empire's cultural diversity and its ostensible blending of East and West. Cf. Fisher Onar, Nora, *Echoes of a universalism lost: Rival representations of the Ottomans in contemporary Turkey* [Paper delivered at the conference 'Echoes of Imperialism'] (Oxford: European Studies Centre, May 2008). Yet even neo-Ottomanism is relatively welcoming towards the Balkan legacy of Empire and rather disinterested in the former Turkey in Asia. See also Onar's chapter in this volume.
35   The Turkish Foreign Ministry commissioned the global public relations company, Wunderman, to embellish the country's international image. Its director for Turkey, Atilla Aksoy, suggests that 'Turkey is not a modern Arabia' and hence has to re-branded with a 'Mediterranean identity'. He suggests that this will help to wipe out the negative impact of the 'Orientalist image' Turkey has been associated with undeservedly. 'Artık yeni imajimiz Akdenizlilik. Biz modern bir Arabistan değiliz [Our new image is Mediterraneanism. We are not a modern Arabia'] (*Dünya*: 01/02/2006) [http://www2.dunyagazetesi.com.tr/news_display.asp?upsale_id=249449].
36   Silverstein: 'France's Mare Nostrum', p. 12.
37   Nocke: 'Ex Occidente', p. 53.
38   Goytisolo, Juan, *Cinema Eden: Essays from the Muslim Mediterranean* (London: Eland, 2003).
39   Troebst: 'Historical region', p. 186.
40   Brown: *Imperial legacy*, p. 9.
41   Davies, Norman, *Europe East and West* (London: Pimlico, 2007), p. 14.

42 Pappé, Ilan, *A History of Modern Palestine: One Land, Two Peoples* (Cambridge: Cambridge University Press, 2004), p. 27.

43 Howe, Marvine, *Morocco. The Islamist Awakening and Other Challenges* (Oxford: Oxford University Press, 2005); Perkins, Kenneth, *A History of Modern Tunisia* (Cambridge: Cambridge University Press, 2004).

44 Ageron, Robert Charles, *Modern Algeria: a History from 1830 to the Present* (London: C. Hurst, 1991).

45 Shlaim, Avi, *War and Peace in the Middle East. A Concise History* (London: Penguin Books, 1994), p. 12.

46 Pappé, Ilan, *The Ethnic Cleansing of Palestine* (Oxford: Oneworld Publications, 2006); *Palestine,* p. 19; Kamrava, Mehran, *The Modern Middle East: a Political History since the First World War* (Berkeley, London: University of California Press, 2005).

47 Shehadeh, Raja, *Palestinian Walks. Notes on a Vanishing Landscape* (London: Profile Books, 2007); Benvenisti, Meron, *Sacred Landscape. The Buried History of the Holy Land since 1948* (Berkeley, Los Angeles, London: University of California Press, 2000).

48 Glenny, Misha, *The Balkans 1804 – 1999. Nationalism, War and the Great Powers* (London: Granta Publications, 1999), p. 2.

49 Mazower, Mark, *The Balkans* (London: Phoenix Press, 2000), pp. 71f.

50 *Ibid., p.* 79.

51 Pavlowitch, Stevan, *The role of the monarchy as a legitimising factor in South East Europe (1830–1940)* [Paper delivered at the seminar series 'Conceptualising political leadership in Greece and Southeast Europe'] (Oxford: European Studies Centre, February 2007).

52 Mazower: *The Balkans,* p. 84.

53 Cf. Maria Todorova, *Imagining the Balkans* (Oxford: Oxford University Press, 1997), pp. 3-21, for the discussion of Balkanism vs. Orientalism.

54 Marx, Anthony, *Faith in Nation: Exclusionary Origins of Nationalism* (Oxford: Oxford University Press, 2003); Mann, Michael, *The Dark Dide of Democracy: Explaining Ethnic Cleansing* (Cambridge: Cambridge University Press, 2004).

55 Bloxham, Donald, *The Great Game of Genocide. Imperialism, Nationalism, and the Destruction of Ottoman Armenians* (Oxford: Oxford University Press, 2005); 'Three imperialisms and a Turkish nationalism: international stresses, imperial disintegration and the Armenian genocide', *Patterns of Prejudice* xxxvi/4 (2002), pp. 37-58.

56 Mazower: *The Balkans,* p. 52.

57 Mazower, Mark, *Salonica: City of Ghosts. Christians, Muslims and Jews 1430 – 1950* (London: Harper Collins, 2004), pp. 324 ff.

58 Clark, Bruce, *Twice a Stranger. How Mass Expulsion Gorged Modern Greece and Turkey* (London: Granta Books, 2006); Hirschon, Renée (ed), *Crossing the Aegean: an Appraisal of the 1923 Compulsory Population Exchange between Greece and Turkey* (New York, Oxford: Berghahn, 2003).

59 Davies: *Europe,* p. 216.

60 Page, Melvin, *Colonialism: An International, Social, Cultural, and Political Encyclopedia* (Santa Barbara, Oxford: ABC-CLIO, 2003), p. 567; also Fromkin, *A peace,* pp. 188ff.

61 Zürcher, Erik Jan, *Turkey: A Modern History* (London: I. B. Tauris, 2004), p. 153.

62 Eldem, Edhem, Daniel Goffman and Bruce Alan Masters, *The Ottoman City between East and West: Aleppo, Izmir, and Istanbul* (Cambridge: Cambridge University Press, 1999); Keyder, Çağlar, Eyup Özveren and Donald Quataert, 'Port-Cities in the Ottoman Empire: Some Theoretical and Historical Perspectives', *Review* xvi/4 (1993) [Special issue on 'Port Cities of the eastern Mediterranean, 1800 – 1914'].

63 Mazower, Mark, *Dark Continent. Europe's Twentieth Century* (New York: Vintage Books, 2000), p. 298.

64 Carr, Raymond, *Modern Spain* (Oxford: Oxford University Press, 1980).

65 Rogan, Eugene and Avi Shlaim (eds), *The War for Palestine. Rewriting the History of 1948* (Cambridge: Cambridge University Press, 2001).

66 King, Stephen, *Liberalization against Democracy. The Local Politics of Economic Reform in Tunisia* (Bloomington: Indiana University Press, 2003), p. 139.

67 An increasing number of scholars, criticizing the Braudelian notion of the Black Sea as a 'Turkish Sea' and a mere annex to the Mediterranean, conceptualize the Black Sea world as economically and demographically distinct, yet integrated part of the Mediterranean. Cf. King, Charles, *The Black Sea: a History* (Oxford: Oxford University Press, 2004); Özveren, 'A Framework for the study of the Black Sea world, 1789-1915', *Review* xx (1997), pp. 77-113.

68 Glenny: *The Balkans,* p. 634.

69 Kasbarian, Sossie, *The 'others' within – the Armenians in Cyprus* [Paper delivered at the Oxford Symposium on Trans-Nationalism] (Oxford: European Studies Centre, May 2006).

70 Pattie, Susan, *Longing and Belonging: Issues of Homeland in the Armenian Diaspora* (Oxford: Institute for Social and Cultural Anthropology, Transnational Communities Programme, Working Paper Series, 1999).

71 Shohat, Ella, 'Notes on the "post-colonial"', *Social Text* xxxi/32 (1992), pp. 99-113; 'Sephardim in Israel: Zionism from the Standpoint of Its Jewish Victims', *Social Text* xix/20 (1988), p. 11.

72 Davies: *Europe,* p. 203.

73 Norris, Harry Thirlwall, *Islam in the Balkans. Religion and Society between Europe and the Arab world* (London: C. Hurst, 1993).

74 *Ibid.*, p. 203.

75 *Ibid.*, p. 209.

76 Silverstein: 'France's Mare Nostrum', p. 8.

77 Woodsworth, Nicholas, *The Liquid Continent – A Mediterranean Trilogy (Alexandria, Venice, Istanbul)* (London: Haus Publishing, 2008).

78 Shohat, Ella, 'Rethinking Jews and Muslims: quincentennial reflections', *Middle East Report* clxxviii (1992), pp. 25-29.

79 Horden: 'Mediterranean excuses', p. 29.

80 De Rato, Rodrigo, 'Economic integration in the Maghreb: the path to prosperity', *International Monetary Fund News* [http://www.imf.org/external/np/vc/2005/061505.htm] (2005).

81 Silverstein: 'France's Mare Nostrum', p. 11.

Chapter II

1   Located between Bir Romane and the southern extremity on the level of Garat El Hamel, better known by the name of border 233, located some 15 kilometres from Ghadamès.

2   Bono, Salvatore, 'Le controversie di frontiera dell'Algeria con il Marocco e con la Tunisia (1950-1970)', *Oriente Moderno*, 10-11(October–November 1970), pp. 602–634.

3   Laroui, Abdallah, *Les origines sociales et culturelles du nationalisme marocain (1830-1912)* (Paris: François Maspero, 1977), p. 11.

4   This is a general crisis experienced in many parts of the world, not just the Maghreb. Cf. Badie, Bertrand, *La fin des territoires. Essai sur le désordre international et sur l'utilité du respect social, l'espace du politique.* (Paris : Fayard, 1995).

5   Baduel, P. Robert, 'La production de l'espace national au Maghreb' in Baduel (ed), *Lieux d'autonomie et centralisation étatique. Etat, territoire et terroirs au Maghreb* (Paris: CNRS, 1985).

6   Badie, Bertrand, *L'Etat importé. L'occidentalization de l'ordre politique* (Paris: Fayard, 1992).

7   Badie, Bertrand, 'Les territoires de l'appartenance', *Qantara, Magazine des cultures arabes et méditerranéennes, monde arabe et musulman* No. 17 (October–December 1995).

8   Nordman, Daniel, 'Problématique historique: des frontières de l'Europe aux frontières du Maghreb (XIXe siècle)' in *Profils du Maghreb. Frontières, figures et territoires (XVIIIe-XXe siècles)* (Rabat: Mohammed V University, 1996).

9   Originally Berber, the Almohad Dynasty (from the Arabic *al-Muwahhidun* meaning monotheists) ruled over large territories in Spain and North Africa from 1121 to 1269.

10 The dynasties in question were: (a) The Hafsids of Tunis. Their territory, known as *Ifriqiya* or *al-Maghreb al-Adna* (the Near Maghreb), spanned from Bougie/Béjaïa (Algeria) in the West to Tripoli (Libya) in the East. (b) The Zayyanid Principality, named *al Maghreb al-Awsat* (the Middle Maghreb), had Tlemcen as a political centre and extended its power until Oran (both in present-day Algeria). (c) The Merinids in Fes, who reigned over an area between the Atlantic and the Zayyanid known as *al-Maghreb al-Aqsa* (the Far Maghreb).

11 According to Ibn Khaldun, as with individuals, states go through a lifecycle which starts with birth followed by childhood and youth, corresponding to the zenith of the state, before entering a period of maturity that ends with old age, corresponding to the decline and fall of power.

12 On the meanings of this vocabulary, see Brauer, Ralph. W., *Boundaries and Frontiers in Medieval Muslim Geography* (Philadelphia: American Philosophical Society, 1995).

13 The Greek word 'zone' means literally 'belt'.

14 Baduel, *op.cit.*

15 Certain dynasties succeeded in accomplishing that goal but their achievement was ephemeral. This was the case with the Merinids, who managed to impose their authority on the entire region twice in the fourteenth century. Similarly, the Hafsids extended their conquests all the way to the Kingdom of Tlemcen. On the attempts to unify the Maghreb, see Laroui, Abdallah, *L'histoire du Maghreb, essai de synthèse* (Paris: Maspero, 1975).

16 Leo Africanus, who crossed the Maghreb from the West to the East around 1516–1517, witnessed the anarchy which raged in the interior parts of the region as well as the uncertainty of its political attachments. See Al-Wazzen Al-Fasi (Leo Africanus), *Wasf Ifriqiya* ('Description of Africa') (Rabat, 1982).

17 Braudel, 'Les espagnols et l'Afrique du Nord de 1492 à 1577', *Revue Africaine* (Alger, 1928).

18 Turner, Frederick Jackson, *The Frontier in American History* (New York: Henry Holt, 1920).

19 See Monchicourt, Charles, *Etudes Kairouanaises. Kairouan et les Chabbia (1450-1592)* (Tunis, 1939).

20 Al-Ifrani, Mohammed Saghir, *Nuzhat Al Hadi fi Akhbar Muluk Al Karn Al Hadi* (Rabat, 1988).

21 Garcia-Arenal, Mercedes, 'Mahdisme et dynastie saadienne', in Abdelmajid Kaddouri (ed), *Mahdisme: crises et changement dans l'histoire du Maroc* (Rabat: Mohammed V University, 1994). pp. 95–117.

22 The document is kept at the National Library of Tunisia, Register 3397.

23 Henia, Abdelhamid, *Propriété et stratégies sociales à Tunis (XVIè-XIXe siècles)* (Tunis: Faculty of Human and Social Sciences, 1999), p. 57.

24 The correspondence is published in Temimi, Abdeljalil, 'Formation administrative et géopolitique des provinces ottomanes du Maghreb (1554-1588)', *Arab Historical Review for the Ottoman Studies* xi-xii (2000).

25 Laroui: *Les origines sociales.*

26 *Ibid.*

27 The Alaouite armies took Maamoura from Spain in 1681, Tanger from the British in 1684, Larache from Spain in 1689, and Arzila from Portugal in 1691. They unsuccessfully besieged Ceuta, too.

28 Al-Ifrani: *Nuzhat Al Hadi*, p. 305.

29 The Alaouite sultan addressed the Ottoman governor of Algiers in the following way : 'I commit before God to do everything in my powers in order not to attack your country or its subjects; I give you my word in the name of God and his prophet not to cross the Tafna *wadi* in your direction, unless to satisfy God and his prophet.' See Berahab, Okacha, 'La notion de frontière dans les documents marocains depuis la conquête d'Alger jusqu'en 1912', in Siraj, Ahmed and Okacha Berahab, *Les espaces frontaliers dans l'histoire du Maroc* (Rabat: Mohammed V University, 1999).

30 Burgat, François and Laronde, André, *La Libye, Que sais-je* (Paris: PUF, 1996), pp. 39–40.

31 Hess, Andrew, *The Forgotten Frontier: A History of the Sixteenth-century Ibero-African Frontier* (Chicago: University of Chicago Press, 1978).

32 See the map of the Moroccan Empire as conceived by Moroccan intellectuals in Laroui: *Les origins sociales*, p. 63.

33 Temimi, Abdeljalil, *Recherches et documents d'histoire maghrébine: L'Algérie, la Tunisie et la Tripolitaine (1816-1871)* (Tunis, 1971).

34 In a book published in 1976 dealing with Moroccan borders, the author writes 'Morocco will not retrieve its original image without a return to the Motherland of its stolen territories in the north and the south.' See Maazouzi, Mohammed, *L'Algérie et les étapes successives de l'amputation du territoire marocain* (Casablanca: Dar Al-Kitab, 1976), p. 101.

35 This was achieved with strategic and economic vehicles such as the construction of a trans-Algerian (or trans-Saharan) railway. See Nordman 'L'armée d'Algérie et le Maroc: le dynamisme de la conquête (fin du XIXe siècle- début du XXe siècle)', in *Profil du Maghreb, op.cit.,* pp. 41–56.

36 Zaïm, Fouad, 'Le Maroc Méditerranéen au XIXe siècle ou la frontière intérieure', in *Le monde musulman à l'épreuve de la frontière, op.cit.,* pp. 61–90; Temimi, *Recherches et documents d'histoire maghrébine: L'Algérie, la Tunisie et la Tripolitaine (1816-1871)* (Tunis, 1971). See also the chapter by Henk Driessen in this volume.

Chapter III

1 Terms which did not stick included 'Crescent of Crisis', 'Arc of Instability', and 'Islamic Revolution'; see Bulliet, Richard W., *The Case for Islamo-Christian Civilization* (New York: Columbia University Press, 2004).

2 Adem, Seifudein, 'Constructing a new imperial order? The war in Iraq and the ideology of clashism', *Alternatives* ii/2. (2003).

3 This is Adem's felicitous phrase. He uses it alongside 'endism', in reference to Francis Fukuyama's rival 'End of History' thesis.

4 Said, Edward, *Culture and Imperialism* (Vintage, New York, 1993), p. xiii

5 Kaya, Ibrahim, *Social Theory and Later Modernities: The Turkish Experience* (Liverpool: Liverpool University Press, 2004).

6 Gaonkar, Dilip Parameshwar, *Alternative Modernities* (Durham: Duke University Press, 2001).

7 'Beyond hegemony?-"Europe" and the politics of non-Western elites, 1900-1930', *Journal of Modern European History* iv/2 (2006).

8 Gaonkar: *Alternative modernities.*

9 Cf. Hurd, Elizabeth Shakman, 'Appropriating Islam: the Islamic Other in the consolidation of Western modernity', *Critique, Critical Middle Eastern Studies* xii/1 (2003), pp. 24–41.

10 Pitts, Jennifer, *A Turn to Empire: the Rise of Imperial Liberalism in Britain and France* (Princeton, Princeton University Press: 2005).

11 Said, Edward, *Orientalism* (New York, Vintage: 1979), pp. 1-3, 95.

12 Scheffler, Thomas, '"Fertile Crescent", "Orient", "Middle East": the changing mental maps of southwest Asia', *European Review of History* x/2. (2003), pp. 261-6.

13 On regional labels, see Kerem Öktem's contribution to this volume.

14 Seminal figures of this era of 'Muslim Enlightenment' have been co-opted by different camps. The ideas of Jamal Al-Din Al-Afghani, for example, inspired Islamic modernists and fundamentalists alike, although Elie Kedourie maintains that both Al-Afghani and his disciple Muhammad Abduh were actually sceptics regarding religion, who saw in Islam the potential for a powerful mobilising political ideology with which to resist the West. *Afghani and 'Abduh, An Essay on Religious Unbelief and Political Activism in Modern Islam* (London, Frank Cass: 1966).

15 Erdem, Hakan, '"Do not think of the Greeks as agricultural labourers": Ottoman responses to the Greek War of Independence', in Faruk Birtek and Thalia Dragonas (eds), *Citizenship and the Nation-State in Greece and Turkey* (New York: Routledge, 2005), p. 81.

204 MEDITERRANEAN FRONTIERS

16 Karpat, Kemal H., 'Historical continuity and identity change or how to be modern Muslim, Ottoman, and Turk', in Kemal H. Karpat (ed), *Ottoman Past and Today's Turkey* (Leiden: Brill, 2000). p. 3.

17 The question is posed by Erik Jan Zürcher in *Turkey: a Modern History* (London: I.B. Tauris, 1994), p. 132.

18 Karpat: 'Historical continuity', p. 4.

19 *Ibid.*, p. 5

20 Zürcher: *Turkey*, p. 59.

21 Karpat: 'Historical continuity', p. 3.

22 The chapter uses the Ottoman-Turkish versions of particular terms rather than the Arabic or Persian originals. Hence *şeriat* instead of *sharia*.

23 Karpat, 'Historical continuity', p. 4.

24 Şentürk, Recep, 'Sociology of rights: "I am therefore I have rights": human rights in Islam between universalistic and communalistic perspectives', *Muslim World Journal of Human Rights* ii/1 (2005).

25 Chambers, Richard L., 'The education of a nineteenth-century Ottoman alim, Ahmed Cevdet Pasha', *International Journal of Middle East Studies*, iv/4 (1973), p. 463.

26 Berktay, Fatmagül, *Tarihin Cinsiyeti* (Istanbul: Metis, 2003), p. 98.

27 Enginün, Inci, 'Turkish literature and self-identity', in Karpat (ed): *Ottoman Past*, p. 214.

28 *Ibid., p.* 216.

29 Karpat: 'Historical continuity', p. 2.

30 Zürcher: *Turkey*, p. 71.

31 Mardin, Şerif, *Jön Türklerin Siyasi Fikirleri 1895-1908* (Istanbul: İletişim, 1989), pp. 81-106.

32 On the institution of *bay'a* in the Maghreb, see Fatma Ben Slimane's chapter in this volume.

33 Zürcher: *Turkey*, pp. 71-2.

34 *Ibid.,* p. 73.

35 Keyder, Çağlar, *Memâlik-i Osmaniye'den Avrupa Birliği'ne* (Istanbul: İletişim, 2004), p. 24.

36 Shaw, Stanford, and Shaw, Ezel, *History of the Ottoman Empire and Modern Turkey: Volume II: Reform Revolution and Republic: the Rise of Modern Turkey, 1808-1975* (Cambridge: Cambridge University Press, 1997), p. 213.

37 Karpat: 'Historical continuity', p. 17.

38 Sayyid observes that Atatürk's abolition of the caliphate actually fed Islamism even more than its evocation of an institution had done in Abdulhamid's time, because 'the master signifier of Islam was no longer fixed to a particular institutional arrangement', making it available for appropriation by political movements across a fragmented Muslim *ümmet* (*umma*). See Sayyid, Bobby, *A Fundamental Fear: Eurocentrism and the Emergence of Islamism* (London: Zed Books, 1997), p. 63.

39 Mardin: *Jön türklerin*, p. 213 and p. 218.

40 Zürcher: *Turkey*, p. 92.

41 Europeans, who traditionally named states for their dominant ethnic group, had called the Ottomans 'Turks' since as early as 1396; the Ottomans themselves,

whilst preserving a range of Turkish customs, let the term fall out of use, given the heterogeneity of their subjects. See Karpat, pp. 20-1.

42 Zürcher believes that contemporary authors overestimate the impact of Akçura's *Üç Tarz-ı Siyaset* on his contemporaries. The piece is referred to as having set forth the basic principles of pan-Turkism (e.g. patriarchy, linguistic and cultural rather than territorial attachments, extreme religious tolerance, powerful leadership circumscribed by law and custom). See Zürcher, 'Young Turks, Ottoman Muslims and Turkish nationalists: identity politics 1908-1938', in Karpat (ed): *Ottoman Past,* p. 153; Findley, Carter Vaughn, 'Continuity, innovation, synthesis, and the state', in Karpat (ed): *Ottoman Past,* p. 29.

43 Zürcher: *Turkey*, p. 13.
44 Karpat: 'Historical continuity', p. 24-5.
45 Zürcher: *Turkey*, p. 134.
46 Karpat: 'Historical continuity', p. 23.
47 Kushner, David, *The Rise of Turkish Nationalism 1876-1908* (London: Frank Cass, 1977), pp. 88-9.
48 Gökalp cited in Davison, Andrew, 'Ziya Gökalp and Provincializing Europe', *Comparative Studies of South Asia, Africa and the Middle East* xxvi/3, 2006. p. 384
49 Çelebi, Nilgün, 'Sociological organizations in Turkey: continuity behind discontinuity', *International Sociology* xvii (2002), p. 256.
50 *Ibid.,* p. 255.
51 Hanioğlu, Şükrü, *The Young Turks in Opposition* (Oxford: Oxford University Press, 1995), pp. 203-12.
52 Turner, Bryan S., *Weber and Islam* (London: Routledge, 1974), p. 167.
53 It has been quipped that 'atheist Jews' and 'atheist Christians' disbelieve in different Gods: the same could be said of 'atheist' or non-practising Muslims.
54 Elias, Norbert, *The Civilizing Process* (Oxford: Blackwell, 1994), p. 3.
55 Cited in Davison: 'Ziya Gökalp', p. 383.

Chapter IV

1 Todorova, Maria, 'The Ottoman legacy in the Balkans', in Carl L. Brown (ed), *Imperial Legacy in the Balkans and the Middle East* (New York: Columbia University Press, 1995), pp. 45–77. See also the rest of the essays included in Brown's volume.
2 See the chapter by Fatma Ben Slimane in this volume.
3 Ferguson, Niall, *Empire: How Britain Made the Modern World* (London: Penguin, 2003); Ignatieff, Michael, *Empire Lite: Nation-Building in Bosnia, Kosovo and Afghanistan* (London: Penguin, 2003). Ironically, Ignatieff's great-grandfather Count Nicholas Ignatieff, Russia's Ambassador to the Sublime Porte, was a signatory to the Treaty of San Stefano (1878) which was a key step in the decline of the Ottoman imperial power in the Balkans.
4 Zielonka, Jan, *Europe as Empire: the Nature of the Enlarged European Union* (Oxford and New York: Oxford University Press, 2006).
5 Motyl, Alexander, *Imperial Ends: the Decay, Collapse, and Renewal of Empires* (New York: Columbia University Press, 2001), pp. 4-5. See also Motyl's critical discussion of the concept of empire in history, political science and the academic discipline of International Relations. For an overview of definitions and ap-

proaches, see Doyle, Michael, *Empires* (Ithaca NY: Cornell University Press, 1986), pp. 19–51.

6   Further on colonial empires, including a comparison with their land-based predecessors, see Darwin, John, *After Tamerlane: the Global History of Empire* (London: Penguin, 2007).

7   There are those who take issue with this distinction. Sebe, Berny, *Celebrating British and French Imperialism: The Making of Colonial Heroes Acting in Africa, 1870-1939,* Unpublished D.Phil thesis, University of Oxford (2007).

8   Iorga, Nicolae, *Byzance après Byzance: continuation de l'histoire de la vie byzantine* (Bucharest: Institut d'Etudes Byzantines, 1971 [1935]).

9   Yurdusev, Nuri (ed), *Ottoman Diplomacy: Conventional or Unconventional* (Basingstoke: Palgrave Macmillan, 2004).

10   Cf. Ben Slimane: *op. cit.*

11   For a discussion of the vicissitudes of nationalising policies in imperial contexts (focusing on Russia, the Ottoman Empire and the Wilhelmine Reich), see Miller, Alexei and Rieber, Alfred J. (eds), *Imperial Rule* (Budapest: Central European University Press, 2004).

12   Spruyt, Hendrik, *The Sovereign State and Its Competitors: an Analysis of Systems Change* (Princeton: Princeton University Press, 1994).

13   Gellner, Ernest, *Nations and Nationalism* (Ithaca NY: Cornell University Press, 1983).

14   See the chapter by Nora Fisher Onar in this volume.

15   See the chapter by Kerem Öktem in this volume.

16   Hobsbawm, Eric, *Age of Empire: 1875-1914* (Vintage Books, 1989).

17   Renan, Ernest, *Qu'est-ce qu'une nation?* (Paris: Presses Pocket, 1992 [1882]).

18   For Smith's conception of national mythology, see *Myths and Memories of the Nation* (Oxford and New York: Oxford University Press, 2000).

19   McNeill, William, 'Mythistory, or Truth, Myth, History, and Historians', *The American Historical Review* xci/1 (1986), p. 6.

20   Schwandner-Sievers, Stephanie, 'Introduction: Capacities of Myth in Albania', in Stephanie Schwandner-Sievers and Bernd Fischer (eds), *Albanian Identities: Myth and History* (London: C. Hurst, 2002); Boia, Lucian, *History and Myth in the Romanian Consciousness* (Budapest: Central European University Press, 2001).

21   The section's title mirrors the title of Jack Snyder's oft-quoted monograph which otherwise has a rather different analytical focus and, unlike this chapter, conceptualizes myth as delusion or untruth. See *Myths of Empire: Domestic Politics and International Ambition* (Ithaca: Cornell University Press, 1991).

22   On the taxonomy of myths see Schöpflin, George, 'The Functions of Myth and Taxonomy of Myths' in Geoffrey A. Hosking and George Schöpflin (eds), *Myths and Nationhood* (London: C. Hurst, 1997), pp. 19–36. Also Smith, *Myths and Memories.*

23   Hroch, Miroslav, *Social Preconditions of National Revival in Europe* (Cambridge: Cambridge University Press, 1985).

24   See the essays in Stephen Graubard (ed), *Eastern Europe … Central Europe … Europe* (Boulder CO: Westview Press, 1993), particularly the contributions by Tony Judt and Timothy Garton Ash. Also Todorova, Maria, *Imagining the Balkans* (New York and Oxford: Oxford University Press, 1997), Chapter 6, pp. 140–161.

25 Koliopoulos, John and Veremis, Thanos, *Greece: the Modern Sequel. From 1831 to the Present* (London: C. Hurst, 2002), Part V: Ideology, pp. 227–277. The prominent political scientist Nikiforos Diamandouros relates the Romaic conception of Greek identity to the so-called 'underdog mentality' which underlies the suspicion of the West felt by parts of the society. Conversely, the Hellenic myth is linked to the pro-European, reformist strands. Of course, this distinction – which reflects essentialist understandings of identity and binary oppositions between progress and backwardness – is open to historical questioning.

26 See the chapter by Bojan Baskar in this volume.

27 Kramer, Martin, 'Arab Nationalism: The Mistaken Identity', *Daedalus* cxxii/3 (1993), p. 173.

28 This was a cornerstone of the Phalange Party established in the 1930s.

29 This was a particularly salient feature of 1930s Kemalist historiography, which coined the so-called 'history thesis' and the 'sun-language theory' in an attempt to establish that the Turks were amongst the most ancient people in the world and their language was the origin of all modern idioms, thus reclaiming their place at the top of the hierarchy of contemporary nations. See Çetin, Zafer M., 'Tales of past, present, and future: Mythmaking and nationalist discourse in Turkish politics', *Journal of Muslim Minority Affairs* xxiv/2 (2004), pp. 347–365. See also the chapter by Nora Onar in the present volume.

30 Ben-Yehuda, Nachman, *The Masada Myth. Collective Memory and Mythmaking in Israel* (Madison: The University of Wisconsin Press, 1995).

31 On the shifting meanings and usages of the *antemurale* myth in Croatia, see Žanić, Ivo, 'The symbolic identity of Croatia in the triangle crossroads – bulwark – bridge', in Pal Kolsto (ed), *Myths and Boundaries in South-Eastern Europe* (London: C. Hurst, 2005), pp. 35–76.

32 On *Megali Idea*, see Koliopoulos and Veremis, *op. cit.*, pp. 227–235.

33 On Aflaq and Baathism, see Devlin, John F., 'The Baath Party: rise and metamorphosis', *The American Historical Review* xcvi/5 (1991), pp. 1396–1407.

34 Of course, the pharaonic reference was problematic in Quranic terms, as Pharaoh, Moses' adversary, represents the unjust and despotic ruler. It is not for nothing that President Anwar Sadat's assassin in October 1981 was shouting that he had killed Pharaoh.

35 See Pamuk's autobiographical journeys imbued by the sense of *hüzün* (melancholy) in *Istanbul: Memories of a City* (London: Faber and Faber, 2005).

36 See Marinov, Tchavdar, 'Multiculturalism in the Balkans: is it necessary? The use of the term in the context of the Balkans', in *Identities-Journal for Politics, Gender, and Culture* (Skopje) v/2, pp. 35–62.

Chapter V

1 See Bertrand, Romain, *Mémoires d'empire. La controverse autour du 'fait colonial'* (Paris: Editions du Croquant, 2006).

2 Joffrin, Laurent, 'Tourner la page' (editorial) and Semo, Marc, 'La repentance vue par les historiens', *Libération*, 5 December 2007.

3 Speech by Jacques Chirac before the Algerian parliament, 3 March 2003.

4 Two opinion polls were carried out by the CSA Institute over a nationally representative sample, the first in October 2003, and the second in October

2004. In the first, 55 per cent of those surveyed responded negatively (37 per cent affirmative) to the question 'Should France ask for an official pardon from Algeria for its 130 years of colonization?' In the second poll, 50 per cent responded negatively and 45 per cent positively to the question 'Does France have to present an official apology to the Algerian people for its behaviour during the Algerian War?' However, in another CSA survey dated March 2002, 50 per cent responded positively to the question 'Following the revelations over the last two years about the acts of violence committed during the Algerian war, do you think that the demands made of the French authorities for an official condemnation of the then government are justified?'. 45 per cent disagreed.

5   Following the widespread riots of October 1988, which were suppressed in a heavy-handed way, Algeria witnessed a period of political liberalization starting from 1989. This heralded a transition to a multi-party system and the appearance of a free press. However, in January 1992, faced with the electoral success of the Islamic Salvation Front (FIS), the military in control of the government decided to annul the two rounds of legislative elections which were on the verge of giving the power to the Islamists.

6   Stora, Benjamin, 'La mémoire retrouvée de la guerre d'Algérie?', *Le Monde*, 19 March 2002, and '1999-2003, guerre d'Algérie, les accélérations de la mémoire', in *Hommes & Migrations*, No. 1244 ('Français et Algériens' edition), July–August 2003, pp. 83–95.

7   See articles in *Le Monde* by Florence Beaugé and the account of her investigation in Beaugé, Florence, *Algérie, une guerre sans gloire. Histoire d'une enquête* (Paris: Calmann-Lévy, 2005; Algiers: Chihab, 2006).

8   See Dutour, Nassera, 'De la Concorde civile à la Charte pour la Paix et la Réconciliation nationale', as well as Gèze, François and Melah, Salima, 'L'impossible justice pour les victimes des "années de sang"', *Mouvements*, No. 53 (special issue 'Vérité, justice, réconciliation. Les dilemmes de la justice transitionnelle'), April–May 2008.

9   Bey, Maïssa, *Bleu blanc vert* (La Tour d'Aigues: Aube, 2006; Alger: Barzakh, 2006).

10   Rousseau, Christine, 'Maïssa Bey. "Je suis le produit de cette histoire"', *Le Monde des Livres*, 4 April 2008, p. 10 [about her latest novel, *Pierre Sang Papier ou Cendre* (Paris: Ed. de l'Aube, 2008), a poetic fresco dealing with the 132 years of French colonialism].

11   *Un rêve algérien* (2003) follows Henri Alleg, former editor of *Alger républicain*, who was arrested and tortured by the French army in 1957 and who wrote *La Question* on his 'return' to Algeria; *Algéries, mes fantômes* (2004) deals with the *harkis* (Algerian loyalists), Jews and *Pieds-Noirs* who were exiled in the 1960s, but also with Algerian intellectuals. Their recollections from 'the country' do not cease to haunt them. Finally, *Algérie, histoires à ne pas dire* (2007) is a response to the previous film, and traces the memories of the Algerians in Algeria 'to commemorate the Absent who left in 1962, and ask whether this tragic end meant that it was impossible to live together'. See the film's website: http://www.algeriehistoiresanepasdire.com

12 Calle-Gruber, Mireille, 'L'amour-dans-la-langue-adverse', in Anny Dayan Rosenman and Lucette Valensi (eds), *La guerre d'Algérie dans la mémoire et l'imaginaire*
   (Saint-Denis: Bouchene, 2004), pp. 247–256.

13 Bonn, Charles, 'Le roman algérien', in Charles Bonn et Xavier Garnier (eds),
   Littérature francophone. Tome 1: Le Roman (Paris: Hatier, 1997), pp. 185–210.

14 Bonn, 'Scénographies coloniales et postcoloniales dans le roman algérien: le
   thème de la guerre comme révélateur d'un fonctionnement littéraire', in Rosenman and Valensi: *La guerre d'Algérie*, p. 263.

15 Hachemaoui, Mohammed, ' Algérie-France: la guerre des mémoires?', *El Watan*, 2 March 2006.

16 Harbi, *FLN. Mirages et réalités* (Paris: Jeune Afrique, 1980); *Une vie debout. Mémoires politiques, tome 1, 1945-1962* (Paris: La Découverte, 2001). Harbi has also co-
   edited a volume with Benjamin Stora: Harbi and Stora (eds), *La Guerre d'Algérie.
   1954-2004, la fin de l'amnésie* (Paris: Robert Laffont, 2004).

17 Manceron, Gilles and Hassan Remaoun, *D'une rive à l'autre, la guerre d'Algérie, de
   la mémoire à l'histoire* (Paris: Syros, 1993). See also CRASC's website: http://www.
   crasc.org/

18 Djerbal, Daho, 'Critique de la subalternité', interviewed by Seloua Luste Boul-
   bina in *Rue Descartes* lviii (2007), p. 89.

19 Lavabre, Marie-Claire, 'Entre histoire et mémoire: à la recherche d'une méthode', in Jean-Clément Martin (ed), *La guerre civile entre histoire et mémoire* (Nantes:
   Ouest Editions, 1994), pp. 45–46.

20 See Lavabre and Chauliac, Marina, 'Identité démocratique et mémoire. Micro-
   sociologie de la transmission intergénérationnelle', in Gesine Schwan, Jerzy
   Holzer, Marie-Claire Lavabre, Birgit Schwelling (eds), *Demokratische politische
   Identität Deutschland, Polen und Frankreich im Vergleich* (Wiesbaden: VS Verlag für
   Sozialwissenschaften, 2006), pp. 317–358.

21 Interviews conducted by Dimitri Nicolaïdis with some 12 respondents. Language constraints meant that it was not possible to interview non-French speak-
   ers, or at least people unable to understand q uestions in French and then answer in Algerian Arabic, for translation by family members. This has obviously
   narrowed the sample to a group where the knowledge of French is still a socio-
   cultural marker of distinction. The social profile is diversified but, undoubtedly,
   the upper and middle class is overrepresented. See following note.

22 Of the 12 interviews, seven are systematically cited in the chapter. Aicha M.
   (b. 1929) is from a modest background (daughter and wife of a *fellah*). She has
   nine children, born between 1950 and 1973, including Kheira D., a high school
   instructor in geography and history, who acted together with one of her sisters
   as an interpreter. Baya YD. (b. 1924) is the cousin of Youssef B. (b. 1934). They
   hail from a notable family (landowners, city businessmen), stress their Turkish,
   Iraqi and Tunisian origins, and were educated at a French school catering for
   the *indigènes*. Youssef later became a teacher. Mohammed B. (b. 1928) is the son
   of a member of the French Army and later a city councillor in Miliana. He has
   worked as a public works official and later in the insurance sector. His daughters, Karima B. (b. 1970) and Hamida B. (b. 1972) grew up in Algiers (during
   the 'the golden age' of the 1970s), before moving to Miliana in 1981, which
   they experienced as an exile. Mohammed A. (b. 1986), whose parents work in

the local hospital, studies English (a subject he did not choose) in the University of Blida.

23　See Stora, *La gangrène et l'oubli. La mémoire de la guerre d'Algérie* (Paris: La Découverte, 1991), pp. 119–184.

24　*Ibid.*

25　The Organization of the Secret Army, which used armed struggle in an attempt to prevent Algeria's independence.

26　A racist term used towards North African Arabs.

27　Lavabre, 'Identité démocratique et mémoire'.

28　Ramdane was a revolutionary leader in the Kabylie region, killed on the orders of the FLN in December 1957.

29　This hypothesis is founded on common knowledge about the socio-economic conditions of Algerian youth.

30　See Revel, Jacques (ed), *Jeux d'échelles. La micro-analyze à l'expérience* (Paris: Gallimard et Le Seuil, 1996).

31　Bloch, Marc, 'Mémoire collective: tradition, coutume', *Revue de Synthèse Historique* xl (1925), p. 79.

32　Bastide, Roger, 'Mémoire collective et sociologie du bricolage', *L'Année sociologique* xxi (1970).

Chapter VI

1　In Dalmatia, Italians were a particularly tiny minority. In 1846, the prominent Dalmatian archaeologist Francesco Carrara held that 340,000 Slavs (or Morlachs) and 16,000 Italians lived in the region. See Carrara, Francesco, *La Dalmazia descritta* (Zadar: Fratelli Battana, 1846). Quoted in Kitzmüller, Hans, *Arcipelago del vento* (Trieste: Lint, 2003), p. 46–47.

2　Doumanis, Nicholas, *Italy* (London: Arnold, 2001), p. 92.

3　One exception is the historian Gabriella Gribaudi, who has pointed out that both national unifications were underpinned by the same set of assumptions about the integrative effects of interaction. She has observed that the conflict between North and South in Italy developed in a similar manner to that in eastern Europe. See Gribaudi, Gabriella, 'Images of the South: The Mezzogiorno as seen by Insiders and Outsiders', in Robert Lumley and Jonathan Morris (eds), *The New History of the Italian South: the Mezzogiorno Revisited* (Exeter: University of Exeter Press), pp. 82–123.

4　Vivante, Angelo, *Irredentismo adriatico: Contributo alla discussione sui rapporti austro-italiani* (Genoa: Graphos, 1997), p. 85. Original edition: 1912.

5　Benussi, Bernardo, *Manuale di geografia dell'Istria* (Trieste: Stabilimento artistico tipografico G. Caprin, 1877); Combi, Carlo, *Istria: Studii storici e politici.* (Milan: Tipografia Bernardoni di C. Rebeschini, 1886).

6　An in-depth account of the conference in Macmillan, Margaret, *Peacemakers. Six Months that Changed the World* (London: John Murray, 2003).

7　Bitelli, Remo, *Claustra Alpium Juliarum, il confine di Rapallo e fascismo: Archeologia come esempio di continuità* (Koper: Znanstveno raziskovalno središče Republike Slovenije, 1999).

8　'Il discorso di Mussolini al 'Ciscutti' entusiasma al delirio l'imponentissima folla', *L'Azione*, 22 September 1920.

9   Burgwyn, H. James, *Empire on the Adriatic: Mussolini's Conquest of Yugoslavia, 1941-1943* (New York: Enigma Books, 2005), p. 10–11.

10   Burgwyn, *op. cit.*, p. 196. See also Rodogno, Davide, 'Italian soldiers in the Balkans: the experience of the occupation (1941-1943), *Journal of Southern Europe and the Balkans* vi/2 (2004), pp. 125–144.

11   Ferenc, Tone (ed), *Promemoria del comandante della Divisione "Granatieri di Sardegna" e dell'XI Corpo d'Armata. Memoria per l'Eccellenza il Commandante della 2° armata. Situazione nella Provincia di Lubiana – Possibilità e modalità di una rapida pacificazione. La provincia "italiana" di Lubiana. Documenti 1941- 1942* (Udine: Istituto friulano per la storia del movimento di liberazione, 1994).

12   The quotations are collected from Pedace Naso, Magda, 'La questione adriatica nella pubblicistica fra le due guerre. L'imperialismo italiano e la Jugoslavia', in Massimo Pacetti (ed), *Atti del convegno italo-jugoslavo. Ancona 14-16 ottobre 1977* (Urbino: Argalia Editore, 1981); Sluga, Glenda, 'Identità nazionale italiana e fascismo: alieni, allogeni e assimilazione sul confine nord-orientale italiano', in Marina Cattaruzza (ed), *Nazionalismi di frontiera: Identità contrapposte sull'Adriatico nord-orientale*, 1850-1950 (Palermo: Rubettino, 2003), pp. 171–202; Gobetti, Eric, *L'occupazione allegra: Gli italiani in Jugoslavia, 1941-1943.* (Rome: Carocci editore, 2007), p. 180; Burgwyn, *op. cit.*; Sirovich, Livio Isaak, *Cime irredente: Un tempestoso caso storico alpinistico* (Turin: Vivalda editori, 1996).

13   See, Todorova, Maria, *Imagining the Balkans* (Oxford: Oxford University Press, 1997), p. 116.

14   *Ibid.*, p. 116. This view is also questioned in Baskar, Bojan, 'Imagining the Balkans in Trieste', *Caietele Echinox / Cahiers de l'Echinox. Les imaginaires européens* x (2006), pp. 190–199. For a somewhat different perspective on the Italian variety of Balkanism, see Patterson, Patrick Hyder, 'On the edge of reason: the boundaries of Balkanism in Slovenian, Austrian, and Italian discourse', *Slavic Review*, lxii/1 (2003), pp. 110–141.

15   Silverman, Sydel, *The Three Bells of Civilization: The Life of an Italian Hilltown* (New York: Columbia University Press, 1975).

16   Quoted in Fuller, Mia, *Moderns Abroad: Architecture, Cities and Italian Imperialism* (London and New York: Routledge, 2007), p. 51.

17   Pitkin, Donald S., 'Mediterranean Europe', *Anthropological Quarterly* xxxvi/3 (1963), p. 122.

18   The context of the *foibe* and exile commemoration is studied in detail in Ballinger, Pamela, *History in Exile: Memory and Identity at the Borders of the Balkans* (Princeton and Oxford: Princeton University Press, 2003); Sluga, 'Italian National Memory, National Identity and Fascism', in J.B. Bosworth and Patrizia Dogliani (eds), *Italian Fascism: History, Memory and Representation* (Basingstoke and New York: Macmillan, 2001), pp. 178–194; Crainz, Guido, *Il dolore e l'esilio: L'Istria e le memorie divise d'Europa* (Rome: Donzelli, 2005).

19   Pupo, Raoul, 'La tragica scelta tra foibe ed esilio', *Il Giornale*, 17 May 2005. www.lefoibe.it/rassegna/raoulpupo.htm (accessed 22 July 2007).

20   Fumich, Sergio, *Il Pozzo e le Parole* (Brembio: La Gattera, 2005), p. 54.

21   Senato della repubblica. XIII legislatura. Giovedi 25 novembre 1999. Resoconto sommario e stenografico. 719a seduta pubblica. www.cittadinolex.kataweb.it/article_view.jsp?idArt=16821&idCat=227 – 127k – (accessed 16 July 2007)

22 *Discorso presidente.* http://www.quirinale.it/Discorsi/Discorso.asp?id=32144 (accessed 23 February 2007)

23 *Delo*, 15 February 2007.

24 Cited in Candreva, Gino, *La verità nel pozzo, ovvero come si costruisce il senso comune fascista.* http://www.cnj.it/documentazione/cuorenelpozzo_candreva.pdf (accessed 13 July 2007) A few years before the screening of *Cuore in pozzo*, the historian Guido Crainz, writing about the RAI documentary production, underlined 'the general character which television programmes have now assumed in a syncretic world in which the borders between fact and fiction, documentary and special investigation, "recreation" and "television special", have become more and more blurred, with the fictional element growing all the time. In this world, history is reduced to a mere pretext, and its 'public use' has reached the lowest level imaginable.' Crainz, 'The Representation of Fascism and the Resistance in the Documentaries of Italian State Television', in Bosworth and Dogliani (eds): *Italian fascism*, pp. 124–140.

25 One may speculate on whether the elevation of this incident to e level of a Holocaust has something to do with the fact that the perpetrators (local Friulian or Italian Partisans) of this massacre, which took place near a village close to the Italian-Slovene border, were obeying orders of Slovene partisans.

26 See for example Goldstein, Ivo, *Croatia: a History* (London: C. Hurst, 2001), p. 156. A recent contribution to the discussion, Pavlowitch, Stevan, *Hitler's New Disorder: the Second World War in Yugoslavia* (London: C. Hurst, 2008).

27 Bleiburg is also being shamelessly referred to as the 'Croat Holocaust'. On (ab)uses of the Holocaust metaphor in former Yugoslav lands, see MacDonald, D.B., *Balkan Holocausts? Serbian and Croatian Victim Centered Propaganda and the War in Yugoslavia* (Manchester: Manchester University Press, 2003); Živković, Marko, 'The wish to be a Jew: the power of the Jewish trope in the Yugoslav conflict', *Cahiers de l'Urmis* vi (2000), pp. 1–16. http://urmis.revues.org/document323.html (accessed 24 January 2008).

28 For a succinct discussion of this topic, see Luzzatto, Sergio, *La crisi del antifascismo* (Turin: Einaudi, 2004); Bosworth and Dogliani, 'Introduction', in Bosworth and Dogliani (eds): *Italian fascism*, pp. 1–9.

29 For a vivid account of such a punitive regime in the Medjugorje district of eastern Herzegovina, where some of worst *Ustaše* mass atrocities against local Serbs took place in 1941, see Bax, Mart, *Medjugorje: Religion, Politics, and Violence in Rural Bosnia* (Amsterdam: VU Uitgeverij, 1995); Bax, 'The celebration of the violent past: about some local sources of the recent war in Bosnia-Herzegovina', *Narodna umjetnost. Hrvatski časopis za etnologiju i folkloristiku* xxxvii/1 (2000), pp. 115–132.

30 Cunningham, Michael, 'Saying Sorry: The Politics of the Apology', *The Political Quarterly* lxx/3 (1999), pp. 285–93. Quoted in Delanty, Gerard and Chris Rumford, *Rethinking Europe: Social Theory and the Implications of Europeanization* (London and New York: Routledge, 2005), p. 98.

31 Ben-Ghiat, Ruth, 'A lesser evil? Italian fascism in/and the totalitarian equation', in Helmut Dubiel and Gabriel Motzkin (eds), *The Lesser Evil: Moral Approaches to Genocide in a Comparative Perspective* (London and New York: Routledge, 2004), pp. 137–153, p. 145.

32 On the role of film in the forging of memory of Italian fascism, see Ben-Ghiat, 'Liberation: Italian cinema and the fascist past, 1945-50', in Bosworth and Dogliani (eds), pp. 83–101; Bosworth, 'Film memories of fascism', pp. 102–123.

33 See Ben-Ghiat and Mia Fuller, 'Introduction', in Ben-Ghiat and Fuller (eds), *Italian Colonialism* (New York: Palgrave Macmillan, 2005), pp. 1–12.

Chapter VII

1 Cf. Nora, Pierre (ed), *Les Lieux de Mémoire, Vol. 1: La République* (Paris: Gallimard, Bibliothèque illustrée des histoires, 1984).

2 Schraút, Sylvia and Sylvia Paletschek, *The Gender of Memory. Cultures of Remembrance in Nineteenth- and Twentieth-Century Europe* (Chicago: Chicago University Press, 2008), pp. 2–3.

3 See Sangster, Joan, 'Telling our stories: feminist debates and the use of oral history', in Robert Perks and Alistair Thomson (eds), *The Oral History Reader* (London: Routledge, 1998); Leydesdorff, Selma, 'Introduction' in Leydesdorff, Luisa Passerini and Paul Thompson (eds), *Gender and Memory* (New Brunswick, NJ: Transaction Publishers, 2005); for an early classic addressing the absence of women's stories, see Rowbotham, Sheila, *Hidden from History: Three Hundred Years of Women's Oppression and the Fight against It* (London: Pluto Press, 1973).

4 This is of course not a phenomenon limited to the Yugoslav wars. See, for example, Diamond, Hannah, *Women and the Second World War in France 1939–1948: Choices and Constraints* (Harlow: Pearson Education, 1999); Grayzel, Susan R., *Women's Identities at War: Gender, Motherhood, and Politics in Britain and France during the First World War* (Chapel Hill NC: University of North Carolina Press, 1999); Summerfield, Penny, *Reconstructing Women's Wartime Lives. Discourse and Subjectivity in Oral Histories of the Second World War* (Manchester: Manchester University Press, 1998); Thom, Deborah, *Nice Girls and Rude Girls. Women Workers in World War One* (London: I.B. Tauris, 1998).

5 See Misztal, Barbara A., *Theories of Social Remembering* (Philadelphia: Open University Press, 2003), p. 61.

6 Banaszak, Klara et al (eds), *Securing the Peace: Guiding the International Community towards Women's Effective Participation throughout Peace Processes* (United Nations Development Fund for Women, 2005); Rodríguez Losada, Carmen and de la Cruz, Carmen (eds), *Contributions to Peace Building in Colombia (2005): Best Practices From a Gender Perspective* (United Nations Development Fund for Women, 2005); *Peace Needs Women and Women Need Justice: Report of the Conference on Gender Justice in Post-Conflict Situations* (United Nations Development Fund for Women, 2004); Banaszak, Klara et al (eds), *Women, Peace and Security: UNIFEM Supporting Implementation of Security Council Resolution 1325* (United Nations Development Fund for Women, 2004).

7 See Rehn, Elisabeth and Ellen Johnson Sirleaf, *Women, War, Peace: The Independent Experts' Assessment on the Impact of Armed Conflict on Women and Women's Role in Peace-Building* (United Nations Development Fund for Women, 2002).

8 See Misztal: *Social Remembering,* pp. 62–65, for an explication of this Foucauldian term ('must record the singularity of events outside of any monotonous finality').

9 Leydesdorff: 'Introduction', p. 5.

10 For a discussion of the ethical dilemmas of feminist studies of collective memories, see Sangster: 'Telling our stories'.

11 Maurice Halbwachs' work on the social conditions of remembering has shown that even though it is the individual who remembers and not the group, individual remembrances do not exist in emptiness, but are always associated with and interpreted according to collective identities, values and broader frameworks that offer meaning to the past and the present. See also Misztal: *Social Remembering*, p. 52, and Gensburger, Sarah and Marie-Claire Lavabre, 'Entre «devoir de mémoire» et «abus de mémoire» : La sociologie de la mémoire comme tierce position', in Bertrand Müller (ed), *L'histoire entre mémoire et épistémologie, autour de Paul Ricoeur* (Lausanne: Editions Payot Lausanne, 2005), p. 87. Also the chapter by Marie-Claire Lavabre and Dimitri Nicolaidis in this volume.

12 As Misztal argues, Halbwachs failed to address 'how individual consciousnesses might relate to those of the collectivities these individuals actually make up'. His assumption that collective identity precedes memory limits dynamic interpretations of the linkages between individuals and collective memories. Misztal: *Social Remembering*, p. 55.

13 Cf. Pető, Andrea and Bela Rasky, *Construction and Reconstruction. Women, Family and Politics in Central Europe 1945-1998*, CEU, The Program on Gender and Culture, Austrian Science and Research Liaison Office, Budapest, OSI Network Women's Program (1999). http://www.nexus.hu/osi-bp/texte/petorask01.PDF

14 Ricoeur, Paul, *La Mémoire, l'Histoire, l'Oubli* (Paris: Editions du Seuil, 2000), p. 1.

15 *Juste mémoire* in its third meaning is understood as memory work with a goal of 'appeasement' of a society, which aims to mediate and, if possible, reconcile the diversity of memories, to create and shape a memory that cannot be captured by a single constituency. As the English term 'appeasement' is historically charged, unlike the French 'apaisement', I will use 'pacification' instead. Gensburger and Lavabre : *Entre devoir*, p. 76.

16 Simona Sharoni, in her account of 'the politics of women's resistance' in the Israeli-Palestinian conflict, relates that 'it was not uncommon for Jewish women, who emigrated to Palestine in the early 1900s, to connect their struggles for equal rights and equal pay to those of Arab workers.' Sharoni, Simona, *Gender and the Israeli-Palestinian Conflict, The Politics of Women's Resistance* (Syracuse: Syracuse University Press, 1995), p. 133.

17 Sharoni: *Gender,* p. 139

18 See, for example, Levinas, Emmanuel, *Altérité et transcendance* (Paris: Fata Morgana, 1995), p. 113–4:

19 See Cédric Parizot's chapter in this volume.

20 http://www.machsomwatch.org/, accessed on 28 May 2007.

21 Trevisan-Semi, Emanuela, 'La traverse des frontières entre Israel et la Palestine: de la métaphore littéraire au militantisme', *A Contrario* iii/2, p. 106.

22 *Ibid.,* p. 107.

23 Minow, Martha, 'The work of re-membering: after genocide and mass atrocity', *Fordham International Law Journal* xxiii (1999), p. 431.

24 Mertus, Julie, with Olja Hocevar and Van Wely, *Women's Participation in the International Criminal Tribunal for the Former Yugoslavia (ICTY): Transitional Justice for Bosnia and Herzegovina*, Women Waging Peace Policy Commission (July 2004), p.vi.

25 *Ibid.,* p.vii.

26 *Ibid.,* p.vii.

27 For a critique of the ICTY and the insufficient integration of its work at the local level, see Hazan, Pierre, *Justice in a Time of War: The True Story Behind the International Criminal Tribunal for the Former Yugoslavia* (College Station: Texas A & M University Press, 2004).

28 Minow: 'The work of re-membering', p. 438.

29 Mertus et al: *Women's Participation,* p.vii; see also Skjelsbæk, Inger, 'Victim and survivor: narrated social identities of women who experienced rape during the war in Bosnia-Herzegovina', *Feminism and Psychology* xvi/4 (2006), pp. 373–403; Centre for Investigation and Documentation of the Association of Former Prison Camp Inmates of Bosnia-Herzegovina (CID), *I Begged Them to Kill Me: Crimes Against the Women of Bosnia-Herzegovina* (Sarajevo: CID, 2002); Drakulić, Slavenka, 'The rape of women in Bosnia', in Miranda Davies (ed), *Women and Peace* (London: Zed, 1994), pp. 176–181; Stiglmayer, Alexandra (ed), *Mass Rape: The War against Women in Bosnia-Herzegovina* (London: University of Nebraska Press, 1994); Vranić, Seada, *Breaking the Wall of Silence: The Voices of Raped Bosnia* (Zagreb: Anti Barbarus, 1996).

30 This is based on interviews conducted by the author in May 2007.

31 On 1 July 2003, the Serbian National Assembly adopted a law establishing a speciaized War Crimes Chamber to prosecute and investigate crimes against humanity and serious violations of international humanitarian law as defined in Serbian law. The War Crimes Chamber's first trial, the Ovčara case, began on 9 March 2004.

32 Interview with the author.

33 Yuval-Davis, Nira, *Gender and Nation* (London: Sage, 1997), p. 125.

34 *Ibid.,* p. 131.

35 On the importance of emotion in remembering see Minow: *Work of re-membering* pp. 429–439.

36 Women in Black, Belgrade, 2 March 2007.

37 Ulasowski, Nina, *Women's Solidarity in the Anti-war Movement,* Honour's thesis, University of Queensland, Australia, to be accessed under: http://www.gilasvirsky.com/femsolidarity.html

38 *Ibid.,*

39 The term *nakba* was first introduced in 1948 by the historian Constantine Zurayk in his book *Ma'nat an-Nakba* ('The significance of the catastrophe') in order to describe the events of 1948. See also the chapters by Cédric Parizot and Kerem Öktem included in this volume.

40 www.nakbainhebrew.org, accessed on 27 May 2007.

41 Since 1948, the State of Israel has expropriated hundreds of thousands of *dunams* of land belonging to the Palestinian Arabs in Israel. On 30 March 1976, in the wake of increasing land expropriation in the Galilee, part of government plans for 'Judaizing' that area, the Palestinian Arabs in Israel held protest demonstrations. At the peak of these demonstrations, seven demonstrators, including one woman, were shot at and killed. Since that day, Palestinian Arabs in Israel have observed 30 March every year as a day commemorating those killed on Land Day, and marking the struggle for equality and justice, against the continued implementation of a discriminatory program of expropriation.

42 http://www.zeneucrnom.org

43 Helman, Sara and Tamar Rapoport, 'Women in Black: challenging Israel's gen-der and socio-political orders', *British Journal of Sociology* viii/4 (1997), pp. 690–694.

44 This is based on interviews by the author in May 2007 with women from Kos-ovo and Serbia.

45 Enloe, Cynthia, *Bananas, Beaches and Bases: Making Feminist Sense of International Politics* (Berkeley: University of California Press, 1990).

46 Luci, Nita and Vjollca Krasniqi, *Politics of Remembrance and Belonging: Life Histories of Albanian Women in Kosova* (Prishtina: Center for Research and Gender Policy, 2006).

47 This is based on interviews conducted by the author in May 2007.

48 Ulasowski: *Women's solidarity.*

49 Presentation by Luljeta Vuniqi at *Gender, Conflict and Memory in the Mediterranean*, Workshop organized by the European Studies Centre, St Antony's College, Ox-ford in co-operation with the Ramses² Network of Excellence on Mediterra-nean Studies, 13–14 June 2007.

50 *Ibid.* Similarly, nobody followed up on the fate of many women resistance par-ticipants who were taken to Serbian jails. Only women's activism brought to the forefront the fact that women were still being jailed, some only being freed in 2002 thanks to their research and lobbying in the public sphere.

51 Bornat, Joanna, 'Oral history as a social movement: reminiscence and older people', in Perks and Thomson (eds): *Oral History Reader,* p. 199.

52 Misztal: *Social Remembering,* p. 56, referring to Hobsbawm and Ranger's *Invention of Tradition.*

53 Sangster: 'Telling our stories', p. 92.

54 *Ibid.,* p. 88.

55 For a discussion of the benefits of 'reminiscence' work, see Bornat: 'Oral his-tory as a social movement'.

56 Humphries, Isabelle and Laleh Khalili, 'Gender of Nakba memory', in Ahmad H. Sa'di and Lila Abu-Lughod (eds), *Nakba: Palestine, 1948, and the Claims of Memory* (New York: Columbia University Press, 2007), p. 224.

57 Geries, Raneen, *Women's Testimonies of the Nakba, Palestinian Women Recount the Stories of the Nakba in their Villages* (Zochrot, 2006), Third Prize, Badil Film Competition.

58 See Misztal: *Social Remembering,* p. 78.

59 Rugova, Igballe, *Blace Story,* written in June 2002.

60 Rugova, *Keeping Spirits Alive,* written in June 2003.

61 Cited in Ulasowski: *Women's solidarity.*

62 *Ibid.*

63 *Ibid.*

64 Cf. Dean, Jodi, *Solidarity of Strangers: Feminism after Identity Politics* (Berkeley: Uni-versity of California Press, 1996).

65 Cf. Mohanty, Chandra Talpade, *Feminism without Borders: Decolonizing Theory, Prac-ticing Solidarity* (Durham and London: Duke University Press, 2003).

66 'The interplay in transversal politics between 'rooting' and 'shifting' assumes that although knowledge and imagination are situated, there is a possibility of transcending the limitations of the specific 'situatedness' of the subject in the

'shifting'. Such transcendence is assumed possible as a result of a combination of firstly, listening to the situated knowledge and fantasy of the other participants in the dialogue, and secondly, empathetic imaginings in which the subject attempts to position herself in the standpoint of the other participants. However, an active act of imagining is involved already in the act of 'rooting'. (…) The aim of the 'rooting' process (or 'centring', as others prefer to call it) is *not* to imagine oneself just in relation to the social category of the Other but also in other ways through which different kinds of relationships with the partners in the transversal dialogue may be developed. That is probably one of the most important differences between identity politics and transversal politics.' Yuval-Davis, Bristol Lecture, 2004.

67 Glasson Deschaumes, Ghislaine, *Women activists' cross-border actions: a caravan to get beyond the warlike peace in the Yugoslavs,* General Conclusions, 25 May – 10 June 2002, Paris (December 2002), p. 1.

68 Royaumont2 refers to a women's meeting organized by the *Transeuropéennes* journal, five months after the NATO intervention in Kosovo. It brought together at the Fondation Royaumont in France about fifty women activists from the former Yugoslavia and Albania, culminating in a political declaration on building peace with women.

69 Misztal: *Social remembering,* p. 56.

70 Mohanty: *Feminism without Borders*, p. 242–245.

71 *Ibid., p.* 55.

72 Cf. Dean: *Solidarity of strangers.*

73 Ulasowski: *Women's solidarity.*

Chapter VIII

1 The author would like to thank Dimitar Bechev, Magali Gravier, Kalypso Nicolaïdis, and Nathalie Tocci for valuable comments and feedbacks on earlier drafts of this chapter.

2 See for example Jellinek, Georg, *Allgemeine Staatslehre*, third edition (Berlin: Springer, 1929).

3 See Kratochwil, Friedrich V., 'Of systems, boundaries and territoriality: an inquiry into the formation of the state system', *World Politics* xxxix/1 (1986), pp. 21–52; Krasner, Stephen D., *Sovereignty, Organized Hypocrisy* (Princeton, NJ: Princeton University Press, 1999); Hurrell, Andrew, 'Order and justice in international relations: what is at stake?', in Rosemary Foot, John Lewis Gaddis and Andrew Hurrell (eds), *Order and Justice in International Relations* (Oxford: Oxford University Press, 2003), p. 41 ff.; Brown, Chris, *Sovereignty, Rights and Justice* (Cambridge: Polity Press, 2002), p. 212 ff.; Stirk, Peter, 'The Westphalian model, sovereignty and law in *fin-de-siècle* German international theory', *International Relations* xix/2 (2005) pp. 153–172.

4 See for example Smith, Anthony D., *National Identity* (London: Penguin, 1991); Anderson, Benedict, *Imagined Communities: Reflections on the Origins and Spread of Nationalism*, second edition (London: Verso, 1991). Particularly in the Middle East and in Africa, nations and states often do not coincide: the examples of the Kurds, the Druze, or of the Turkish Cypriots are cases in point. See for

example, Lewis, Bernard, *The Multiple Identities of the Middle East* (New York: Schocken, 1998).

5   Newman, David, 'On borders and powers: a theoretical framework', *Journal of Borderland Studies* xviii/1 (2003), p. 139.

6   Although this contribution focuses on borders in the Euro-Mediterranean context, a similar argument could obviously also be made regarding EU policies *vis-à-vis* its *eastern* 'neighbourhood'.

7   See Del Sarto, Raffaella A. and Tobias Schumacher, 'From EMP to ENP: what's at stake with the European Neighbourhood Policy towards the Southern Mediterranean?', *European Foreign Affairs Review* x/1 (2005), pp. 17–38. See also Comelli, Michele, Ettore Greco and Nathalie Tocci, 'From boundary to borderland: transforming the meaning of borders through the European Neighbourhood Policy', *European Foreign Affairs Review* xii/2 (2007), pp. 203-218.

8   See Zielonka, Jan, *Europe as Empire: The Nature of the Enlarged European Union* (Oxford: Oxford University Press, 2006); Gravier, Magali, 'The Next European Empire?', unpublished manuscript (obtained by the author), 2007.

9   This chapter does not deal with the identity function of borders in the Euro-Mediterranean context, although I assume that such an analysis would further sustain the argument on the blurring of boundaries in the Euro-Mediterranean context.

10 For the different typologies of borders, see for example Newman, 'On borders and powers'; Newman, 'Borders and bordering: towards an interdisciplinary dialogue', *European Journal of Social Theory* ix/2 (2006), pp. 171–186; Anderson, Malcolm, *Frontiers, Territories and State Formation in the Modern World* (Cambridge: Polity, 1996); Smith, Michael, 'The European Union and a changing Europe: establishing the boundaries of order', *Journal of Common Market Studies* xxxiv/1 (1996), pp. 5–28; Cassarino, Jean-Pierre, 'Approaching borders and frontiers: notions and implications', Research Report of the Euro-Mediterranean Consortium for Applied Research on International Migration (CARIM), Carim RR-2006/03 (Florence: European University Institute, 2006); Zielonka, Jan, 'How new enlarged borders will reshape the EU', *Journal of Common Market Studies* xxxix/3 (2001), pp. 507–36; Zielonka, Jan 'Introduction', in *idem* (ed), *Europe Unbound: Enlarging and Reshaping the Boundaries of the European Union* (London: Routledge, 2001), pp. 1–16.

11 See Newman, David and Anssi Paasi, 'Fences and neighbours in the postmodern world: boundary narratives in political geography', *Progress in Human Geography* xxii/2 (1998), pp. 187; Newman: 'On borders and power', pp. 13-25; Anderson: *Frontiers*, p. 1.

12 Newman: 'On borders and power', p. 18.

13 Balibar, Etienne, 'Europe as Borderland', The Alexander von Humboldt Lecture in Human Geography, University of Nijmegen, 10 November 2004, at http://www.ru.nl/socgeo/colloquium/Europe%20as%20Borderland.pdf, accessed 11 April 2008.

14 See Hassner, Pierre, 'Fixed borders or moving Borderlands? A new type of border for a new type of entity', in Zielonka (ed): *Europe Unbound*, p. 39.

15 See Newman: 'On borders and power'.

16 See Zielonka: *Europe as Empire*; Gravier: 'The next European empire?'. On fuzzy EU borders, see also Christiansen, Thomas, Fabio Petito, and Ben Tonra,

'Fuzzy politics around fuzzy borders: the European Union's "Near Abroad"', *Cooperation and Conflict* xxxv/4 (2000), pp. 389–415.

17 Hassner: 'Fixed Borders', p. 43.

18 Zielonka: 'Introduction', p. 7.

19 See for example Anderson, Malcolm and Eberhart Bort, *The Frontiers of the European Union* (Basingstoke: Palgrave, 2001); Zielonka: 'How new Enlarged Borders'.

20 The academic literature on borders reflects international developments over the last decades: during much of the 1990s, the literature focused on the gradual disappearance of borders, including in the EU context. Conversely, the focus of attention shifted to the increasing closure of (external) borders in the post-9/11 era. For an excellent overview of the literature, see Newman, 'The lines that continue to separate us: borders in our "borderless" world', *Progress in Human Geography* xxx/2 (2006), pp. 1–19; see also Newman: 'Borders and Bordering'. For a counter-argument regarding the securitization of EU migration politics after 9/11 see Boswell, Christina 'Migration control in Europe after 9/11: explaining the absence of securitization', *Journal of Common Market Studies* xlv/3 (2007), pp. 589–610.

21 Schengen started as an intergovernmental agreement between five EC member states in 1985. The Schengen area currently comprises all EU member states except Britain, Ireland, Cyprus, Romania and Bulgaria, as well as non-EU members Norway and Iceland. For nine of the ten member states that joined the EU in 2004, interim agreements towards the full implementation of the Schengen *acquis* (which is expected in March 2008) are in place. See Council of the European Union, 'Information sheet: enlargement of the Schengen area', Rev 1, Brussels, 8 November 2007.

22 Bilateral interim agreements regulate the rights of these citizens to work and reside in the 'old' EU members. See, for example, Commission of the European Communities, 'Report on the Functioning of the Transitional Arrangements set out in the 2003', Brussels, 8 February 2006, COM(2006) 48 final.

23 Interestingly, at the border control of London's Gatwick airport, this category is termed 'Rest of World'.

24 Additional technical barriers to the free movement of people within the EU's internal market include taxation, social policy, health insurance, and the recognition of professional certificates and qualifications, to mention a few.

25 See Zielonka: *Europe as Empire*, p. 145.

26 See for example Wallace, William, 'Where does Europe end? Dilemmas of inclusion and exclusion', in Zielonka (ed): *Europe Unbound*, pp. 78–94; Maier, Charles S., 'Does Europe need a frontier? From territorial to redistributive community', in Zielonka (ed): *Europe Unbound*, pp. 17–37.

27 See European Council, 'Tampere European Council, Presidency Conclusions', 15–16 October 1999.

28 See Cassarino, *Europe's Migration Policy in the Mediterranean: An Overview*, San Domenico di Fiesole (Florence): European University Institute, Robert Schuman Centre for Advanced Studies (2005), available at http://www.eui.eu/RSCAS/e-texts/CARIM-AS05_10-Cassarino.pdf, accessed 20 February 2008; see also Geddes, Andrew, 'Europe's Border Relationships and International Migration Relations', *Journal of Common Market Studies* xliii/4 (2005), pp. 787–806.

29   See for example the Commission's Justice and Home Affairs website, at http://
     ec.europa.eu/justice_home/fsj/intro/fsj_intro_en.htm, accessed 18 February
     2008.
30   See Castle, Stephen, 'EU executive calls for creation of a European border
     patrol', *International Herald Tribune*, 13 February 2008, online edition at www.iht.
     com, accessed 13 February 2008.
31   See, for example, Commission of the European Communities, 'Towards more
     accessible, equitable and managed asylum system', Brussels, 3 June 2003,
     COM(2003) 315 final; see also Wolff, Sarah, 'La dimension méditerranéenne
     de la politique Justice et Affaires intérieures', *Cultures et Conflits* lxvi (2007), pp.
     77–99.
32   Commission of the European Communities, 'Communication from the Com-
     mission to the Council and the European Parliament in View of the European
     Council of Thessaloniki on the Development of a Common Policy on Illegal
     Immigration, Smuggling and Trafficking of Human Beings, External Borders
     and the Return of Illegal Residents, Brussels, 3 June 2003, COM(2003) 323
     final, p. 12; see also *idem*, 'A strategy on the external dimension of the area
     of freedom, security, and justice', Brussels, 12 October 2005, COM(2005) 491
     final, p. 10.
33   See Lavenex, Sandra, 'EU external governance in "Wider Europe"', *Journal of
     European Public Policy* xi/4 (2004), pp. 680–700; see also Cassarino: *Europe's Mi-
     gration Policy in the Mediterranean.*
34   Balibar: *Europe as Borderland*, p. 16; italics in the original.
35   See European Council, 'Santa Maria de Feira Council presidency conclusions',
     19-20 June 2000, Annex V.
36   The rather complicated name of this programme is 'Regional Cooperation
     Programme in the Field of Justice, Combating Drugs, Organised Crime, and
     Terrorism as well as Co-operation in the Treatment of Issues Relating to the
     Social Integration of Migrants, Migration and Movement of People'. See Coun-
     cil of the European Union, 'Presidency conclusions: Valencia Action Plan, fifth
     Euro-Mediterranean conference of foreign ministers, Valencia, 2002.
37   Readmission agreements have become the standard method of ensuring that
     persons are expelled from EU member states or from the EU as a whole. These
     agreements stipulate a state's acceptance of the re-entry of an individual (which
     may be its own national, but also third-country national or stateless person)
     who has been found illegally entering, being present in or residing in another
     state (in this case, the EU or its member states). The contracting parties must
     also permit the transit of persons back to a non-contracting party if neces-
     sary. See for example Peers, Steve, 'Readmission agreements and EC external
     migration law', Statewatch Analysis No. 17, May 2003, available at http://www.
     statewatch.org/news/2003/may/readmission.pdf, accessed 2 April 2008.
38   See Cassarino: *Europe's Migration Policy in the Mediterranean*, pp. 8–9.
39   See Commission, 'Communication from the Commission to the Council and
     the European Parliament in view of the European Council of Thessaloniki',
     COM(2003) 323 final, p. 13; *idem*, 'Wider Europe – neighbourhood: a new
     framework for relations with our eastern and southern neighbours', Brussels,
     11 March 2003, COM(2003) 104 final; *idem*, 'European Neighbourhood Policy:
     strategy paper', Brussels, 12 March 2004, COM(2004) 373 final. EU incentives

under the ENP include integration into the internal market and extension of regulatory structures, preferential trade relations and the opening of markets, integration into the EU's transport, telecommunications, energy and research networks, instruments for promoting foreign investments, support for integration into the global trading system, enhanced financial and technical assistance, and perspectives for lawful immigration.

40 Commission, 'Communication from the Commission to the Council and the European Parliament in view of the European Council of Thessaloniki', COM(2003) 323 final, p. 14.

41 See Cassarino: 'Approaching borders and frontiers', p. 1.

42 Commission, 'EU Strategy for Africa: towards a Euro-African path to accelerate Africa's development', Brussels, 12 October 2005, COM (2005) 489 final, p. 37. See also the chapter by Henk Driessen in this volume.

43 See Brothers, Caroline, 'Obscurity and confinement for migrants in Europe', *International Herald Tribune,* 30 December 2007, online edition, at <http://www.iht.com/articles/2007/12/30/europe/greece.php>, accessed 27 February 2008. Migrant detention centres have also been set up in the EU's eastern periphery, such as in the Ukraine. See also the chapter by Henk Driessen in this volume.

44 See Commission, 'EU Technical Mission to Libya on Illegal Immigration 27 November – 6 December 2004: Report 7753/05', available at <http://www.statewatch.org/news/2005/may/eu-report-libya-ill-imm.pdf>, accessed 26 February 2008.

45 See Brothers: 'Obscurity and confinement for migrants in Europe'. Libya has not signed the Geneva Convention on refugees, which is of particular concern. In March 2008, the European Commission proposed to negotiate a 'Framework Agreement' with Libya.

46 See Council of the European Union 'Inventory of Readmission Agreements, Note from the General Secretariat to the Expulsion Working Party [*sic*]', Brussels, 24 November 1999, 11486/2/99, available at <http://register.consilium.eu.int/pdf/en/99/st11/11486-r2en9.pdf>, accessed 26 February 2008. For updated data on formal and informal readmission agreements see the website of the MiRem (Return Migration to the Maghreb) project based at the European University Institute, at <http://mirem.eu/datasets/agreements>, accessed 8 April 2008.

47 Rome and Tripoli signed a cooperation agreement on combating drugs, terrorism, organised crime, and illegal migration on 13 December 2000; the Italian government has been rather reluctant to publicise the matter. See Commission, 'EU Technical Mission to Libya on Illegal Immigration 27 November – 6 December 2004'; Brothers: 'Obscurity and Confinement for Migrants in Europe'.

48 On this issue, see for example Geddes: 'Europe's border relationships'.

49 I am grateful to Kalypso Nicolaïdis for bringing this point to my attention.

50 Commission, 'European Neighbourhood and Partnership Instrument: Cross-Border Cooperation. Strategy Paper 2007–2013, Indicative Programme 2007-2010', n.d. (probably 2006), available at http://ec.europa.eu/world/enp/documents_en.htm, accessed 1 March 2008.

51 For the development of the EU's Mediterranean policy, see Del Sarto, *Contested State Identity and Regional Security in the Euro-Mediterranean Area* (New York: Pal-

grave Macmillan, 2006), chapter 3; and Bicchi, Federica, *European Foreign Policy Making towards the Mediterranean* (New York: Palgrave Macmillan, 2007).

52 Free trade agreements have been ratified and are in force with Tunisia (since 1998), Morocco (since 2000), Israel (since 2000), Jordan (since 2002) and Egypt (since 2004). Interim Euro-Mediterranean Association Agreements with the PLO (1997) and Lebanon (2003) are in force. The agreement with Syria was initialled in 2004, but has not been signed yet. The agreement with Algeria was signed in 2002 and is in the process of ratification. Mauritania has been accepted as new 'southern' member of the Barcelona Process in November 2007 and has therefore not yet entered into negotiations with Brussels.

53 Council, 'Information note: Euro-Mediterranean Partnership: fifth Euro-Mediterranean ministerial conference on energy (Cyprus, 17 December 2007)', Brussels, 18 December 2007, 16707/07.

54 Commission, 'Developing external energy policy for the EU', Brussels, 30 November 2007, MEMO/07/233, available at <http://europa.eu/rapid/press-ReleasesAction.do?reference=MEMO/07/533&format=HTML&aged=1&language=EN&guiLanguage=en#fnB1>.

55 Algeria eventually gave in. See for example 'Algeria's Sonatrach bows to EU pressure to open up gas supply contracts', *International Herald Tribune*, 11 July 2007; see also Commission, 'Commission and Algeria reach agreement on territorial restrictions and alternative clauses in gas supply Contracts', 11 July 2007, IP/07/1074.

56 A natural gas pipeline linking Algerian gas fields to Spain and Portugal through Morocco and the Strait of Gibraltar became operational in 1996.

57 The planned Arab Gas Pipeline explains the importance of Jordan as a transit country in the EU's energy policy.

58 Council, 'Information note: Euro-Mediterranean Partnership: fifth Euro-Mediterranean ministerial conference on energy (Cyprus, 17 December 2007)', Brussels, 18 December 2007, 16707/07, p. 17.

59 The Energy Community Treaty entered into force in 2006. It aims at creating a legal and economic framework in the energy sector which is capable of attracting investments, developing electricity and gas market competition on a broader geographical scale, enhancing supply security, and tackling environmental issues. Information on the treaty is available at <http://www.energy-community. org/>, accessed 28 March 2008. All states in the Balkan states have joined this initiative, but Ankara has so far preferred to keep its observer status, since it could use its strategic importance as an asset in the accession negotiations with the EU. See Barysch, Katinka, *Turkey's Role in European Energy Security,* Centre for European Reform Essays (London: Centre for European Reform, 2007), available at <http://www.cer.org.uk/pdf/essay_turkey_energy_12dec07.pdf>, accessed 28 March 2008.

60 See Commission, 'Reinvigorating the Barcelona Process', Brussels, 6.9.2001, COM(2000) 497 final; *idem,* 'Euro-Mediterranean Partnership: The European Commission Calls for Enhanced Cooperation on Transport and Energy', 21 March 2003, IP/01/425.

61 *Ibid.* See also Commission, 'Development of a Euro-Mediterranean transport network', Brussels, 24 June 2003, COM(2003) 376 final.

62 Council, 'Agreed conclusions of the 9th Euro-Mediterranean meeting of ministers of foreign affairs, Lisbon, 5-6 November 2007', 14743/07 (Presse 255), p. 11; see also Euro-Mediterranean Transport Forum, 'Blue Paper: Towards an Integrated Euro-Mediterranean transport forum, Communication from the Euro-Mediterranean transport forum to the first Euro-Mediterranean conference of transport ministers', November 2005.

63 See Commission, 'Wider Europe – Neighbourhood', COM(2003) 104 final; *idem,* 'European Neighbourhood Policy: strategy paper', COM(2004) 373 final.

64 Commission, 'Developing the agenda for the Community's external aviation policy', Brussels, 11 March 2005, COM(2005) 79 final, p. 8.

65 See the website of DG Transport of the European Commission, at http://ec.europa.eu/transport/air_portal/international/pillars/common_aviation_area/morocco_en.htm, accessed 28 March 2008.

66 See Commission, 'Developing a common aviation area with Israel', Brussels, 9.11. 2007, COM(2007) 691 final.

67 See the website of the EC's DG Transport at http://ec.europa.eu/transport/air_portal/international/pillars/common_aviation_area/israel_en.htm

68 See Maier: 'Does Europe need a frontier?, pp. 21 ff.

69 See Council, 'Agreed conclusions of the 9th Euro-Mediterranean meeting of ministers of foreign affairs, Lisbon, 5–6 November 2007', 14743/07 (Presse 255), p. 13.

70 See Zielonka: *Europe as Empire,* p. 155.

71 See, for example, Adler, Emanuel, Federica Bicchi, Beverly Crawford, and Raffaella A. Del Sarto (eds), *The Convergence of Civilizations: Constructing a Mediterranean Region* (Toronto: University of Toronto Press, 2006); see also Bechev, Dimitar, 'Hegemonic Europe? Centres, peripheries, and regional order', paper presented at the Faculty Seminar, Department of Politics and International Relations, University of Oxford, 7 March 2008.

Chapter IX

1 This chapter is based on a paper given in a workshop on 'Transnationalism in the Mediterranean' at St Antony's College, Oxford, 26–28 May 2006.

2 For local coverage of these events, see *Melilla Hoy,* 26 December 2006 and 2 January 2007.

3 Sahel is the region south of the Sahara desert, stretching from Senegal all the way to Eritrea.

4 This is drawn from a report on the assaults in Melilla in *El País,* 29 September 2005.

5 This summary of events in the autumn of 2005 is based on reports from Spanish, Moroccan and Dutch newspapers, BBC News, and Human Rights Watch. I have conducted eighteen months of field work and archival research in the Spanish enclaves over the past twenty years. My publications include Driessen, Henk, *On the Spanish-Moroccan Frontier: A Study in Ritual, Power, and Ethnicity* (Oxford: Berg, 1992); 'The politics of religion on the Hispano-African frontier: a historical-anthropological view', in Eric R. Wolf (ed), *Religious Regimes and State Formation: Perspectives from European Ethnology* (Albany, NY: State University of New York Press, 1991), pp. 237–260; and 'The "new immigration" and the

transformation of the European-African frontier', in Thomas M. Wilson and Hastings Donnan (eds), *Border Identities: Nation and State at International Frontiers* (Cambridge: Cambridge University Press, 1998), pp. 96–117.

6   For a general discussion of trans-Mediterranean migration see King, Russell (ed), *The Mediterranean Passage. Migration and New Cultural Encounters in Southern Europe* (Liverpool: Liverpool University Press, 2001); also Suárez-Navaz, Liliana, *Rebordering the Mediterranean: Boundaries and Citizenship in Southern Europe* (New York and Oxford: Berghahn Books, 2004); Ribas-Mateos, Natalia, *The Mediterranean in the Age of Globalization* (New Brunswick & London: Transaction Publishers, 2005).

7   On the difficult relationship with Morocco, see Magone, José M, *Contemporary Spanish Politics* (London: Routledge, 2004).

8   Gold, Peter, *Europe or Africa? A Contemporary Study of the Spanish North African Enclaves of Ceuta and Melilla* (Liverpool: Liverpool University Press, 2000). Also, see my review of this study in *Journal of Ethnic and Migration Studies* xxviii/4 (2002), p. 758.

9   See Stoller, Paul, *Money Has No Smell: The Africanization of New York City* (Chicago and London: University of Chicago Press, 2002). Also consider the case of diasporic Tongans in the United States, New Zealand and Australia, Tongan migration being part of the same global trend. See Lee, Helen Morton, *Tongans Overseas: Between Two Shores* (Honolulu: University of Hawaii Press, 2003).

10   See Howe, Marvine, *Morocco: the Islamist Awakening and Other Challenges.* (Oxford: Oxford University Press, 2005).

11   Braudel, Fernand, *The Mediterranean and the Mediterranean World in the Age of Philip II,* Vols. 1 and 2 (Glasgow: Fontana/Collins, 1976).

12   Driessen: *On the Spanish-Moroccan frontier,* Chapter Two.

13   The contradictions and ironies of the management of borders at Ceuta and Melilla are also dealt with by Xavier Ferrer-Gallardo in the draft paper 'Theorizing the Spanish-Moroccan Rebordering' (2005).

14   Ferrer-Gallardo correctly reads the reconfiguration of the Spanish-Moroccan border as a process of geopolitical, functional and symbolic reshaping. See also the chapter by Raffaella A. Del Sarto in this volume.

15   See Haas, Hein de, 'Trans-Saharan migration to North Africa and the EU: historical roots and current trends', http://www.migrationinformation.org (November 2006); see also Haas, 'Morocco: from emigration country to Africa's migration passage to Europe', *ibid.* (October 2005).

16   There are also several realistic literary representations of the clandestine passage from Morocco to Spain. See, for example, Binebine, Mahi, *Cannibales* (Paris: Fayard, 1999); Ben Jelloun, Tahar, *Partir* (Paris: Gallimard, 2006). See also Marko Juntunen's excellent multi-sited ethnography *Between Morocco and Spain: Men, Migrant Smuggling and a Dispersed Moroccan Community* (Helsinki: University Printing House, 2002).

Chapter X

1   For their comments and assistance, I wish to thank Noa Shuval (Université Paris 5), Adriana Kemp (Tel Aviv University), Eyal Ben Ari (Hebrew University of Jerusalem), Dganit Manor (Ben Gurion University), Richard Ratcliffe (St

Antony's College, Oxford), Nadia Abu Zahra (St Antony's College, Oxford), Karima Direche (TELEMME, CNRS), Myriam Catusse (IREMAM, CNRS), Françoise Lorcerie (IREMAM, CNRS), Eric Gobe (IREMAM, CNRS). I would also like to thank John Krivine for his editing assistance, and Shadrock Roberts and Marjolaine Barazani (CRFJ) for the maps.

2   I use alternatively the terms "Fence", "Wall" and "Barrier" to describe the barrier Israel has been building around the West Bank since 2002. I use the three terms because this structure is constituted a complex sets of concrete walls, electronic fences, patrol roads, and razor wires. For instance, around Jerusalem it is mainly a 8 meter concrete wall, while between the southern West Bank and the Northern Negev, the barrier (still partially unachieved in 2008) is constituted of electronic fences and patrol roads.

3   In this article, I do not use the term border to refer to internationally acknowledged limits between states. The only recognized limits in this context were those established during the implementation of the Oslo agreements (1994–2000). Yet, since the outbreak of the Second Intifada (September 2000), these limits have been constantly challenged by Israel. West Bank Palestinian enclaves were first invaded by the Israeli army during Operation Defensive Shield (spring 2002), and have subsequently been subject to regular Israeli incursions. Nevertheless, the absence of an internationally recognized border does not mean an absence of limits. As Adriana Kemp (Tel Aviv University) put it in one of our discussions, in the Israeli-Palestinian space, the absence of border leads to the proliferation of limits. The Second Intifada (2000–) witnessed a proliferation of checkpoints, barriers, earth mounds and trenches built by the Israeli authorities in the West Bank to reassert control over Palestinian enclaves. In February 2005, 600 obstacles were listed by the United Nations Office for the Coordination of Humanitarian Affairs (UN OCHA 2005). Finally, the construction of the Wall since June 2002 established new limits and created new Palestinian enclaves inside the West Bank (see Palestinian Environmental NGOs Network (ed), *The Wall in Palestine: Facts, Testimonies, Analysis and Call to Action* (Jerusalem: PENGON, 2003). Hence when using the term borders or borderlands, I refer to the zones and limits surrounding the Palestinian enclaves inside the West Bank that are defined both by the juxtaposition of administrative limits, set during the Oslo period and after 2000 by the Israeli army, and by infrastructures such as checkpoints, earth mounds, and barriers. These borders or borderlands are not separating two continuous territorial entities. Rather, they surround islands of semi autonomy of the Palestinian enclaves inside the West Bank that remain 60 per cent controlled by Israel.

4   Bornstein, Avraham, *Crossing the Green Line Between the West Bank and Israel* (Philadelphia: University of Pennsylvania Press, 2002).

5   Kemp and Raijman, 'Labor migration, managing the ethno-national conflict, and client politics in Israel', in Sarah S. Willen (ed), *Transnational Migration to Israel in Global Comparative Context* (Lanham: Lexington, 2007).

6   Ben Ari, Eyal et al, *From checkpoints to flowpoints: sites of friction between the Israel Defense Forces and Palestinians,* Final report submitted to the Friedrich Ebert Foundation (Israel, 2004).

7   Palestinian Central Bureau of Statistics, *Labour Force Survey (July-September, 2005) Round (Q3/2005)*, Press Conference on the Labour Force Survey Results (Ramallah: PCBS, 2005) p. 9.

8   Andreas, Peter, *Border Games: Policing the US-Mexico Divide* (Ithaca: Cornell University Press, 2001). Santibañez-Romellon, Jorge, 'La frontière Mexique-États-Unis à l'heure de la mondialisation', Lecture at the Maison Méditerranéenne des Sciences de l'homme, Aix en Provence, 31 January 2005.

9   Marx, Emanuel, *The Bedouin of the Negev* (Manchester: Manchester University Press, 1967); Parizot, Cédric, 'Crossing and constructing borders within daily contacts', *Notes de Recherche du CER* cclxxxvii (2004).

10 Marx, Emanuel, 'Land and work: Negev Bedouin struggle with Israeli bureaucracies', *Nomadic Peoples* iv/2 (2000), pp. 107–121.

11 Meir, Avinoam, *As Nomadism Ends: The Israeli Bedouin of the Negev* (Boulder: Westview Press, 1997).

12 Abu Rabia, Aref, 'Employment and unemployment among the Negev Bedouin', *Nomadic Peoples* iv/2 (2000), pp. 84–94; Jakubowska, Longina, 'Finding Ways to Make a Living', *Nomadic Peoples* iv/2 (2000), pp. 94–105.

13 Parizot, 'Gaza, Beer-Sheva, Dahriyya: another approach to the Negev Bedouin in the Israeli-Palestinian space' *Bulletin du Centre de Recherche Français de Jérusalem* ix (2001), pp. 98–110.

14 The Green Line was the Armistice Line of 1949. It functioned as a de facto border between Israel and the neighbouring Arab countries until 1967.

15 Abu Rabia, *The Negev Bedouin and Livestock Rearing: Social, Economic and Political Aspects* (Oxford: Berg, 1994); Parizot: 'Crossing and constructing Borders'.

16 Arnon, Arie, Israel Luski, Avia Spivak and Jimmy Weinblatt, *The Palestinian Economy: Between Imposed Integration and Voluntary Separation* (Leiden, New York, Köln: Brill, 1997); Bornstein: *Crossing the Green Line*.

17 Arnon, Israel, Spivak and Weinblatt, *The Palestinian Economy*.

18 Ruppert Bulmer, Elizabeth, *The Impact of future labor policy options on the Palestinian labor market*, Discussion paper (2001), p. 657.

19 Parizot: 'Crossing and Constructing Borders'.

20 Regarding marriage celebrations, see for example Lewando-Hundt, Gillian, *Women's Power and Settlement: the Effect of Settlement on the Position of Negev Bedouin Women*, MA Thesis, University of Edinburgh (1978); for, religious beliefs see (Jakubowska, Longina. *Urban Bedouin: Social Change in a Settled Environment*, PhD Thesis, State University of New York, 1985) for genealogical techniques and models of authorities (Parizot, Cédric, *Le mois de la bienvenue: ré-appropriations des mécanismes électoraux et réajustements de rapports de pouvoir chez les Bédouins du Néguev (Israël)*. PhD Thesis, EHESS, Paris, 2001, p. 80-81 and p. 135-143)

21 Eshkolot and Tene, East and South of ad-Dhahriyya; Shim'a and Otni'el, on the road 60 between Dhahriyya and Sammu', and finally, Shani, Karmel, Metzadot Yehuda, Susiya and Ma'on south and South East of Sammu' and Yatta.

22 By 2004, the population of settlers in the southern Hebron Hills amounted to approximately than 4000 people.

23 Bornstein, Avraham: *Crossing the Green Line*.

24 Kemp and Raijman: 'Labor migration, managing the ethno-national conflict'.

25 Hass, Amira 'Israel's closure policy: an ineffective strategy of containment and repression' *Journal of Palestine Studies* xxxi/3 (2002), pp. 5-20.; Hertzog, Sergio

"The relationship between economic hardship and crime: the case of Israel and the Palestinians" *Sociological Perspectives* xlviii/2 (2005), pp. 189-211.

26 Kemp and Raijman: 'Labor migration, managing the ethno-national conflict', note 28.

27 Farsakh, Leila 'Under siege: closure, separation and the Palestinian economy', *Middle East Report, No. 217, Beyond Oslo: the New Uprising* (Winter 2000), pp. 22-25.; Bucaille, Laetitia. *Générations Intidada* (Paris: Hachette, 2002), 118-122.

28 Amir, Shmuel. *Overseas foreign workers in Israel: policy aims and labour market outcomes. Discussion Paper A00-01* Jerusalem: The Maurice Falk Insititute for Economic Research in Israel. Quoted in Farsakh, Leila. *Palestinian Labour Migration to Israel: Labour, Land and Occupation* (London: Routledge, 2006), p. 140.

29 Arnon, Arie, Israel Luski, Avia Spivak and Jimmy Weinblatt. *The Palestinian Economy. Between Imposed Integration and Voluntary Separation* (Leiden, New York, Köln: Brill, 1997), p. 76-77

30 Farsakh: *Palestinian labour migration to Israel,* p. 141.

31 Kemp and Raijman: 'Labor migration, managing the ethno-national conflict', note 10.

32 Parizot, Cédric: "Crossing and constructing borders'.

33 http://www.iris.org.il/cartheft.htm, consulted on 6 February 2006

34 Abu Moailek, Yasser, 'Ex-car thief aims to revive business in Gaza', *The Electronic Intifada*, 9 November 2005, http://electronicintifada.net/v2/article4286.shtml, site consulted on February 6, 2006; Hertzog: 'The Relationship between economic hardship and crime'.

35 In February 2005, the number of earth mounds, checkpoints, trenches and barriers set in the West Bank to monitor the movement of the Palestinian population rose to 600 (Cf. United Nations Office for the Coordination of Humanitarian Affairs, March 2005) http://www.humanitarianinfo.org/opt/docs/UN/OCHA/OCHABarRprt05_Full.pdf, site accessed on 16 February 2006.

36 During the Second Intifada, the number of work permits dropped from 60,000 in 2000, to less than 10,000 in the third quarter of 2005, cf. United Nations Office for the Coordination of Humanitarian Affairs, OCHA protection of civilians. Weekly briefing notes, Jerusalem: *OCHA*, 7-13 September 2005 and 30 November-6 December 2005.

37 Palestinian Media Centre, http://www.palestine-pmc.com, consulted on 11 April 2002.

38 During the Oslo period (1994-2000), in order to ease the movements of Israeli settlers between the West bank and Israel proper, as well as to increase the separation between Palestinians and Israelis, the Israeli authorities built in this region a networks of 200 km of roads by-passing main Palestinian villages and cities.

39 Such as that close to the Jewish settlement of Shim'a (route 60), that of Rifa'iyya, North of Yatta on the road 356 (June-August 2004), or that of al-Fawwâr.

40 Between September 2000 and December 2002, according to the Office for the Coordination of Humanitarian Affairs in the Occupied Palestinian Territories (OCHA), the damages caused by the conflict on the Palestinian infrastructures amounted to $ 1.7 billion. Poverty reached almost 47 per cent of the population.

41 World Bank. *Poverty in the West Bank and Gaza, Report No. 22312-GZ*, 18 June 2001.

42 NIS = New Isreali Shekels.

43 Hass, Amira, 'Down in the dumps', *Haaretz*, 16 November 2004, www.kavlaoved.org.il/katava_main.asp?news_id=1156&sivug_id=4, consulted on 7 February 2006.

44 This number refers to the number of individual trips and not workers who enter Israel. It is hard to evaluate how many workers cross the Green Line through this mean as many come back few times per month.

45 Parizot: 'Constructing'.

46 Vila, Pablo, 'Conclusion: The limits of American border theory'', in *Idem* (ed) *Ethnography at the Border* (Minneapolis: University of Minnesota Press, 2003), pp. 306-341; Van Dijk, Teun A., 'Stories and racism', in Mumby, D.K. (ed), *Narrative and Social Control: Critical Perspectives* (Newbury Park CA: Sage, 1993), p. 126.

47 The expression 'delocalization in situ' (*délocalisation en place*) is borrowed from Emmanuel Terray 'Le travail des étrangers en situation irrégulière ou la délocalisation sur place', in Etienne Balibar, Monique Chemillier-Gendreau, Jacqueline Costa-Lascoux, and Emmanuel Terray, *Sans Papiers : l'archaïsme fatal* (Paris: La découverte (1999), pp. 15-17.

48 Hass: 'Israel's closure policy', p. 14-15.

49 Vila: 'Conclusion', p. 325:

50 Abu Moailek: 'Ex-car thief aims'.

51 Andreas: *Border games.*

NOTES ON CONTRIBUTORS

Bojan Baskar is Professor of Social Anthropology and Mediterranean Studies at the University of Ljubljana.

Fatma Ben Slimane is Lecturer in History at the University of Tunis.

Franziska Brantner is a researcher affiliated with the Heinrich Boell Foundation.

Raffaella A. Del Sarto is the Pears-Rich Research Fellow in Israel Studies, a joint post at the Middle East Centre, St Antony's College, Oxford and the Oxford Centre for Hebrew and Jewish Studies.

Henk Driessen is Professor of Cultural Anthropology at Radbout University, Nijmegen.

Thierry Fabre is Professor of Mediterranean Studies at the Maison Méditerranéenne des Sciences de l'Homme in Aix-en-Provence. He is the Academic Coordinator of RAMSES2, a Network of Excellence of Mediterranean Studies, and editor in chief of the journal *La pensée de midi*.

Marie-Claire Lavabre is a Research Director at the Centre for Political Research (CEVIPOF) at the Institut d'Etudes Politiques (Sciences Po) in Paris.

Dimitri Nicolaidis is a French historian and a research associate at the Maison Méditerranéenne des Sciences de l'Homme in Aix-en-Provence.

Kerem Öktem is Research Fellow at the European Studies Centre, St Antony's College, Oxford.

Nora Fisher Onar is Research Associate at the European Studies Centre, St Antony's College, Oxford and Assistant Professor in International Relations at Sabancı University, Istanbul.

Cédric Parizot is Fellow at the Centre de Recherche Français in Jerusalem.

BIBLIOGRAPHY

Abu Rabia, Aref, 'Employment and Unemployment among the Negev Bedouin', *Nomadic Peoples* iv/2 (2000).

_____, *The Negev Bedouin and Livestock Rearing: Social, Economic and Political Aspects* (Oxford: Berg Publishers, 1994).

Adem, Seifudein, 'Constructing a new imperial order? The war in Iraq and the ideology of clashism', *Alternatives* ii/2 (2003).

Adler, Emanuel, 'A Mediterranean canon and an Israeli prelude to a long peace', in Emmanuel Adler, *Communitarian International Relations: the Epistemic Foundations of International Relations* (London: Routledge, 2005).

Adler, Emanuel, Federica Bicchi, Beverly Crawford and Raffaella A. Del Sarto (eds), *The Convergence of Civilizations: Constructing a Mediterranean Region* (Toronto: University of Toronto Press, 2006).

Ageron, Robert Charles, *Modern Algeria: a History from 1830 to the Present* (London: C. Hurst, 1991).

Aliboni, Roberto, Ahmed Driss, Tobias Schuhmacher and Alfred Tovias, *Putting the Mediterranean Union in Perspective* (Lisbon: Euromesco, 2008).

Al-Ifrani, Mohammed Saghir, *Nuzhat Al Hadi fi Akhbar Muluk Al Karn Al Hadi* (Rabat, 1988).

Al-Wazzen Al-Fasi (Leo Africanus), *Wasf Ifriqiya* ('Description of Africa') (Rabat, 1982).

Albert, Mathias, David Jacobson and Yosef Lapid (eds), *Identities, Borders, Orders: Rethinking International Relations Theory* (Minneapolis: Minnesota University Press, 2001).

Anderson, Benedict, *Imagined Communities: Reflections on the Origins and Spread of Nationalism*, second edition, (London: Verso, 1991).

Anderson, Malcolm, *Frontiers, Territories and State Formation in the Modern World* (Cambridge: Polity, 1996).

Anderson, Malcolm and Eberhart Bort, *The Frontiers of the European Union* (Basingstoke: Palgrave, 2001).

Andreas, Peter, *Border Games: Policing the US-Mexico Divide* (Ithaca: Cornell University Press, 2001).

Arnon, Arie, Israel Luski, Avia Spivak and Jimmy Weinblatt, *The Palestinian Economy: Between Imposed Integration and Voluntary Separation* (Leiden, New York, Köln: Brill, 1997).

Ayubi, Nazih, *Overstating the Arab State: Politics and Society in the Middle East* (London: I.B. Tauris, 1995).

Badie, Bertrand, *La fin des territoires. Essai sur le désordre international et sur l'utilité du respect social, l'espace du politique* (Paris: Fayard, 1995).

——————, *L'Etat importé. L'occidentalisation de l'ordre politique* (Paris: Fayard, 1992).

——————, 'Les territoires de l'appartenance', *Qantara, Magazine des cultures arabes et méditerranéennes, monde arabe et musulman* xvii (October–December 1995).

Baduel, P. Robert, 'La production de l'espace national au Maghreb' in Robert Baduel (ed), *Etat, territoire et terroirs au Maghreb* (Paris: CNRS, 1985).

Balibar, Etienne, 'Europe as Borderland', The Alexander von Humboldt Lecture in Human Geography, University of Nijmegen, 10 November 2004.

Ballinger, Pamela, *History in Exile: Memory and Identity at the Borders of the Balkans* (Princeton and Oxford: Princeton University Press, 2003).

Barysch, Katinka, *Turkey's Role in European Energy Security, Centre for European Reform Essay* (London: Centre for European Reform, 2007).

Baskar, Bojan, 'Imagining the Balkans in Trieste', *Caietele Echinox / Cahiers de l'Echinox. Les imaginaires européens* x (2006).

Bax, Mart, 'The celebration of the violent past: about some local sources of the recent war in Bosnia-Herzegovina', Narodna umjetnost. Hrvatski časopis za etnologiju i folkloristiku xxxvii/1 (2000).

——————, *Medjugorje: Religion, Politics, and Violence in Rural Bosnia* (Amsterdam: VU Uitgeverij, 1995)

Bechev, Dimitar, *Hegemonic Europe? Centres, peripheries, and regional order*, paper presented at the Faculty Seminar, Department of Politics and International Relations, University of Oxford, 7 March 2008.

Ben Ari, Eyal, Meirav Maymon, Nir Gazit and Ron Shatzberg, *From checkpoints to flowpoints: sites of friction between the Israel Defense Forces and Palestinians*, Final report submitted to the Friedrich Ebert Foundation (Israel: 2004).

Ben Jelloun, Tahar, *Partir* (Paris: Gallimard, 2006).

Ben-Ghiat, Ruth, 'Liberation: Italian cinema and the fascist past, 1945-50', in J.B. Bosworth and Patrizia Dogliani (eds), *Italian Fascism: History, Memory and Representation* (Basingstoke and New York: Macmillan, 1999).

——————, 'A Lesser Evil? Italian Fascism in/and the totalitarian equation', in Helmut Dubiel and Gabriel Motzkin (eds), *The Lesser Evil: Moral Approaches to Genocide in a Comparative Perspective* (London and New York: Routledge, 2004).

Benussi, Bernardo, *Manuale di geografia dell'Istria* (Trieste: Stabilimento artistico tipografico G. Caprin, 1877).

Benvenisti, Meron, *Sacred Landscape. The buried history of the Holy Land since 1948* (Berkeley, Los Angeles, London: University of California Press, 2000).

Ben-Yehuda, Nachman, *The Masada Myth. Collective Memory and Mythmaking in Israel* (Madison: The University of Wisconsin Press, 1995).

Berahab, Okacha, 'La notion de frontière dans les documents marocains depuis la conquête d'Alger jusqu'en 1912', in Ahmed Siraj and Okacha Berahab, *Les espaces frontaliers dans l'histoire du Maroc* (Rabat: University Mohammed V, 1999).

Berktay, Fatmagul, *Tarihin Cinsiyeti* (Istanbul: Metis, 2003).

Bertrand, Romain, *Mémoires d'empire. La controverse autour du 'fait colonial'* (Paris: Editions du Croquant, 2006).

Bey, Maïssa, *Bleu blanc vert* (Algiers: Barzakh, 2006).

Bicchi, Federica, *European Foreign Policy Making towards the Mediterranean*, (New York: Palgrave Macmillan, 2007).

Binebine, Mahi, *Cannibales* (Paris: Fayard, 1999).

Bitelli, Remo, *Claustra Alpium Juliarum, il confine di Rapallo e fascismo: Archeologia come esempio di continuità* (Koper: ZRSRS, 1999).

Bloxham, Donald, 'Three Imperialisms and a Turkish Nationalism: International Stresses, Imperial Disintegration and the Armenian Genocide', *Patterns of Prejudice* xxxvi/4 (2002).

_____, *The Great Game of Genocide. Imperialism, Nationalism, and the Destruction of Ottoman Armenians* (Oxford: Oxford University Press, 2005).

Boia, Lucian, *History and Myth in the Romanian Consciousness* (Budapest: Central European University Press, 2001).

Bonn, Charles, 'Scénographies coloniales et postcoloniales dans le roman algérien: le thème de la guerre comme révélateur d'un fonctionnement littéraire', in Anny Dayan Rosenman and Lucette Valensi (eds), *La guerre d'Algérie dans la mémoire et l'imaginaire* (Saint-Denis: Bouchene, 2004).

_____, 'Le roman algérien', in Charles Bonn and Xavier Garnier (eds), *Littérature francophone. Tome 1: Le Roman* (Paris: Hatier, 1997).

Bono, Salvatore, 'Le controversie di frontiera dell'Algeria con il Marocco e con la Tunisia (1950-1970)', Oriente Moderno x-xi (October–November 1970).

Bornat, Joanna, 'Oral History as a Social Movement: Reminiscence and Older People', in Robert Perks and Alistair Thomson (eds), *Oral History Reader* (London: Routledge, 1998).

Bornstein, Avraham, *Crossing the Green Line Between the West Bank and Israel* (Philadelphia: University of Pennsylvania Press, 2002).

Boswell, Christina 'Migration control in Europe after 9/11: explaining the absence of securitization', *Journal of Common Market Studies* xlv/3 (2007).

Bosworth, J.B., 'Film Memories of Fascism', in J.B. Bosworth and Patrizia Dogliani (eds), *Italian Fascism: History, Memory and Representation* (Basingstoke and New York: Macmillan, 1999).

Brandell, Inga (ed), *State Frontiers: Borders and Boundaries in the Middle East* (London: I.B. Tauris, 2006).

Braudel, Fernand, 'Les espagnols et l'Afrique du Nord de 1492 à 1577', *Revue Africaine* (Algiers, 1928).

_____, *The Mediterranean and the Mediterranean World in the Age of Philip II* (Glasgow: Fontana/Collins, 1976).

Brauer, Ralph. W., *Boundaries and Frontiers in Medieval Muslim Geography* (Philadelphia: American Philosophical Society, 1995).

Brown, Carl (ed) *Imperial Legacy: the Ottoman Imprint on the Balkans and the Middle East* (New York: Columbia University Press, 1996).

Brown, Chris, *Sovereignty, Rights and Justice* (Cambridge: Polity Press, 2002).

Bucaille, Laetitia, *Générations Intifada* (Paris: Hachette, 2002).

Bulliet, Richard W., *The Case for Islamo-Christian Civilization* (New York: Columbia University Press, 2004).

Burgat, François and Laronde, André, *La Libye* (Paris: PUF, 1996).

Burgwyn, H. James, *Empire on the Adriatic: Mussolini's Conquest of Yugoslavia, 1941-1943* (New York: Enigma Books, 2005).

Calle-Gruber, Mireille, 'L'amour-dans-la-langue-adverse', in Anny Dayan Rosenman and Lucette Valensi (eds), *La guerre d'Algérie dans la mémoire et l'imaginaire* (Saint-

Denis: Bouchene, 2004).

Carr, Raymond, *Modern Spain* (Oxford: Oxford University Press, 1980).

Carrara, Francesco, *La Dalmazia descritta* (Zadar: Fratelli Battana, 1846).

Cassarino, Jean-Pierre, *Approaching borders and frontiers: notions and Implications*, Research Report of the Euro-Mediterranean Consortium for Applied Research on International Migration (CARIM), CARIM RR-2006/03, (Florence: European University Institute, 2006).

——————, *Europe's migration policy in the Mediterranean: an overview*, San Domenico di Fiesole (Florence): European University Institute, Robert Schuman Centre for Advanced Studies (2005).

Çelebi, Nilgün, 'Sociological organizations in Turkey: continuity behind discontinuity', *International Sociology* xvii/2 (2002).

Centre for Investigation and Documentation of the Association of Former Prison Camp Inmates of Bosnia-Herzegovina (CID), I *Begged Them to Kill Me: Crimes Against the Women of Bosnia-Herzegovina* (Sarajevo: CID, 2002).

Çetin, Zafer M., 'Tales of past, present, and future: mythmaking and nationalist discourse in Turkish politics', *Journal of Muslim Minority Affairs* xxiv/3 (2004).

Chambers, Richard L., 'The education of a nineteenth-century Ottoman alim, Ahmed Cevdet Pasa', *International Journal of Middle East Studies* iv/4 (1973).

Christiansen, Thomas, Fabio Petito and Ben Tonra, 'Fuzzy politics around fuzzy borders: the European Union's "near abroad"', *Cooperation and Conflict* xxxv/4 (2000).

Clark, Bruce, *Twice a Stranger. How Mass Expulsion Forged Modern Greece and Turkey* (London: Granta Books, 2006).

Combi, Carlo, *Istria: Studii storici e politici* (Milan: Tipografia Bernardoni di C. Rebeschini, 1886).

Comelli, Michele, Ettore Greco and Nathalie Tocci, 'From boundary to borderland: transforming the meaning of borders through the European Neighbourhood Policy', *European Foreign Affairs Review* xii/2 (2007).

Crainz, Guido, 'The representation of fascism and the resistance in the documentaries of Italian state television', in Bosworth and Dogliani (eds), *Italian Fascism: History, Memory and Representation* (Basingstoke and New York: Macmillan, 1999).

——————, *Il dolore e l'esilio: L'Istria e le memorie divise d'Europa* (Rome: Donzelli, 2005).

Cunningham, Michael, 'Saying sorry: the politics of the apology', *The Political Quarterly* lxx/3 (1999).

Darwin, John, *After Tamerlane: The Global History of Empire* (London: Penguin, 2007).

Davies, Norman, *Europe East and West* (London: Pimlico, 2007).

Davison, Andrew, 'Ziya Gökalp and provincializing Europe', *Comparative Studies of South Asia, Africa and the Middle East* xxvi/3(2006).

Dean, Jodi, *Solidarity of Strangers: Feminism after Identity Politics* (University of California Press, 1996).

Del Sarto, Raffaella, *Contested State Identity and Regional Security in the Euro-Mediterranean Area* (New York: Palgrave Macmillan, 2006).

Del Sarto, Raffaella A. and Tobias Schumacher, 'From EMP to ENP: what's at stake with the European Neighbourhood Policy towards the Southern Mediterranean?', *European Foreign Affairs Review* x/1 (2005).

Delanty, Gerard and Chris Rumford, *Rethinking Europe: Social Theory and the Implications of Europeanization* (London and New York: Routledge, 2005).

Devlin, John F., 'The Baath Party: Rise and Metamorphosis', *The American Historical Review* xcvi/5 (December 1991).

Diamond, Hannah, *Women and the Second World War in France 1939–1948: Choices and Constraints* (Harlow: Pearson Education, 1999).

Doumanis, Nicholas, *Italy* (London: Arnold, 2001).

Doyle, Michael, *Empires* (Ithaca NY: Cornell University Press, 1986).

Drakulić, Slavenka, 'The rape of women in Bosnia', in Miranda Davies (ed), *Women and Peace* (London: Zed, 1994).

Driessen, Henk, 'The "new immigration" and the transformation of the European-African frontier', in Thomas M. Wilson and Hastings Donnan (eds), *Border Identities: Nation and State at International Frontiers* (Cambridge: Cambridge University Press, 1998).

_____, 'The politics of religion on the Hispano-African frontier: a historical-anthropological view', in Eric R. Wolf (ed), *Religious Regimes and State Formation: Perspectives from European Ethnology* (Albany, NY: State University of New York Press, 1991).

_____, *On the Spanish-Moroccan Frontier: A Study in Ritual, Power, and Ethnicity* (Oxford: Berg, 1992).

_____, Review: 'Europe or Africa? By Peter Gold', *Journal of Ethnic and Migration Studies* xxviii/4 (2002).

Eldem, Edhem, Goffman, Daniel and Bruce Alan Masters, *The Ottoman City between East and West: Aleppo, Izmir, and Istanbul* (Cambridge: Cambridge University Press, 1999).

Elias, Norbert, *The Civilizing Process* (Oxford: Blackwell, 1994).

Emanuel, Marx, 'Land and work: Negev Bedouin struggle with Israeli bureaucracies', *Nomadic Peoples* iv/2 (2000).

Enginun, Inci, 'Turkish Literature and Self-Identity' in Kemal Karpat (ed), *Ottoman Past and Today's Turkey* (Leiden, Brill: 2000).

Erdem, Hakan, '"Do not think of the greeks as agricultural labourers": Ottoman responses to the Greek war of independence', in Faruk Birtek and Thalia Dragonas (eds), *Citizenship and the Nation-State in Greece and Turkey* (New York, Routledge: 2005).

Ferenc, Tone (ed), *Promemoria del comandante della Divisione «Granatieri di Sardegna» e dell'XI Corpo d'Armata. Memoria per l'Eccelenza il Commandante della 2° armata. Situazione nella Provincia di Lubiana – Possibilità e modalità di una rapida pacificazione. La provincia "italiana" di Lubiana. Documenti 1941- 1942* (Udine: Istituto friulano per la storia del movimento di liberazione, 1994).

Ferguson, Niall, *Empire: How Britain Made the Modern World* (London: Penguin, 2003).

Findley, Carter Vaughn, 'Continuity, Innovation, Synthesis, and the State', in Kemal Karpat (ed), *Ottoman Past and Today's Turkey* (Leiden, Brill: 2000).

Florence Beaugé, *Algérie, une guerre sans gloire. Histoire d'une enquête* (Paris: Calmann-Lévy, 2005; Algiers: Chihab, 2006).

Fromkin, David, *A Peace to End all Peace. The Fall of the Ottoman Empire and the Creation of the Modern Middle East* (London: Phoenix Press, 2000).

Fuller, Mia, *Moderns Abroad: Architecture, Cities and Italian Imperialism* (London and New York: Routledge, 2007).

Fumich, Sergio, *Il Pozzo e le Parole* (Brembio: La Gattera, 2005).

Gaonkar, Dilip Parameshwar, *Alternative Modernities* (Durham: Duke University Press, 2001).

Garcia-Arenal, Mercedes, 'Mahdisme et dynastie saadienne', in Abdelmajid Kaddouri (ed), *Mahdisme: crises et changement dans l'histoire du Maroc* (Rabat: Mohammed V University, 1994).

Geddes, Andrew, 'Europe's border relationships and international migration relations', *Journal of Common Market Studies* xliii/4 (2005).

Gellner, Ernest, *Nations and Nationalism* (Ithaca NY: Cornell University Press, 1983).

Gensburger, Sarah and Lavabre, Marie-Claire, 'Entre «devoir de mémoire» et «abus de mémoire»: La sociologie de la mémoire comme tierce position', in Müller, Bertrand (ed), *L'histoire entre mémoire et épistémologie, autour de Paul Ricœur* (Lausanne: Editions Payot Lausanne, 2005).

Glenny, Misha, *The Balkans 1804 – 1999. Nationalism, War and the Great Powers* (London: Granta Publications, 1999).

Gobetti, Eric, *L'occupazione allegra: Gli italiani in Jugoslavia, 1941-1943* (Rome: Carocci editore, 2007).

Gold, Peter, *Europe or Africa? A Contemporary Study of the Spanish North African Enclaves of Ceuta and Melilla* (Liverpool: Liverpool University Press, 2000).

Goldstein, Ivo, *Croatia: A History* (London: Hurst and Company, 2001).

Goytisolo, Juan, *Cinema Eden: Essays from the Muslim Mediterranean* (London: Eland, 2003).

Graubard ,Stephen (ed), *Eastern Europe … Central Europe … Europe* (Boulder CO: Westview Press, 1993).

Grayzel, Susan R., *Women's Identities at War: Gender, Motherhood, and Politics in Britain and France during the First World War* (Chapel Hill, NC and London: University of North Carolina Press, 1999).

Gribaudi, Gabriella, 'Images of the South: The Mezzogiorno as seen by insiders and outsiders', in Robert Lumley and Jonathan Morris (eds), *The New History of the Italian South: The Mezzogiorno Revisited* (Exeter: University of Exeter Press, 1997).

Haas, Hein de, 'Morocco: From Emigration Country to Africa's Migration Passage to Europe', http://www.migrationinformation.org (October 2005).

———————, 'Trans-Saharan Migration to North Africa and the EU: Historical Roots and Current Trends', http://www.migrationinformation.org (November 2006).

Hanioğlu, Şükrü, *The Young Turks in Opposition* (Oxford: Oxford University Press, 1995).

Harbi, Mohamed, *FLN. Mirages et réalités* (Paris: Jeune Afrique, 1980).

———————, *Une vie debout. Mémoires politiques*, Vol 1, 1945-1962 (Paris: La Découverte, 2001).

Harbi, Mohamed and Benjamin Stora (eds), *La Guerre d'Algérie. 1954-2004, la fin de l'amnésie* (Paris: Robert Laffont, 2004).

Hartog, François and Jacques Revel, 'Historians and the present conjuncture', *Mediterranean Historical Review* xvi/1 (2001).

Hass, Amira, 'Israel's Closure Policy: An Ineffective Strategy of Containment and Repression', *Journal of Palestine Studies* xxxi/3 (Spring 2002).

Hassner, Pierre, 'Fixed borders or moving borderlands? a new type of border for a new type of entity', in Jan Zielonka (ed), *Europe Unbound: Enlarging and Reshaping the Boundaries of the European Union* (London: Routledge, 2001).

Hazan, Pierre, *Justice in a Time of War: The True Story Behind the International Criminal Tribunal for the Former Yugoslavia* (College Station: Texas A & M University Press, 2004).

Helman, Sara, and Tamar Rapoport, 'Women in Black: challenging Israel's gender and socio-political orders', *British Journal of Sociology* viii/4 (1997).

Henia, Abdelhamid, *Propriété et stratégies sociales à Tunis* (XVIè-XIXe siècles) (Tunis: Faculty of Human and Social Sciences, 1999).

Hertzog, Sergio, 'The relationship between economic hardship and crime: the case of Israel and the Palestinians', *Sociological Perspectives* xlviii/2 (2005).

Herzfeld, Michael, 'The horns of the Mediterraneanist dilemma', *American Ethnologist* xi/3 (1984).

————, Practical Mediterraneanism: excuses for everything, from epistemology to eating, in William V. Harris (ed), *Rethinking the Mediterranean* (Oxford: Oxford University Press: 2005)

Hess, Andrew, *The Forgotten Frontier: A History of the Sixteenth-Century Ibero-African Frontier* (Chicago: University of Chicago Press, 1978).

Hirschon, Renée (ed), *Crossing the Aegean: An Appraisal of the 1923 Compulsory {opulation Exchange between Greece and Turkey* (New York, Oxford: Berghahn, 2003).

Hobsbawm, Eric, *Age of Empire: 1875-1914* (Vintage Books, 1989).

Horden, Peregrine, 'Mediterranean excuses: historical writing in the Mediterranean since Braudel', *History and Anthropology* xvi/1 (2005).

Howe, Marvine, *Morocco. The Islamist Awakening and Other Challenges* (Oxford: Oxford University Press, 2005).

Hroch, Miroslav, *Social Preconditions of National Revival in Europe* (Cambridge: Cambridge University Press, 1985).

Humphries, Isabelle and Khalili, Laleh, 'Gender of Nakba memory', in Ahmad H. Sa'di and Lila Abu-Lughod (eds), *Nakba: Palestine, 1948, and the Claims of Memory* (New York: Columbia University Press, 2007).

Hurd, Elizabeth Shakman, 'Appropriating Islam: the Islamic Other in the consolidation of Western modernity', *Critique, Critical Middle Eastern Studies* xii/1 (Spring 2003).

Hurrell, Andrew, 'Order and justice in international relations: what is at stake?', in Rosemary Foot, John Lewis Gaddis and Andrew Hurrell (eds), *Order and Justice in International Relations* (Oxford: Oxford University Press, 2003).

Ignatieff, Michael, *Empire Lite: Nation-Building in Bosnia, Kosovo and Afghanistan* (London: Penguin, 2003).

Iorga, Nicolae, *Byzance après Byzance: Continuation de l'Histoire de la Vie Byzantine* (Bucharest: Institut d'Etudes Byzantines, 1971[1935]).

Jakubowska, Longina, 'Finding Ways to Make a Living', *Nomadic Peoples* iv/2 (2000).

————, *Urban Bedouin: Social Change in a Settled Environment*, PhD Thesis. State University of New York (1985)

Jellinek, Georg, *Allgemeine Staatslehre*, third edition (Berlin: Springer, 1929).

Juntunen, Marko, *Between Morocco and Spain: Men, Migrant Smuggling and a Dispersed Moroccan Community* (Helsinki: University Printing House, 2002).

Kamrava, Mehran, *The Modern Middle East: A Political history since the First World War* (Berkeley, London: University of California Press, 2005).

Karpat, Kemal H., *Ottoman Past and Today's Turkey* (Leiden: Brill, 2000).

_____, 'Historical continuity and identity change or how to be modern Muslim, Ottoman, and Turk', in Kemal Karpat (ed), *Ottoman Past and Today's Turkey*, (Leiden, Brill: 2000).

Kasbarian, Sossie, '*The 'Others' within – the Armenians in Cyprus.*' Paper delivered at the Oxford Symposium on Trans-Nationalism (Oxford: European Studies Centre, May 2006).

Kaya, Ibrahim, *Social Theory and Later Modernities: The Turkish Experience* (Liverpool: Liverpool University Press, 2004).

Kedourie, Elie, *Afghani and 'Abduh, An Essay on Religious Unbelief and Political Activism in Modern Islam* (London, Frank Cass: 1966).

Kemp, Adriana and Rebecca Raijman, 'Labor migration, managing the ethno-national conflict, and client politics in Israel', in Sarah S. Willen (ed), *Transnational Migration to Israel in Global Comparative Context* (Lanham: Lexington, 2007).

Kemp, Adriana, David Newman, Uri Ram and Oren Yiftachel (eds) *Israelis in Conflict. Hegemonies, Identities and Challenges* (Brighton: Sussex University Press, 2004).

Keyder, Çaglar, Eyup Özveren and Donald Quataert, 'Port-Cities in the Ottoman Empire: Some Theoretical and Historical Perspectives', *Review* xvi/4 (1993) [Special issue on 'Port Cities of the eastern Mediterranean, 1800 – 1914'].

Keyder, Çağlar, *Memâlik-i Osmaniye'den Avrupa Birliği'ne* (Istanbul: İletişim, 2004).

King, Charles, 'The new Near East', *Survival* xliii/2 (2001).

_____, The Black Sea: a History (Oxford: Oxford University Press, 2004).

King, Russell (ed), *The Mediterranean Passage. Migration and New Cultural Encounters in Southern Europe* (Liverpool: Liverpool University Press, 2001).

_____, 'Ants and frogs round a pond: interpretations of mediterranean historical geography', *Journal of Historical Geography* xxvii/4 (2001).

King, Stephen, *Liberalization against Democracy. The Local Politics of Economic Reform in Tunisia* (Bloomington: Indiana University Press, 2003).

Koliopoulos, John and Thanos Veremis, *Greece: the Modern Sequel. From 1831 to the Present* (London: Hurst, 2002).

Kramer, Martin, 'Arab Nationalism: The Mistaken Identity', *Daedalus* (Summer 1993).

Krasner, Stephen D., *Sovereignty, Organized Hypocrisy* (Princeton, NJ: Princeton University Press, 1999).

Kratochwil, Friedrich V., 'Of Systems, Boundaries and Territoriality: An Inquiry into the Formation of the State System', World *Politics* xxxix/1 (1986).

Kushner, David, *The Rise of Turkish Nationalism 1876-1908* (London: Frank Cass, 1977).

Laroui, Abdallah, *L'histoire du Maghreb, essai de synthèse* (Paris: Maspero, 1975).

_____, *Les origines sociales et culturelles du nationalisme marocain* (1830-1912) (Paris: François Maspero, 1977).

Lavabre, Marie-Claire and Marina Chauliac, 'Identité démocratique et mémoire. Micro-sociologie de la transmission intergénérationnelle', in Gesine Schwan, Jerzy Holzer, Marie-Claire Lavabre and Birgit Schwelling (eds), *Demokratische politische Identität Deutschland, Polen und Frankreich im Vergleich* (Wiesbaden: VS Verlag für Sozialwissenschaften, 2006).

Lavabre, Marie-Claire, 'Entre histoire et mémoire: à la recherche d'une méthode', in Jean-Clément Martin (ed), *La guerre civile entre histoire et mémoire* (Nantes: Ouest Editions, 1994).

_____, 'Un exemple d'utilisation de méthode projective en sociologie', in Jean-Marie Donegani, Sophie Duchesne and Florence Haegel (eds), *Aux frontières des attitudes entre le politique et le religieux, Hommage à Guy Michelat* (Paris: L'Harmattan, 2002).

Lavenex, Sandra, 'EU External Governance in "Wider Europe"', *Journal of European Public Policy* xi/4 (2004).

Lee, Helen Morton, *Tongans Overseas: Between Two Shores* (Honolulu: University of Hawaii Press, 2003).

Levinas, Emmanuel, *Altérité et transcendance* (Paris: Fata Morgana, 1995).

Lewando-Hundt, Gillian, *Women's Power and Settlement: the Effect of Settlement on the Position of Negev Bedouin Women*, MA Thesis, University of Edinburgh (1978)

Lewis, Bernard, *The Multiple Identities of the Middle East* (New York: Schocken, 1998).

Leydesdorff, Selma, 'Introduction' in Leydesdorff, Luisa Passerini and Paul Thompson (eds), *Gender and Memory* (New Brunswick, NJ: Transaction Publishers, 2005).

Luci, Nita and Vjollca Krasniqi, *Politics of Remembrance and Belonging: Life Histories of Albanian Women in Kosova* (Prishtina: Center for Research and Gender Policy, 2006).

Luzzatto, Sergio, *La crisi del antifascismo* (Turin: Einaudi, 2004).

Maazouzi, Mohammed, *L'Algérie et les étapes successives de l'amputation du territoire marocain* (Casablanca: Dar Al-Kitab, 1976).

MacDonald, D.B., *Balkan Holocausts? Serbian and Croatian Victim Centered Propaganda and the War in Yugoslavia* (Manchester: Manchester University Press, 2003).

Magone, José M, *Contemporary Spanish Politics* (London: Routledge, 2004).

Maier, Charles S., 'Does Europe need a frontier? from territorial to redistributive community', in Zielonka (ed), *Europe Unbound: Enlarging and Reshaping the Boundaries of the European Union* (London: Routledge, 2001).

Manceron, Gilles and Hassan Remaoun, *D'une rive à l'autre, la guerre d'Algérie, de la mémoire à l'histoire* (Paris: Syros, 1993).

Mann, Michael, *The Dark Side of Democracy: Explaining Ethnic Cleansing* (Cambridge: Cambridge University Press, 2004).

Mardin, Şerif, *Jön Türklerin Siyasi Fikirleri 1895-1908* (Istanbul: İletişim, 1989).

Marinov, Tchavdar, 'Multiculturalism in the Balkans: Ii it necessary? The use of the term in the context of the Balkans', *Identities-Journal for Politics, Gender, and Culture* v/2 (2006).

Marx, Anthony, *Faith in Nation: Exclusionary Origins of Nationalism* (Oxford: Oxford University Press, 2003).

Marx, Emanuel, *The Bedouin of the Negev* (Manchester: Manchester University Press, 1967).

Matvejević, Predrag, *Mediterranean: A Cultural Landscape* (Los Angeles: University of California Press, 1999).

Mazower, Mark, *Dark Continent. Europe's Twentieth Century* (New York: Vintage Books, 2000).

_____, *The Balkans* (London: Phoenix Press, 2000).

_____, *Salonica: City of Ghosts. Christians, Muslims and Jews 1430 – 1950* (London: HarperCollins, 2004).

McNeill, William, 'Mythistory, or Truth, Myth, History, and Historians', *The American Historical Review* xci/1 (February 1986).

Meir, Avinoam, *As Nomadism Ends: The Israeli Bedouin of the Negev* (Boulder: Westview Press, 1997).

Mertus, Julie, with Olja Hocevar and Van Wely, Women's Participation in the International Criminal Tribunal for the Former Yugoslavia (ICTY): Transitional Justice for Bosnia and Herzegovina, Women Waging Peace Policy Commission (July 2004).

Migdal, Joel (ed), *Boundaries and Belonging: States and Societies in the Struggle to Shape Identities and Local Practices* (Cambridge: Cambridge University Press, 2004).

Miller, Alexei and Alfred J. Rieber (eds), *Imperial Rule* (Budapest: Central European University Press, 2004).

Minow, Martha, 'The work of re-membering: after genocide and mass atrocity', *Fordham International Law Journal* xxiii (1999).

Misztal, Barbara A., *Theories of Social Remembering* (Philadelphia: Open University Press, 2003).

Mohanty, Chandra Talpade, *Feminism without Borders: Decolonizing Theory, Practicing Solidarity* (Durham and London: Duke University Press, 2003).

Monchicourt, Charles, *Etudes Kairouanaises. Kairouan et les Chabbia (1450-1592)* (Tunis, 1939).

Motyl, Alexander, *Imperial Ends: The Decay, Collapse, and Renewal of Empires* (New York: Columbia University Press, 2001).

Müller, Dietmar 'Southeastern Europe as a historical meso-region: constructing space in twentieth-century German historiography', *European Review of History* x/2 (2003).

Newman, David, 'On borders and powers: a theoretical framework', *Journal of Borderland Studies* xviii/1 (2003).

——————————, 'Borders and bordering: towards an interdisciplinary dialogue', *European Journal of Social Theory* ix/2 (2006).

——————————, 'The lines that continue to separate us: borders in our "borderless" world', *Progress in Human Geography* xxx/2 (2006).

Newman, David and Anssi Paasi, 'Fences and neighbours in the postmodern world: boundary narratives in political geography', *Progress in Human Geography* xxii/2 (1998).

Nicolaidis, Kalypso and Dimitri Nicolaidis, 'The EuroMed beyond civilizational paradigms,' in Emanuel Adler, Emanuel et al. (eds), *The Convergence of Civilizations: Constructing a Mediterranean Region* (Toronto: University of Toronto Press, 2006).

Nocke, Alexandra, 'Ex Occidente Lux?', Mare. Die Zeitschrift der Meere lxvii (2008).

——————————, 'Israel and the Emergence of Mediterranean Identity: Expressions of Locality in Music and Literature', *Israel Studies* xi/1 (2006).

Nora, Pierre (ed), *Les Lieux de Mémoire, Vol. 1: La République* (Paris: Gallimard, Bibliothèque illustrée des histoires, 1984).

Nordman, Daniel, *Profils du Maghreb. Frontières, figures et territoires (XVIIIe-XXe siècles)* (Rabat: Mohammed V University, 1996).

Norris, Harry Thirlwall, *Islam in the Balkans. Religion and Society between Europe and the Arab World* (London: C. Hurst, 1993).

Oktem, Kerem, 'Faces of the city: poetic, mediagenic and traumatic images of a multi-cultural city In Southeast Turkey', *Cities* xxii/3 (2005).

Onar, Nora, 'Echoes of a universalism lost: Rival representations of the Ottomans in contemporary Turkey,' paper delivered at the conference 'Echoes of Imperialism' (Oxford: European Studies Centre, May 2008).

Özveren, Eyup, 'A Framework for the Study of the Black Sea World, 1789-1915', *Review* 20 (1997).

Pace, Michelle, *The Politics of Regional Identity: Meddling with the Mediterranean* (London: Routledge, 2005).

Page, Melvin, *Colonialism: An International, Social, Cultural, and Political Encyclopedia* (Santa Barbara, Oxford: ABC-CLIO, 2003).

Palestinian Environmental NGOs Network (ed), *The Wall In Palestine: Facts, Testimonies, Analysis and Call to Action* (Jerusalem: PENGON, 2003).

Pamuk, Orhan, *Istanbul: Memories of a City* (London: Faber and Faber, 2005).

Pappé, Ilan, *A History of Modern Palestine: One Land, Two Peoples* (Cambridge: Cambridge University Press, 2004).

_____, *The Ethnic Cleansing of Palestine* (Oxford: Oneworld Publications, 2006).

Parizot, Cédric, 'Gaza, Beer-Sheva, Dahriyya: Another Approach of the Negev Bedouin in the Israeli Palestinian Space', Bulletin du Centre de Recherche Français de Jérusalem, No. 9 (Autumn 2001).

_____, 'Crossing and Constructing Borders within Daily Contacts', Notes de Recherche du CER, No. 287 (2004).

_____, *Le mois de la bienvenue: ré-appropriations des mécanismes électoraux et réajustements de rapports de pouvoir chez les Bédouins du Néguev* (Israël), PhD Thesis, EHESS, Paris (2001).

Patten, S. N., Review: 'The Nearer East. By D. G. Hogarth', *The Annals of the American Academy of Political and Social Science* xxii/115 (1903).

Patterson, Patrick Hyder, 'On the edge of reason: the boundaries of Balkanism in Slovenian, Austrian, and Italian Discourse', *Slavic Review* lxii/1 (2003).

Pattie, Susan, *Longing and belonging: issues of homeland in the Armenian diaspora* (Oxford: Institute for Social and Cultural Anthropology, Transnational Communities Programme, Working Paper Series, 1999).

Pavlowitch, Stevan, 'The role of the monarchy as a legitimising factor in South East Europe (1830–1940)'. Paper delivered at the seminar series 'Conceptualising political leadership in Greece and Southeast Europe' (Oxford: European Studies Centre, February 2007).

Pedace Naso, Magda, 'La questione adriatica nella pubblicistica fra le due guerre. L'imperialismo italiano e la Jugoslavia', in Massimo Pacetti (ed), *Atti del convegno italo-jugoslavo. Ancona 14-16 ottobre 1977* (Urbino: Argalìa Editore, 1981).

Perkins, Kenneth, *A History of Modern Tunisia* (Cambridge: Cambridge University Press, 2004).

Pirenne, Henri, *Mohammed and Charlemagne* (New York: Barnes and Noble, 1956[1935]).

Pitkin, Donald S., 'Mediterranean Europe', *Anthropological Quarterly* xxxvi/3 (1963).

Pitts, Jennifer, *A Turn to Empire: The Rise of Imperial Liberalism in Britain and France* (Princeton, Princeton University Press: 2005).

Renan, Ernest, *Qu'est-ce qu'une nation?* (Paris: Presses Pocket, 1992[1882]).

Ribas-Mateos, Natalia, *The Mediterranean in the Age of Globalization* (New Brunswick & London: Transaction Publishers, 2005).

Ricœur, Paul, *La Mémoire, l'Histoire, l'Oubli* (Paris: Editions du Seuil, 2000).

Rodogno, Davide, 'Italian soldiers in the Balkans: the experience of the occupation

(1941-1943)', *Journal of Southern Europe and the Balkans* vi/2 (2004).

Rogan, Eugene and Avi Shlaim (eds), *The War for Palestine. Rewriting the History of 1948* (Cambridge: Cambridge University Press, 2001).

Rowbotham, Sheila, *Hidden from History: Three Hundred Years of Women's Oppression and the Fight against It* (London: Pluto Press, 1973).

Said, Edward, *Orientalism* (New York, Vintage: 1979).

―――――――, *Culture and Imperialism* (Vintage, New York, 1993).

Sangster, Joan, 'Telling our stories: feminist debates and the use of oral history', in Robert Perks and Alistair Thomson (eds), *The Oral History Reader* (London: Routledge, 1998).

Sayyid, Bobby, *A Fundamental Fear: Eurocentrism and the Emergence of Islamism* (London: Zed Books, 1997).

Scheffler, Thomas, '"Fertile Crescent", "Orient", "Middle East": the changing mental maps of Southwest Asia', European Review of History x/2 (2003).

Schöpflin, George, 'The Functions of myth and taxonomy of myths' in Geoffrey A. Hosking and George Schöpflin (eds), *Myths and Nationhood* (London: Hurst, 1997).

Schraút, Sylvia and Paletschek, Sylvia, *The Gender of Memory. Cultures of Remembrance in Nineteenth- and Twentieth-Century Europe* (Chicago: Chicago University Press, 2008).

Schwandner-Sievers, Stephanie, 'Introduction: capacities of myth in Albania', in Stephanie Schwandner-Sievers and Bernd Fischer (eds), *Albanian Identities: Myth and History* (London: Hurst, 2002).

Sebe, Berny, *Celebrating British and French Imperialism: The Making of Colonial Heroes Acting in Africa, 1870-1939*, Unpublished D.Phil thesis, University of Oxford (2007).

See Ben-Ghiat and Mia Fuller, 'Introduction', in Ben-Ghiat and Fuller (eds), *Italian Colonialism* (New York: Palgrave Macmillan, 2005).

Senturk, Recep, 'Sociology of Rights: "I Am Therefore I Have Rights": Human Rights in Islam Between Universalistic and Communalistic Perspectives', *Muslim World Journal of Human Rights* ii/1 (2005).

Sharoni, Simona, *Gender and the Israeli-Palestinian Conflict. The Politics of Women's Resistance* (Syracuse: Syracuse University Press, 1995).

Shaw, Stanford and Ezel Shaw, *History of the Ottoman Empire and Modern Turkey: Volume II: Reform Revolution and Republic: The Rise of Modern Turkey, 1808-1975* (Cambridge: Cambridge University Press, 1997).

Shehadeh, Raja, *Palestinian Walks. Notes on a Vanishing Landscape* (London: Profile Books, 2007).

Shlaim, Avi, *War and Peace in the Middle East. A Concise History* (London: Penguin Books, 1994).

Shohat, Ella, 'Notes on the "post-colonial"', *Social Text* xxxi/xxxii (1992).

―――――――, 'Rethinking Jews and Muslims: quincentennial reflections', Middle East Report clxxviii (1992).

―――――――, 'Sephardim in Israel: Zionism from the standpoint of Its Jewish victims', *Social Text* xix/xx (1988).

Silverman, Sydel, *The Three Bells of Civilization: The Life of an Italian Hilltown* (New York: Columbia University Press, 1975).

Silverstein, Paul, 'France's mare nostrum: colonial and post-colonial constructions of the French Mediterranean', *The Journal of North African Studies* vii/4 (2002).

Sirovich, Livio Isaak, *Cime irredente: Un tempestoso caso storico alpinistico* (Turin: Vivalda editori, 1996).

Skjelsbæk, Inger, 'Victim and survivor: narrated social identities of women who experienced rape during the war in Bosnia-Herzegovina', *Feminism and Psychology* xvi/4 (2006).

Sluga, Glenda, 'Italian national memory, national identity and fascism', in J.B. Bosworth and Patrizia Dogliani (eds), *Italian Fascism: History, Memory and Representation* (Basingstoke and New York: Macmillan, 1999).

_____, 'Identità nazionale italiana e fascismo: alieni, allogeni e assimilazione sul confine nord-orientale italiano', in Marina Cattaruzza (ed), *Nazionalismi di frontiera: Identità contrapposte sull'Adriatico nord-orientale, 1850-1950* (Palermo: Rubettino, 2003).

Smith, Anthony D., *National Identity* (London: Penguin, 1991).

_____, *Myths and Memories of the Nation* (Oxford and New York: Oxford University Press, 2000).

Smith, Michael, 'The European Union and a changing Europe: establishing the boundaries of order', Journal of Common Market Studies xxxiv/1 (1996).

Snyder, Jack. *Myths of Empire: Domestic Politics and International Ambition* (Ithaca: Cornell University Press, 1991).

Spruyt, Hendrik, *The Sovereign State and Its Competitors: An Analysis of Systems Change* (Princeton: Princeton University Press, 1994).

Stiglmayer, Alexandra (ed), *Mass Rape: The War against Women in Bosnia-Herzegovina* (London: University of Nebraska Press, 1994).

Stirk, Peter, 'The Westphalian Model, Sovereignty and Law in Fin-de-siècle German International Theory', *International Relations* xix/2 (2005).

Stoller, Paul, *Money Has No Smell: The Africanization of New York City* (Chicago and London: University of Chicago Press, 2002).

Stora, Benjamin, *La gangrène et l'oubli. La mémoire de la guerre d'Algérie* (Paris: La Découverte, 1991).

Suárez-Navaz, Liliana, *Rebordering the Mediterranean: Boundaries and Citizenship in Southern Europe* (New York & Oxford: Berghahn Books, 2004).

Summerfield, Penny, *Reconstructing Women's Wartime Lives. Discourse and Subjectivity in Oral Histories of the Second World War* (Manchester: Manchester University Press, 1998).

Sundhaussen, Holm, 'Was ist Südosteuropa und warum beschäftigen wir uns (nicht) damit?' *Südosteuropa Mitteilungen* (2002).

Temimi, Abdeljalil, 'Formation administrative et géopolitique des provinces ottomanes du Maghreb (1554-1588)' *Arab Historical Review for the Ottoman Studies* xi-xii (2000).

_____, *Recherches et documents d'histoire maghrébine: L'Algérie, la Tunisie et la Tripolitaine (1816-1871)* (Tunis, 1971).

Terray, Emmanuel, 'Le travail des étrangers en situation irrégulière ou la délocalisation sur place', in E. Balibar, M. Chemillier-Gendreau, J. Costa-Lascoux, and E. Terray (eds), *Sans Papiers: l'archaïsme fatal* (Paris: La découverte, 1999).

Thom, Deborah, *Nice Girls and Rude Girls. Women Workers in World War One* (London: I.B. Tauris, 1998).

Todorova, Maria, 'The Ottoman Legacy in the Balkans', in Carl L. Brown (ed), *Imperial Legacy in the Balkans and the Middle East* (New York: Columbia University Press, 1995).

_____, *Imagining the Balkans* (New York and Oxford: Oxford University Press, 1997).

Trevisan-Semi, Emanuela, 'La traverse des frontières entre Israel et la Palestine: de la métaphore littéraire au militantisme', *A contrario* iii/2 (2005).

Troebst, Stefan, 'What's in a historical region? a teutonic perspective', *European Review of History* x/2 (2003).

Turner, Bryan S., *Weber and Islam* (London: Routledge, 1974).

Turner, Frederick Jackson, *The Frontier in American History* (New York: Henry Holt, 1920).

Van Dijk, Teun A., 'Stories and racism', in D.K. Mumby (ed), *Narrative and Social Control: Critical Perspectives* (Newbury Park, California: Sage, 1993).

Vila, Pablo, 'Conclusion: the limits of American border theory', in Pablo Vila (ed), *Ethnography at the Border* (Minneapolis: University of Minnesota Press, 2003).

Vivante, Angelo, *Irredentismo adriatico: Contributo alla discussione sui rapporti austro-italiani* (Genoa: Graphos, 1997[1912]).

Vranić, Seada, *Breaking the Wall of Silence: The Voices of Raped Bosnia* (Zagreb: Anti Barbarus, 1996).

Walker, Rob B.J., *Inside/Outside: International Relations as Political Theory* (Cambridge: Cambridge University Press, 1992).

Wallace, William, 'Where Does Europe End? Dilemmas of Inclusion and Exclusion', in Jan Zielonka (ed), *Europe Unbound: Enlarging and Reshaping the Boundaries of the European Union* (London: Routledge, 2001).

Wolff, Sarah, 'La dimension méditerranéenne de la politique Justice et Affaires intérieures', *Cultures et Conflits* 66 (2007).

Woodsworth, Nicholas, *The Liquid Continent – A Mediterranean Trilogy (Alexandria, Venice, Istanbul)*, (London: Haus Publishing, 2008).

Yılmaz, Suhnaz and Ipek K. Yosmaoğlu, 'Fighting the specters of the past: dilemmas of Ottoman legacy in the Balkans and the Middle East', *Middle East Studies* xliv/5 (2008).

Youngs, Richard, *Europe and the Middle East. In the Shadow of September 11* (Boulder CO: Lynne Renner, 2006).

Yurdusev, Nuri (ed), *Ottoman Diplomacy: Conventional or Unconventional* (Basingstoke: Palgrave Macmillan, 2004).

Yuval-Davis, Nira, *Gender and Nation* (London: Sage, 1997).

Žanić, Ivo, 'The symbolic identity of Croatia in the triangle crossroads – bulwark bridge', in Pal Kolsto (ed), *Myths and Boundaries in South-Eastern Europe* (London: Hurst, 2005).

Zielonka, Jan, 'How new enlarged borders will reshape the EU', *Journal of Common Market Studies* xxxix/3 (2001).

_____, *Europe as Empire: the Nature of the Enlarged European Union* (Oxford and New York: Oxford University Press, 2006).

_____, *Europe as Empire: The Nature of the Enlarged European Union* (Oxford: Oxford University Press, 2006).

Zorob, Anja, *Projekt 'Mittelmeerunion' – 'neuer Schub' für die EU-Mittelmeerpolitik?* (Hamburg: German Institute for Global and Area Studies, 2008).

Zürcher, Erik Jan, 'Young Turks, Ottoman Muslims and Turkish nationalists: identity politics 1908-1938', in Kemal Karpat (ed), *Ottoman Past and Today's Turkey* (Leiden, Brill: 2000).

_____, *Turkey: A Modern History* (London: I. B. Tauris, 2004).

INDEX